THE
INTELLIGENT
INVESTOR

OTHER FINANCIAL BOOKS BY BENJAMIN GRAHAM

The Interpretation of Financial Statements
(*with Spencer B. Meredith*)

THROUGH CHANCES VARIOUS,

THROUGH ALL VICISSITUDES

WE MAKE OUR WAY. . . .

—AENEID

THE
INTELLIGENT
INVESTOR

The classic text on
Value Investing

By Benjamin Graham

HARPER
BUSINESS

HarperCollins books may be purchased for educational, business, or sales promotional use. For information, please write to: Special Markets Department, HarperCollins Publishers Inc., 10 East 53rd Street, New York, New York 10022.

Designed by Kathryn Parise

Library of Congress Cataloging-in-Publication has been applied for.

ISBN 0-06-075261-0

24 25 26 27 28 LBC 38 37 36 35 34

To E. M. G.
and to the many friends
who helped with this book

FOREWORD

———◆◇◆———

BY JOHN C. BOGLE

What Would Benjamin Graham Write Today?

THE FIRST EDITION of *The Intelligent Investor* was published in 1949. It quickly became a classic, endorsed by Warren Buffett as "by far the best book on investing ever written." Over the years, the slim 304 page initial edition that you are now holding was revised and expanded. By the fourth edition, published in 1973, it had grown to 340 pages. In that final edition,[1] Benjamin Graham acknowledged that he was "greatly aided by my collaborator, Warren Buffett, whose counsel and practical aid have proved invaluable."

By curious coincidence, my own long investment career also began in 1949, when an article in *Fortune* magazine introduced me to the mutual fund industry. My first encounter with the Graham book didn't take place until 1965, when I bought (for $5.95, new!) the third revised edition. There, Graham recognized the extraordinary changes that had taken place in the investment environment over the previous half century, yet took comfort in the fact that "through all its vicissitudes and casualties, as earthshaking as they were unforeseen, it remained true that sound investment principles produced generally sound results. We must act on the assumption that they will continue to do so."

As an eyewitness to the earthshaking vicissitudes and casualties of *this* past half century, coincident with the life of Graham's investment classic, I'm honored to contribute this foreword, for it gives me the opportunity to re-

---

[1] In 2003, *Money* journalist Jason Zweig used the 1973 edition as a platform on which he added a contemporaneous commentary, a total of 640 pages.

flect on my own experience with sound investment principles during this long span. I often muse, sort of whimsically, that "a lot can happen in fifty years," and despite another fifty years of mind-boggling change, Ben Graham's assumption was again borne out: *Sound investment principles produced generally sound investment results.*

What might Benjamin Graham write today, nearly thirty years after his death? Of course we can't be sure. But he was well aware that change was inevitable, warning us on the first page of the first edition that "the precepts crystallized out of past experience" many become obsolete with the passage of time. As a long-time student of his investment philosophy, I have allowed myself the temerity to reflect on what he might have to say were he to look down from above, which would surely be his vantage point. While the activities of investors, the investments of choice, and the ownership of stocks today bear little resemblance to those that characterized the world of investing when Graham wrote this original edition in 1949, the basic principles of intelligent investing that he set forth there have remained virtually intact and unassailable.

The Ebb and Flow of Investment Values

During the past half century, by almost every standard, the financial markets have changed. Begin with the vast increase of the importance of stocks in our economy. In 1949, the total value of listings on the New York Stock Exchange was $150 billion. (The over-the-counter market was tiny, perhaps $6 billion.) Today, the value of Big Board listings are $20 *trillion*, with another $3 trillion of stocks listed on NASDAQ.

Stock valuations had changed, too. In the appendix, Graham takes readers through a methodology for determining the "central value" of the Dow Jones Industrial Average, using as a guide its annualized earnings for the previous ten years, divided by twice the corporate bond yield. In 1949, with the Dow at 177 and a value range of 158–236, the market appeared fairly valued. Looking back, this methodology showed that the stock market was clearly overvalued in the late 1920s and undervalued in the mid-1930s, the early 1950s, and during most of the mid-1970s. The system worked!

Alas, however, when the Great Bull Market began in 1982, it also showed the market about 70% overvalued. Under the central-value system, stocks were fully 550% overvalued at the 2000 high, only to fall to a mere 195% overvalued at the 2002 low, just before the rebound. Clearly, Graham had found a good indicator of relative value over the near term. But he had also found yet one more indication of how valuation standards can change with the times.

Bond valuations also changed sharply. In 1949, with a 2.6% yield on AAA corporate bonds and a 2.1% yield on long-term U.S. Treasury bonds, Graham came down firmly in favor of U.S. savings bonds, then yielding 2.9%, as a "boon to investors . . . and a satisfactory answer to every problem of (fixed income) investment." Today savings bonds have little attraction, and the 2% yield on long bonds has vanished. After rising to a high of 14.8% in 1981, the yield on Treasury bonds gradually eased back to its current 5% level.

On balance, even as bond yields soared, stock yields plummeted. Graham cites the 1949 dividend yield on the Dow Jones Industrials at 5.5%, and the price-earnings multiple at 8 times. Currently, the dividend yield on the Dow is 2.1%, and the price-earnings multiple is 18.1 times. (The Dow has now been eclipsed by the Standard and Poor's 500 Stock Index as the accepted measure of the broad stock market; its yield is 1.7%, its multiple 21.2 times.)

"Mr. Market," Trading, and Institutionalization

As market valuations changed, market volumes changed as well. In 1949, one million shares were traded each day on the New York Stock Exchange; in 2004, 1.5 *billion* shares changed hands daily (another 2 billion shares were traded on NASDAQ). Graham was not keen about all that trading, warning investors not to succumb to the wiles of his metaphorical "Mr. Market," who drops by every day and "tells you what he thinks your interest (in your business) is worth and furthermore offers either to buy you out or sell you an additional interest on that basis."

Graham cautioned that, unless the price Mr. Market offers is either ridiculously high or ridiculously low, the prudent investor would be wise to ignore the market's continual bids and offers and form his own ideas of the value of his holdings. But with Mr. Market now persuading investors to do 1500 *times* (!) as much business with him as they did a near-half-century ago, most investors have failed abjectly to follow Graham's sound advice.

This explosion in trading activity reflects, in part, another vast change: the "democratization," if you will, of the world of investing. In 1949, stocks were owned by about two million investors, almost solely individuals of well-above-average means. Today, some 90 million Americans from all walks of life own shares of stock. Even more astonishing, the lion's share of those holdings is owned not directly but indirectly through financial institutions—mutual funds, pension funds, endowment funds, hedge funds, and the like. The mutual fund industry has led the way, growing from a mere $2 billion of assets into a colossus managing $7.6 *trillion* of other people's money, including $4 trillion of equities.

This institutionalization has left the last-line investor in stocks a step removed from ownership, relying on his managers to be faithful stewards in fulfilling the responsibilities of good corporate citizenship. At the same time, as a trading mentality came to dominate the market, a new *rent-a-stock* philosophy came to hold sway over the former tried and true *own-a-stock* philosophy. Together, these two trends have served to sharply dilute the role of the investor as a business owner.

Stockholders and Management

Graham would not have been amused. His first edition includes fully thirty-seven pages of discussion on the optimal relationship between stockholders and management. He makes his point unequivocally: [investors] are owners of the country's larger enterprises. They make money not out of each other but out of these businesses. Hence their major energies and wisdom as investors should—in theory at least—be directed toward assuring themselves of the best operating results from their corporations. This in turn means assuring themselves of fully honest and competent managements.

"Nothing in finance is more fatuous and harmful, in our opinion, than the firmly established attitude of common stock investors and their Wall Street advisers regarding questions of corporate management. That attitude is summed up in the phrase: 'If you don't like the management, sell the stock.' Obviously such action does nothing at all to improve bad management; it only puts down the price of the stock and shifts the ownership to someone else. . . . Investors as a whole . . . seem to have abandoned all claim to control over the paid superintendents of their property."

He held the conviction that "the best opportunity for demonstrating investor intelligence is in the field of stockholder-management relationships; for here investors can act as a class and not as individuals ... a novel but important branch of the science of investment." Surely Graham would have been discouraged, if not disgusted, by the failure of today's investors—especially our giant financial institutions—to assume the rights and respon sibilities of stock ownership and corporate citizenship.

The Defensive Investor

In his original edition, Graham makes an important and timeless distinction, one that in a sense prefigured this vast institutionalization of investing. The two distinct types of investor that he described endure to this day.

The Defensive Investor, following a "simple portfolio policy—the purchase of bonds, plus a diversified list of leading common stocks—which any investor can carry out with a little expert assistance." The lay investor can achieve "a creditable, if unspectacular, result with a minimum of effort and capability ... since anyone—by just buying and holding a representative list—can equal the performance of the market averages, it would seem a comparatively simple matter to 'beat the averages.' "

Alas, he warned, "the proportion of smart people who try this and fail is surprisingly large, [including] many of the investment funds, [which] with all their experienced personnel, have not performed as well over the years as the stock market ... The real money in investing will have to be made—as most of it has been in the past—not out of buying and selling, but out of owning and holding securities, receiving interest and dividends, and benefiting from their long-term increase in value."

The Enterprising Investor

"The adventure beyond this safe and sound territory" occupied by the Defensive Investor is recommended only to the *Enterprising Investor*, who, Graham warned, should "have a clear concept of the differences between market price and underlying value ... [and] should firmly base his stock selection on the margin-of-safety principle." Such an investor, he emphasized, "cannot enter the arena of the stock market with any real hope of success unless he is armed with mental weapons that distinguish him in *kind*—not in a fancied superior *degree*—from the trading public."

Even before he advised enterprising investors how to go about their risky task, Graham warned them about what *not* to do. "At the risk of alienating many of our readers, let us say categorically that we do not consider that either general trading—anticipating moves in the market as a whole—or selective trading—picking out stocks which will do better than the market in the short term—has any place in investment practice. Both of them are essentially speculative in character because they depend for success not only on the ability to foretell specifically what is going to happen, but on the ability also to do this more cleverly than a host of competitors in the field."

He then laid out four areas in which the enterprising investor might practice his aggressive policies:

(1) *Formula Timing.* Buying in low markets and selling in high, although he warned, "that no simple or fool-proof formula could be counted on." In retrospect, the "central value" concept noted above was ample proof of the wisdom of his caution.

(2) *Growth-Stock Approach.* Buying carefully chosen "growth stocks" (quotation marks in original), a policy complicated, he noted, by the fact that "stocks with good records and apparently good prices sell at correspondingly high prices, and that the investor's judgment about the future might be wrong. Unusually rapid growth cannot keep up forever; a brilliant expansion makes a repetition of its achievement more difficult . . . as its growth curve flattens out, and in many cases turns downward." Purchasing a growth stock when it's most favored, he warned, "would have disastrous consequences."

(3) *Bargain Issues*, defined by whether a stock is worth more than it is selling for—"an indicated value at least 50 percent more than the price, . . . [based on] estimating future earnings and then multiplying these by an appropriate factor . . . or on the value of the business to a private owner." He urged, "the inexperienced investor to eschew these issues completely," but since market declines are often overdone, "the group as a whole offers an especially rewarding invitation to careful and courageous analysis."

(4) *Special Situations*, including sales of businesses, mergers, recapitalizations, reorganizations, and liquidations, which Graham described as "a technical branch of investment which requires a somewhat unusual mentality

and equipment, [and in which] only a small percentage of [even] enterprising investors should engage."

While Benjamin Graham is best known by far for his focus on the kind of value investing represented by the category of stocks he describes as "bargain issues," he cautioned that, "the aggressive investor must have a considerable knowledge of security values—enough, in fact, to warrant viewing his security operations as equivalent to a business enterprise . . . It follows from this reasoning that *the majority of security owners should elect the defensive classification.* They do not have the time, or the determination, or the mental equipment to embark upon such investing as a quasi-business. They should therefore be satisfied with the reasonably good return obtainable from a defensive portfolio, and they should stoutly resist the recurrent temptation to increase this return by deviating into other paths."

Graham on Investment Advisers and Mutual Funds

For the defensive investor who required assistance, Graham recommended professional investment advisers who rely on "normal investment experience for their results . . . and who make no claim to being brilliant, (but) pride themselves on being careful, conservative, and competent . . . whose chief value to their clients is in shielding them from costly mistakes." He cautioned about expecting too much from stock-exchange houses, arguing that while "the Wall Street brokerage fraternity has probably the highest ethical standards of any *business*, it is still feeling its way toward the high standards and standing of a *profession.*" (A half century later, the quest remains far from complete.)

He also noted, profoundly if obviously, that Wall Street is "in business to make commissions, and that the way to succeed in business is to give customers what they want, trying hard to make money in a field where they are condemned almost by mathematical law to lose." (Later on, in 1976, Graham described his opinion of Wall Street as, "highly unfavorable . . . a Falstaffian joke that frequently degenerates into a madhouse . . . a huge laundry in which institutions take in large blocks of each other's washing.")

As an alternative to creating their own portfolios, Graham commended the use by investors of leading investment funds. (He thought the term "investment trust" was inaccurate and the term "investment company" ambiguous.) Of course, he was describing what we now have come to know as mutual funds (though that term, too, is ambiguous and not entirely forthright). Graham described the well-established mutual funds of that era as "competently managed, making fewer mistakes than the typical small investor," carrying a reasonable expense, and performing a sound function by acquiring and holding an adequately diversified list of common stocks.

But he was bluntly realistic about what fund managers might accomplish. He illustrated this point with data showing that during 1937–1947, when the Standard & Poor's 500 Index provided a total return of 57%, the average mutual fund produced a total return of 54%. Conclusion: "The figures are not very impressive in either direction . . . on the whole, the managerial ability of invested funds has been just about able to absorb the expense burden and the drag of uninvested cash."

How Much in Stocks?

In *The Intelligent Investor*, Graham clearly recognized the importance of controlling risk, recommending in the first edition a cautious equity position that "would range ordinarily from, say, 20% to as high as 50% . . . *a revolutionary change* [i.e., increase] *from a former conservative practice*" (italics added for emphasis). By his third edition in 1965, he had raised the range to 25% to 75% in stocks, suggesting that the "simplest choice would be to maintain a 50–50 proportion, periodically restoring the equality as market conditions indicate," a position he reaffirmed in the final edition in 1973.

In that later edition, his confidence that funds would produce the market's return, less costs, had been somewhat shaken. "Unsoundly managed" funds, he noted, "can produce spectacular but largely illusionary profits for a while, followed inevitably by calamitous loses." He was describing the so-called "performance funds" of the Go-Go Era of the mid-1960s, in which a "new breed that had a spectacular knack for coming up with winners . . . bright, energetic, young people who promised to perform miracles with other people's money . . . (but) who have inevitably brought losses to their public in the end." He could have as easily been presciently describing the hundreds of "New Era" mutual funds formed during the great bull market of 1997–2000, and their utter collapse in the subsequent 50% market crash that no doubt inevitably followed.

He also would have been appalled, not only by the enormous (100%-plus) increase in those once-reasonable fund expenses, but also by the rapid trading of mutual funds during the recent era, averaging more than 100% per year. Graham would surely, and accurately, describe such an approach as speculation. His timeless lesson for the intelligent investor, as valid today as when he prescribed it in his first edition, is clear: "the real money in investment will have to be made—as most of it has been in the past—not out of buying and selling but of owning and holding securities, receiving interest and dividends and increases in value."

The Index Fund

With those words, Benjamin Graham came close to describing the modern-day stock index fund—a fund that essentially buys the entire U.S. stock market and holds it forever. His buy-and-hold philosophy as well as his admonition to "strictly adhere to standard, conservative, and even unimaginative forms of investment" eerily echo the concept of market indexing. Indeed, he pointed out that "choosing the 'best' stocks is highly controversial. Our advice to the defensive investor is that he let it alone and emphasize diversification more than individual selection."

Later in his life, Graham candidly acknowledged the inevitable failure of individual investment managers to outpace the market. In an interview published in the *Financial Analysts Journal* in its issue dated September/October 1976 (coincidentally, at the very moment that the first index fund—First Index Investment Trust, now Vanguard 500 Index Fund—was beginning its operations), he was asked, "Can the average manager obtain better results than the Standard and Poor's Index over the years?" Graham's blunt response: *"No."* (Italics added for emphasis.) Then he explained: "In effect that would mean that the stock market experts as a whole could beat themselves— a logical contradiction."

The interviewer's next question was whether investors should be content with earning the market's return. Graham's answer: "Yes. Not only that, but I think they should require approximately such results over, say, a moving five-year average period as a condition for paying standard management fees to advisors."

Then, he was asked about the objection made against so-called index funds—that different investors have different requirements. Again, Graham responded bluntly: "At bottom that is only a convenient cliche or alibi to justify the mediocre record of the past. All investors want good results from their investments, and are entitled to them to the extent that they are actually obtainable. I see no reason why they should be content with results inferior to those of an indexed fund or pay standard fees for such inferior results."

While these unequivocal comments may not *quite* add up to an endorsement of a low-cost index fund tracking the Standard and Poor's 500 Index or the Dow Jones Wilshire 5000 Composite Index, they surely come close to an endorsement. But it remained for his collaborator, whose counsel and practical aid Graham acknowledged as invaluable in the final edition of *The Intelligent Investor*, to produce the coup de grace for hyperactive, high-cost portfolio management: In 1993, Warren Buffett wrote, "By periodically investing in an index fund, the know-nothing investor can actually outperform most investment professionals. Paradoxically, when 'dumb' money acknowledges its limitations, it ceases to be dumb." A decade later, he reaffirmed that advice: "those index funds that are very low cost . . . are investor-friendly by definition and are the best selection for most of those who wish to own equities."

A Changing World

More than a half century ago, on the very first page of his introduction to *The Intelligent Investor*, Benjamin Graham cautioned that, "just as the standard works on financial practice current before the First World War could make strange reading today," so he warned that "our present views, based on the experience of 1914–1948, may not stand the test of future developments."

Yet he correctly intuited that the rules that would fail would "relate mainly to *types of securities*: the ones that would survive apply mainly to *human nature and human conduct* [italics added for emphasis] . . . copybook maxims such as: If you speculate you will (most probably) lose your money in the end. Buy when most people are pessimistic and sell when they are actively optimistic. Investigate, then invest. [Rely on] the time-tested principle of insurance, with wide diversification of risk."

An interesting sidelight: The name Benjamin Graham is intimately connected, indeed almost synonymous, with "value investing" and the search for undervalued securities. But, in fact, his classic book gives far more attention to the down-to-earth basics of portfolio policy—the straightforward, uncomplicated principles of diversification and rational long-term expectations— than to solving the sphinx-like mystery of selecting superior stocks through careful security analysis.

It is fair to say that, by Graham's demanding standards, most mutual funds, largely because of their high costs and speculative behavior, have failed to live up to their promise. As a result, a new type of fund—the index fund—is now in the ascendancy. Why? Both because of what it *does*— providing the broadest possible diversification—and because of what it *doesn't* do—neither assessing high costs nor engaging in high turnover. These paraphrases of Graham's copybook maxims are an important part of his legacy to that vast majority of shareholders whom, he believed, should follow the principles he outlined for the defensive investor.

Graham also recognized that the circumstances he described for the aggressive investor and the types of securities he recommended for such an investor would also inevitably change. In his 1976 interview, he confirmed one change, and it was a landmark change: "I am no longer an advocate of elaborate techniques of security analysis in order to find superior value opportunities. This was a rewarding activity, say, forty years ago, but the situation has changed a great deal since then. In the old days, any well-trained security analyst could do a good professional job of selecting undervalued issues through detailed studies; but in the light of the enormous amount of research now being carried on, I doubt whether in most cases such extensive efforts will generate sufficiently superior selections to justify their cost. To that very limited extent, I'm on the side of the 'efficient market' school of thought now generally accepted by the professors."

An Honorable Epitaph

It is Benjamin Graham's common sense, clear thinking, simplicity, and sense of financial history—along with his willingness to hold fast to the sound principles of long-term investing even as he was willing to change with the times with respect to the types of securities employed—that constitute his lasting legacy. His final words as he concluded *The Intelligent Investor* serve as an honorable and fitting epitaph:

For the Enterprising Investor: "Have the courage of your knowledge and experience. If you have formed a conclusion from the facts and if you know your judgment is sound, act on it—even though others may hesitate or differ. (You are neither right nor wrong because the crowd disagrees with you. You are right because your data and reasoning are right.) Similarly, in the world of securities, courage becomes the supreme virtue after adequate knowledge and a tested judgment are at hand."

For the Defensive Investor: "Fortunately for the typical investor, it is by no means necessary for his success that he bring these qualities to bear upon his program—provided he limits his ambition to his capacity and confines his activities within the safe and narrow path of standard, defensive investment. *To achieve satisfactory investment results is easier than most people realize; to achieve superior results is harder than it looks*" (italics added for emphasis).

—John C. Bogle
Valley Forge, Pennsylvania, 2005

CONTENTS

—◆◇◆—

INTRODUCTION

—◆◇◆—

What This Book Expects
to Accomplish

THE PURPOSE OF this book is to supply, in a form suitable for laymen, guidance in the adoption of an investment policy. Some of the material is derived from a larger work—*Security Analysis* by Benjamin Graham and David L. Dodd—intended mainly for working analysts and advanced students. Comparatively little will be said here about the technique of analyzing securities; attention will be paid chiefly to investment principles and investors' attitudes.

The policies suggested will be grounded on intensive observation of and active participation in the securities markets over a period of thirty-five years. During this span of experience many changes have developed in concepts of sound investment. Indeed, the standard works on financial practice current in 1914 would make strange reading today. There is a warning here that, just as the precepts crystallized out of experience before the First World War became largely obsolete in later years, so our present views, based on the experience of 1914–1948, may not stand the test of future developments.

That risk cannot be avoided. But by bearing it clearly in mind we may succeed in reducing it. Much of the investment wisdom of those distant days lay in easy generalizations or in prejudices and partialities that seemed justified by past history rather than by careful thought. For example, "A bond is a safer investment than a stock," "A railroad bond is safer than an industrial bond," "A first-mortgage bond is safer than an unsecured issue" and many other similar clichés are today either untrue or subject to so many exceptions as to be useless.

Our present ideas may escape a like fate if we keep before us the element of *quantity* or *measurement* as an inseparable part of every investment rule that relates to securities rather than to people. For example, in the year 1949 we make the strong and striking statement that the individual investor is foolish to buy high-grade bonds and preferred stocks, because he can do much better with United States Savings Bonds. That advice is good and useful in the light of the comparative yields obtaining in 1949, and it will be as long thereafter as these continue substantially unchanged. If in the future years it again becomes possible to buy high-grade corporate issues with an income yield appreciably better than that offered by United States Savings Bonds, then the change in conditions will warrant a change in policy.

Going back to the rules of 1914, we find that, though many are obsolete, others have retained their validity. Is there a clue that distinguishes one set from the other? We think there is. The rules that have failed relate mainly to types of securities; the ones that survive apply mainly to human nature and human conduct. The latter are familiar copybook maxims, but extremely useful ones. Take these three as illustrations:

(1) If you speculate you will (most probably) lose your money in the end.

(2) Buy when most people (including experts) are pessimistic; and sell when they are actively optimistic.

(3) Investigate, then invest.

What this means is that, though business conditions may change, corporations and securities may change, and financial institutions and regulations may change, human nature remains essentially the same. Thus the important and difficult part of sound investment, which hinges upon the investor's own temperament and attitude, is not much affected by the passing years.

Another encouraging element for the preceptor is found in the strong warp of continuity that seems to underlie the pattern of financial change. Important developments affecting broad groups of security values do not come suddenly or in one piece. An excellent example is found in the long-term course of the stock market; this has never moved to permanently higher levels without retreating at least once to former territory. Hence investors who sold out representative stocks at what seemed a high price as judged by past history have always had a chance to buy them back at substantially lower levels at some later time. This proved true in spite of the inflationary effects of the First World War and again of the Second World War, and it also was notoriously true after the extreme market advance of 1928–29.

Investors have lost a great deal of money in bonds that turned "sour"—especially in the field of railroads and real estate. Yet even here, if in the first instance the investments had been made with an eye to their ability to withstand adverse change and if their position had been reexamined at regular intervals, either there would have been no great shrinkage at all or most of the loss could have been shifted to less alert and intelligent investors. (The convenient impersonality of the securities markets relieves such a transfer of ethical taint.)

When we contemplate the immense financial changes of the past it seems at first that the main requisite for successful investment is foresight in anticipating new conditions. But that is a quality vouchsafed only to the few, and no one individual can rely with safety on the foresight of another. The everyday investor, we believe, can deal best with the factor of change by safeguarding himself against it—that is, by requiring his securities to meet specific standards of strength which will carry them through possible adversity.

Thus investment can be grounded largely on the time-tested principle of insurance—which combines an adequate safety factor in each individual commitment with a wide diversification of risk. Thus, also, successful investment may become substantially a matter of techniques and criteria that are learnable, rather than the product of unique and incommunicable mental powers.

Let us now define with more clarity those to whom this book is addressed and those to whom it is not.

It is not intended for speculators—persons whose chief objective is to anticipate stock-market movements, whether in the general list or in specific securities. But there are certain kinds of speculative purchases which are justified after an intelligent measurement of the gain and loss factors in the security itself; these operations fall within the scope of our study.

The present book is primarily directed toward two kinds of investors—

the "defensive" and the "enterprising." It should help the defensive investor to conserve his capital, avoid serious mistakes of commission, obtain a reasonable income return, and protect himself to some extent against inflation. In addition, it should help the enterprising investor to take advantage of the many and recurrent opportunities to purchase securities at well under their fair value, or intrinsic value, as determined by competent analysis.

To a third type of investor—one who places his main emphasis on looking forward to important changes in an industry or a company—this book may be of only limited use. He may, for example, be a buyer of air-transport stocks, because he believes their future is even more brilliant than the trend the current market level already reflects. For this class of investor the value of our book will lie more in its warnings against the pitfalls lurking in this favorite investment approach than in any positive technique that will help him along his path.

One thing badly needed by investors—and a quality they rarely seem to have—is a sense of financial history. In nine companies out of ten the factor of fluctuation has been a more dominant and important consideration in the matter of investment than has the factor of long-term growth or decline. Yet the market tends to greet each upsurge as if it were the beginning of an endless growth and each decline in earnings as if it presaged ultimate extinction. We shall trace typical patterns of earnings and price behavior for various kinds of securities over a period of twenty-five years or more.

Investments may be soundly made with either of two alternative intentions: (a) to carry them determinedly through the fluctuations that are reasonably to be expected in the future; or (b) to take advantage of such fluctuations by buying when confidence and prices are low and by selling when both are high. Neither policy can be followed with intelligence unless the investor, or his adviser, has a broad comprehension of the effects of the economic alternations of the past, and unless he takes them fully into account in planning to meet the future.

The art of investment has one characteristic which is not generally appreciated. A creditable, if unspectacular, result can be achieved by the lay investor with a minimum of effort and capability; but to improve this easily attainable standard requires much application and more than a trace of wisdom. If you merely try to bring *just a little* extra knowledge and cleverness to bear upon your investment program, instead of realizing a little better than normal results, you may well find that you have done worse.

Since anyone—by just buying and holding a representative list—can equal the performance of the market averages, it would seem a comparatively simple matter to "beat the averages"; but as a matter of fact the proportion of smart people who try this and fail is surprisingly large. Even many of the investment funds, with all their experienced personnel, have not performed as well over the years as has the general market. Allied to the foregoing is the record of the published stock-market predictions of the brokerage houses, for there is strong evidence that their calculated forecasts have been somewhat less reliable than the simple tossing of a coin.

In writing this book we have tried to keep this basic pitfall of investment in mind. We have emphasized the virtues of a simple portfolio policy—the purchase of United States Savings Bonds plus a diversified list of leading common stocks—which any investor can carry out with a little expert assistance. The adventure beyond this safe and sound territory has been presented as fraught with challenging difficulties, especially in the area of temperament. Before attempting such a venture the investor should feel sure of himself and of his advisers—particularly as to whether they have a clear concept of the differences between investment and speculation and between market price and underlying value.

A strong-minded approach to investment, firmly based on the margin-of-safety principle, can yield handsome rewards. But a decision to try for these emoluments rather than for the assured fruits of defensive investment should not be made without much thought.

A final retrospective thought. In 1900 none of us had any inkling of what the next fifty years were to do to the world. Now, in 1949, we have deeper apprehensions but no more knowledge of the future. Yet if we confine our attention to American investment experience there is some comfort to be gleaned from the last half-century. Through all its vicissitudes and casualties, as earth-shaking as they were unforeseen, it remained true that sound investment principles produced generally sound results. We must act on the assumption that they will continue to do so.

Note to the Reader: Specific securities are discussed in this book for purposes of illustration only, and without regard to any possible interest therein on the part of the author or of Graham-Newman Corporation.

THE
INTELLIGENT
INVESTOR

PART I

General Approaches
to Investment

1

◆◇◆◇◆

What the Intelligent
Investor Can Accomplish

THIS CHAPTER will outline the viewpoints that will be set forth in the remainder of the book. In particular, we wish to develop at the outset our concept of appropriate portfolio policy for the individual and non-professional investor.

First, however, the title of the book requires definition. What do we mean by "investor"? Here the term will be used in contradistinction to "speculator." In our textbook *Security Analysis* we attempted a precise formulation of the difference between the two as follows: "An investment operation is one which, upon thorough analysis, promises safety of principal and a satisfactory return. Operations not meeting these requirements are speculative."

This definition has some implications of a non-traditional sort. It permits us, for example, to include under the title of "investment" the purchase of non-dividend-paying stocks, or even defaulted bonds, if the buyer is sure that they will eventually work out at a value well above their cost to him. In such a case the "satisfactory return" would come in the form of a capital gain rather than of regular income.

Such an operation would be exceptional, however. For the most part we shall deal with the concept of investment in the familiar sense. Thus our typical investor will emphasize safety of principal; he will buy securities outright; he will usually hold these for a considerable period; he will be more interested in annual income than in *quick* price changes.

But in one respect the modern investor differs significantly from his predecessor of a generation ago. Intelligent investment today cannot ignore price changes entirely. The security owner must pay attention to them at least to the extent of endeavoring to protect himself against adverse changes of substantial size. It is also appropriate—for tax and other reasons—that an investor place his prime emphasis, if he chooses, upon an increase in principal value over a period of time rather than upon annual income; but this should not be understood to mean an emphasis upon a quick profit as in the ordinary trading operation. (Incidentally, even before the First World War there were bona fide investors who concentrated on low-yielding bank stocks and similar issues, expecting them to increase largely in value over the years.)

The word "intelligent" in our title will be used throughout the book in its common and dictionary sense as meaning "endowed with the capacity for knowledge and understanding." It will not be taken to mean "smart" or "shrewd," or gifted with unusual foresight or insight. Actually the intelligence here presupposed is a trait more of the character than of the brain. This is particularly true of that major class of investors whom we shall call the defensive—or the conservative, in the sense of conserving capital. Such an investor—whom we may envisage, typically, as a widow who must live on the money left her—will place her chief emphasis on the avoidance of any serious mistakes or losses. Her second aim will be freedom from effort, annoyance, and the need for making frequent decisions.

Yet nowadays a woman in this position, with substantial funds, will not be satisfied to leave her financial affairs entirely in the hands of others. She will want to understand—at least in general terms—what is being done with her money, and why. She will probably want to participate to the extent of approving the broad policy of investment, of keeping track of its results, and of judging independently whether or not she is being competently advised. This will be equally true of men who wish to throw the major burden of their investment operations on the shoulders of others. For all these defensive investors, intelligent action will mean largely the exercise of firmness in the application of relatively simple principles of sound procedure.

We shall deal also with a second category of investors, to be termed "aggressive" or "enterprising." These are not distinguished from the others by their willingness to take risks—for in that case they should be called speculators. Their determining trait is rather their willingness to devote time and care to the selection of sound and attractive investments. It is not suggested that the enterprising investor must be a fully-trained expert in the field. He may well derive his information and ideas from others, particularly from security analysts. But the decisions will be his own, and in the last reckoning he must rely upon his own understanding and judgment. The first rule of intelligent action by the enterprising investor must be that he will never embark on a security purchase which he does not fully comprehend and which he cannot justify by reference to the results of his personal study or experience.

Investment Before World War I and Today

It is interesting and enlightening to hark back for a moment to 1914, when the writer first came to Wall Street. At that time the idea of investment began and virtually ended in the field of corporation bonds, most of which were railroad issues. Preferred stocks—then as now—played a minor and not-too-well-understood role in investment portfolios. There was admittedly such a thing as investment in common stocks; but for the ordinary investor it was either taboo or practiced on a small scale and restricted to a limited number of choice issues.

The retired businessman or the widow, seeking to live on a capital fund of say $100,000 in those easy days, would be fitted out with an assortment of fifteen to twenty high-quality corporate bonds, yielding an annual return of between 4½ to 5½ per cent. He or she could then carry on in comparative luxury with the resulting $5,000 per year.

The investor's situation today is different in two important respects. In the first place, one cannot live in any kind of comfort on the income from a $100,000 fund invested in high-grade bonds. The situation was well presented in a little article in the *Commercial & Financial Chronicle*, July 10, 1947, which shows that you need a capital of no less than $500,000 as a *rentier* today to be as well off as you would have been with $100,000 in 1914. A comparison of the income and buying power in the two periods is shown in Table I. In the second place, the standard investment pattern in 1948 is—or should be—different from that of 1914. For the ordinary individual investor, corporation bonds no longer make sense; he can do much better with United States Savings Bonds. For reasons explained in a later chapter, it is now as unwise for the widow to put her money in corporate bonds as it would have been twenty years ago for her to buy tax-exempt municipals if she paid no income tax.

TABLE I. INCOME AND BUYING POWER: 1913 VS. 1947

	1913	1947
Total Investment	$100,000	$500,000
Rate of Return	5%	2¾%
Gross Income	$5,000	$13,750
Income Tax (3 dependents)	none	$3,140
Net Income	$5,000	$10,610
Buying Power of Dollar (1913 base)	100%	45%
Buying Power of Income	$5,000	$4,775

"The moral to be drawn from the above situation is that unless you have more than half a million dollars today, you had better forget about retiring and keep on working."

To the extent that United States Savings Bonds may now replace corporate issues in the investor's portfolio, the problems of investment have become simplified. In fact they have disappeared, since a United States Savings Bond program presents neither difficulties nor financial risks. By contrast, most of the carefully selected corporate-bond lists of a generation ago developed more than one headache for the owner as new conditions arose.

The other side of the coin shows the advent of common stocks as an integral and important part of a sound investment program. The proportion of the total funds to be placed in common stocks will now range ordinarily from, say, 20 per cent to as high as 50 per cent. There are several reasons for this revolutionary change from former conservative practice. The least valid excuse is the desire to increase the present diminished yield from bonds. If common stocks as a whole carry the increased risks of loss of principal that are assumed to go with high yields—and they certainly do so in some cases and at some times—then the larger income return would be deceptive and the venture into common stocks basically unsound. A number of investors have been attracted to the common-stock field by tax considerations. Profits made on the sale of securities held for more than six months are taxed at one-half, or less, of the rate applicable to dividends and interest. It is possible to select common stocks in such a manner as to emphasize the possibilities of capital gains at the expense of current income. Here, of course, there is the real danger that paying attention to appreciation of principal may lead the investor into speculative attitudes and operations, with resultant financial damage. Obviously there can be no real tax advantage unless the ownership of common stocks results in an over-all profit.

A more solid support can be found for the inclusion of common stocks by reference to long-term investment experience rather than to the mere desire for higher income or for tax savings. The history of the past fifty years, and longer, indicates that a diversified holding of representative common stocks will prove more profitable over a stretch of years than a bond portfolio, with one important proviso—that the shares must be purchased at reasonable market levels, that is, levels that are reasonable in the light of fairly well-defined standards derived from past experience.

The chief and compelling reason that has turned the minds of conservative investors in recent years toward common stocks has been a new factor—the fear of inflation. It is generally agreed that the rise of 50 per cent in the general price level between 1913 and the 1920's was the direct result of the deficit financing of the First World War. With an enormously greater increase in our government debt and in our "fiat wealth" resulting from the Second World War—plus the preceding deficits of the 1930's—the possibility, if not the probability, of a still larger permanent rise in the price level has been acknowledged by most thoughtful investors. Although common stocks are by no means a perfect protection or hedge against inflationary developments, they are certain to do more for the investor in that direction than bonds or money in the bank—which will do nothing at all. This reasoning supplies a strong logical basis for the inclusion of a fair-sized proportion of common stocks in any substantial investment portfolio. (The logic is less compelling if the investor has other types of assets—for example, his own business, or commercial real-estate holdings—which themselves are partial inflation hedges.)

The development of the common-stock principle in conservative invest-ment may best be traced in the history of the endowment funds of the large universities. Originally many of these were restricted by law or tradition to the purchase of bonds and real estate. In the 1930's Stanford University pe-titioned the court for permission to add common stocks to its portfolio as a partial safeguard against inflation; Herbert Hoover, as a university trustee, appeared in support of this application. A recent study by Scudder, Stevens & Clark, a well-known firm of investment counselors, reveals that over one-third of the endowment funds of leading universities are now held in com-mon stocks.

Nevertheless, just as the change-over from corporate bonds into United States Savings Bonds greatly simplifies the problems of the investor, so the decision to devote part of his funds to common stocks adds serious complica-tions and hazards. Common stocks can be dynamite. In theory it is not too difficult to invest in common stocks soundly, conservatively, and with a min-imum of excitement and regrets. In practice, however, the common-stock in-vestor finds himself beset with confusions and temptation—both external and internal. The French say it is only a step from the sublime to the ridicu-lous. So too it seems only a step from common-stock investment to common-stock speculation. A great deal of the language and literature of Wall Street has the effect, if not the design, of breaking down the fine but essential dis-tinction between the investment and the speculative approach. On the other side of the picture—in the investor's own mind and temperament—there is likely to be an urge, frequently unconscious, toward speculation, toward making money quickly and excitedly, toward participating in the moods and aberrations of the crowd.

Let us repeat, therefore, that the genuine investor in common stocks does not need a great equipment of brains and knowledge, but he does need some unusual qualities of character.

Results to Be Expected by the Defensive Investor

We have already defined the defensive investor as one interested chiefly in safety plus freedom from bother. Let us assume that this person is pre-pared to follow our prescription and to divide his portfolio between United States Savings Bonds and a diversified list of leading common stocks. A suitable list of this kind can be readily prepared by any competent security analyst or investment adviser. Actually, the choice of high-grade common stocks today is not vastly different from the process of selecting high-grade corporate bonds a generation ago—except for one additional and necessary caution of a highly important character. The buyer of common stocks must assure himself that he is not making his purchases at a time when the general market level is a definitely high one, as judged by established standards of common-stock values.

This investor can obtain a 2.90 per cent return on his Series E Savings Bonds, of which enough may be purchased to fill the needs of the great majority of our readers. If the funds available are unusually large, it will be necessary to buy Series G Savings Bonds, yielding 2.50 per cent. On these investments there is not only complete freedom from risk of eventual loss but also the privilege—potentially of great value—of turning back the bonds for cash at any time, with an appropriate downward adjustment of the income yield to correspond to the shorter period of investment.

The income return on United States Savings Bonds is at least as good as that obtainable from corporate bonds of first quality ("AAA" issues). In other respects—inherent safety, protection against price decline, and so forth—the government issues are clearly superior. It follows that the investor should limit his bond-type investment to United States Savings Bonds exclusively, until a substantially higher yield can be obtained from the best corporates. It is even less sensible to attempt to "sweeten the yield" by buying bonds or preferreds of second quality. In this area the risk of various sorts far outweigh the small gains in income.

The dividend return on leading common stocks cannot be forecast as precisely as that on United States Savings Bonds. In the year 1949 it is running over 5 per cent, and for the past ten years it has averaged at least 4½ per cent on the market price. To the annual income received the holder has the right to add some assumed increment for the value of the undistributed and reinvested profits. This means that, unless unexpectedly adverse conditions develop in the future, there should be a steady increase in the underlying *value* of a representative common-stock list, and this should reflect itself in a corresponding increase in the *average* or "normal" market price. (This fact, plus the impact of inflationary influences, is the reason why the various charts of stock prices going back as far as the Civil War show a definite upward trend in the central value.)

If we assume that the defensive investor places as much as 40 per cent of his portfolio in common stocks, with the rest in Series E bonds, his indicated income return will be about 3.50 per cent. He should also have a sufficient equity in undistributed earnings to bring his true result up to at least 4 per cent. This return is far from being a brilliant achievement, but it is obtainable with only a slight expenditure of intelligent effort. It carries with it a modicum of protection against any loss of purchasing power caused by extreme inflation, and there is a fair chance that even without further inflation the over-all return from the stock component may turn out better than our estimate. Thus the result promised to the defensive investor is by no means unsatisfactory.

At this point let us mention briefly three supplementary concepts or practices for the defensive investor. The first is the purchase of shares of the leading investment funds as an alternative to creating his own common-stock portfolio. (We shall use the term "investment fund" rather than the now inaccurate "investment trust" or its official but ambiguous successor, "investment company.") Alternatively, he may utilize one of the "common trust funds," or "commingled funds," now operated by trust companies and banks in many states. This will give him professional administration of his investment program along standard lines. The second is the device of "dollar averaging," which means simply that the investor invests in common stocks the same number of dollars each month or quarter. By this means he buys more shares in low markets than in high markets and thus is likely to end up with a satisfactory average price for all his holdings. The third is known as "formula timing." This is a positive effort to take advantage of the broad swings of the market by selling out, on some gradual and automatic basis, as the market advances and repurchasing as it declines. All these ideas have merit for even the defensive investor, and they will be discussed more amply in later chapters.

Tax-Exempt Bonds: State and Municipal

It is logical for a wealthy investor to consider the purchase of state and municipal bonds in preference to United States government securities, because the former are tax-free and the latter are not. The average yield of standard municipal obligations in early 1949 was about 2.25 per cent. The value of their tax-exemption feature varies with the income of the purchaser. For a married couple with about $20,000 of taxable income the net yield on a 2.25 per cent municipal issue is currently about the same as from the taxable 2.90 per cent on Series E Savings Bonds. (For a single person the corresponding income figure is only $9,000.) As the income advances above these levels the tax-free bonds show a greater advantage in their net yield.

The selection of state and municipal securities requires expert guidance. We shall not treat the subject in this book, because it would be of interest to only a small proportion of investors. Those with large incomes are advised to explore the matter fully in consultation with one or more leading investment firms. We ask such readers to bear in mind that our future references to a United States government bond program should be considered as including tax-free bonds for them to whatever extent their income and tax position will warrant. This statement applies to both defensive and aggressive investors.

A summary of the important tax rules relating to investment income and security transactions appears at the end of this chapter.

Results to Be Expected by the Aggressive Investor

Our enterprising security buyer, of course, will desire and expect to attain better over-all results than his defensive or passive companion. But first he must make sure that his results will not be worse. It is no difficult trick to bring a great deal of energy, study, and native ability into Wall Street and to end up with losses instead of profits. These virtues, if channeled in the wrong directions, become indistinguishable from handicaps. Thus it is most essential that the enterprising investor start with a clear conception as to which courses of action offer reasonable chances of success and which do not.

We may list five standard methods by which more than ordinary profits may conceivably be made by the aggressive investor:

1. General Trading—that is, anticipating or participating in the moves of the market as a whole, as reflected in the familiar "averages."
2. Selective Trading—that is, picking out issues which, over a period of a year or less, will do better in the market than the average stock.

3. Buying Cheap and Selling Dear—that is, coming into the market when prices and sentiment are depressed and selling out when both are exalted.

4. Long-Pull Selection—that is, picking out companies which will prosper over the years far more than the average enterprise. (These are often referred to as "growth stocks.")

5. Bargain Purchases—that is, selecting issues which are selling considerably below their true value, as measured by reasonably dependable techniques.

At the risk of alienating many of our readers, let us say categorically that we do not consider that either general trading or selective trading has any place in investment practice. Both of them are essentially speculative in character, because they depend for success not only on the ability to foretell specifically what is going to happen but on the ability also to do this more cleverly than a host of competitors in the field. Investment also deals with the future and depends on future developments for its vindication. But the term is meaningless unless it implies that the investor seeks to obtain full present value for his money, that he judges this value in the light of the past record and experience, and that he deals with the future more as a hazard to be guarded against than as a source of profit through prophecy.

Investment requires and presupposes a margin of safety to protect against adverse developments. In market trading, as in most other forms of speculation, there is no real margin for error; you are either right or wrong, and if wrong you lose money. Consequently, even if we believed that the ordinary intelligent reader could learn to make money by trading in the market, we should send him elsewhere for his instruction. But everybody knows that most people who trade in the market lose money at it in the end. The people who persist in trying it are either (a) unintelligent, or (b) willing to lose money for the fun of the game, or (c) gifted with some uncommon and incommunicable talent. In any case they are not investors.

The third form of endeavor—the famous buy-cheap-sell-dear principle commonly ascribed to the original Rothschild—may seem at first blush to be only a special case of trading in the market. Actually it differs in a fundamental sense from what we have just been discussing, because this approach lays its first emphasis on value received rather than on the expected next movement of the market. The buyer at low market levels can be quite satisfied with his results, particularly the earnings and dividends on his holdings, even if prices refuse to advance. Of course the latter has not been true in the past; buyers in depressed markets have invariably been able to sell out later at a handsome profit.

Thus a program of waiting for buying opportunities until the price level is clearly a low one properly belongs under the title of investment. The difficulty with it lies in the irregular nature of the market's wider fluctuations, especially those of the past twenty-five years, and in the consequent risk of miscalculation if the investor seeks to follow it in the future. Hence our verdict on this technique must be inconclusive. Promising though it appears, we are by no means sure that it will prove successful, both financially and psychologically, for the average intelligent investor. (The various formula-timing plans are, at bottom, compromise applications of the buy-low-sell-high principle, devised to secure some of its advantages without running its inherent risk of completely "missing the market.")

Whether the investor should attempt to buy low and sell high, or whether he should be content to hold sound securities through thick and thin—subject only to periodic examination of their intrinsic merits—is one of the several choices of policy which the individual must make for himself. Here temperament and personal situation may well be the determining factors. A person close to business affairs, who is in the habit of forming judgments as to the economic outlook and of acting on them, will be inclined naturally to make similar judgments about the general level of stock prices. It would be logical for such investors to be attracted to the buy-low-sell-high technique. But professional men and wealthy people not active in business can more easily immunize their thinking from the influence of year-to-year fluctuations. For this group the more attractive choice may be the simpler one of buying carefully when funds are available and laying the chief stress on the income return over the years.

More will be said about the investor and market movements in the next chapter.

With respect to our fourth method, it is appropriate for investors to select their securities—especially common stocks—with an eye to their long-term prospects. A well-chosen company can triple its earnings and quadruple the price of its stock over a period of years while badly-chosen ones are losing a good part of their value. Most enterprising investors, therefore, will be inclined to view as the chief role for their intelligence and judgment the correct appraisal of the future possibilities of the many companies they examine. How well can this be done?

When it is done well, the success is not due to following any simple, foolproof rules or even any complicated but well-defined techniques. The long-term future of a company is at best "an educated guess." Some of the best-educated guesses, derived from the most painstaking research, have turned out to be abysmally wrong. Furthermore, the chief obstacle to success lies in the stubborn fact that if the favorable prospects of a concern are clearly apparent they are almost always reflected already—and often overdiscounted—in the current price of the stock. Buying such an issue is like betting on a topheavy favorite in a horse race. The chances may be on your side, but the real odds are against you. You may take it as an axiom that you cannot profit in Wall Street by continuously doing the obvious or the popular thing.

Conversely, by following your independent judgment, in which the majority does not concur, you do have a chance to gain handsomely—provided you are right. But this ability to judge rightly about future prospects, when most others are judging wrongly, is necessarily granted to few. Such foresight cannot properly be regarded as a normal attribute of intelligent investment.

Thus, even in this suitable area for the exercise of investment skill, we are inclined to emphasize the dangers rather more than the possibilities. Select stocks with the best prospects, if you wish, but take care that you are not paying too much for the promise of the future. In sum, the balance in favor of the "growth stock" philosophy may not be so clear-cut as it is made out to be in the current literature of finance. In this field there are chances of loss as well as good possibilities of profit.

Our final category of opportunities for enterprising investment lies in the field of undervalued or "bargain" issues. These are the direct antitheses of growth stocks. If the latter may often sell too high because they are too popular, may not non-growth stocks often sell too low because they are too unpopular? We believe the answer to this question is definitely "yes." A sound analogy may be drawn between a depressed general market and a stock that is individually unpopular. Just as declines of the whole market tend to go too far because public sentiment is generally pessimistic, so the price of many single issues may fall unduly low because their future is considered to be relatively unpromising. In both cases unfavorable circumstances are present—as actual developments, or perhaps only as prospects—and in both cases the response may be excessive and thus create a genuine opportunity for the intelligent and courageous investor. In the depths of a depressed or "bear" market the average person can see no ray of light ahead and can think only in terms of worse to come. So too, when an individual company or industry begins to lose ground in the economy, Wall Street is quick to assume that its future is entirely hopeless and it should be avoided at any price. The two types of reasoning are similar, and equally fallacious.

If buying individual securities that appear undervalued is a sound procedure, it has an important advantage over buying solely at depressed levels of the general market. The former type of opportunity can be found at all periods in the market, whereas the latter occurs at widely separated intervals. Our experience of many years leads us to affirm that the field of undervalued securities is in fact a promising one for the enterprising investor.

Since the selection of these issues naturally requires more than a little skill and good judgment, it is no business for the tyro or the superficial practitioner. It is desirable and perhaps necessary that such transactions be passed upon by a competent security analyst who is free from some of the besetting prejudices of his guild. But their distinctive feature, as we see it, is this: Once a competent analysis has been made and the salient facts presented, the intelligent investor will have the material needed to satisfy his own mind that the commitment is sound and attractive. He will not have to subordinate his own judgment to that of his advisers—which is often required of him in other types of security operations.

The field of undervalued securities may well include corporate bonds and preferred stocks as well as common stocks. In fact, our reasoning leads us to the rather extreme conclusion that the *only* kinds of corporate bonds and preferreds suitable for the investor under present conditions are those which are depressed in price to the point of being definitely undervalued. For, as already pointed out, neither first-grade senior issues nor ordinary types of second-grade issues are as attractive as are United States Savings Bonds. The tendency of second-grade issues to fall to excessively low levels at times is both a reason to avoid them at their ordinary prices and an indication that they *sometimes* present remarkably attractive buying opportunities.

For the sake of completeness, let us mention finally that sometimes an unusually favorable purchase may be made in a convertible bond or a preferred stock, even though it sells at a full price—that is, at about par. We must add that convertible issues do not work out nearly so well in practice as theoretically they should.

This quick survey of the various kinds of activity open to the aggressive investor has been at least as full of warnings as of positive suggestions. The apparently simple job of "doing somewhat better than the averages" is in fact both difficult and not devoid of risk. Let us hazard a guess, however, as to what may be accomplished by an alert student of the investment art, who (a) is of average intelligence, (b) proceeds on sound principles, and (c) is advised by a competent security analyst, of whom he asks the right questions. With this equipment we think he should be able to double the average annual return obtained by his easy-going friend, the passive or defensive investor.

"Yes" and "No" Table for the Investor

It may be useful at this point to summarize in tabular form the kinds of investments which we have found to be suitable for our two classes of investor.

A. The defensive investor will buy:

1. United States Savings Bonds (and/or tax-exempt securities)
2. A diversified list of leading common stocks, at prices that seem reasonable in the light of past market experience—or
2a. Shares of leading investment funds

B. The enterprising investor will buy:

1, 2, 2a—as above

3. Growth stocks, but with caution
4. Also, or alternatively, representative common stocks when the general market is historically low
5. Secondary common stocks, corporate bonds, and preferred stocks, at bargain levels
6. Some exceptional convertible issues, even at full prices

If we accept our reasoning with respect to what today's intelligent individual investor will buy, we are led to several wide and important categories of securities which he will not buy. These are shown as follows:

1. Investment-grade corporate bonds and preferred stocks as long as current yield differentials continue; or foreign government issues at full prices

2. Leading common stocks when the market is at high levels as judged by past experience

3. Secondary common stocks, except at temptingly low prices

4. As a corollary of 3, he will not buy new issues of common stocks, with infrequent exceptions. (This does not refer to the exercise of subscription rights on leading issues.)

The general caveat against buying corporate bonds and preferreds and most new common issues undoubtedly has some disconcerting implications. It would seem to call into question the established economic processes by which the businesses of the country come into our capital market for the funds they need. Our answer is simply that intelligent investors should not support new security financing except on terms which offer them proportionately as attractive a combination of income and safety as is obtainable by the purchase of United States Savings Bonds plus common stocks of leading corporations at normal market prices.

The Investor as Security Owner

There is another field of accomplishment for the intelligent investor—and that is for him to act in an alert and businesslike fashion *after* he has become a security owner. This aspect has been much neglected; yet it is of major importance, especially when we look at investors as a class rather than singly. For let us assume that all, or nearly all, investors (having read and pondered this volume) are now ready to act intelligently. At that time all the real money in investment will have to be made—as most of it has been in the past—not out of buying and selling but out of owning and holding securities, receiving interest and dividends thereon, and benefiting from their long-term increases in value. There cannot be real opportunities for the trader or bargain hunter when everyone is equally sound and sensible in his attitude toward securities.

Investors as a *whole* are not and cannot be dealers or traders in securities.

They are owners of the country's larger enterprises. They make money not out of each other but out of these businesses. Hence their major energies and wisdom as investors should—in theory at least—be directed toward assuring themselves of the best operating results from their corporations. This in turn means assuring themselves of fully honest and competent managements.

Nothing in finance is more fatuous and harmful, in our opinion, than the firmly established attitude of common stock investors and their Wall Street advisers regarding questions of corporate management. That attitude is summed up in the phrase: "If you don't like the management, sell your stock." Obviously such action does nothing at all to improve bad management; it only puts down the price of the stock and shifts the ownership to someone else. Because of that ingrained view, investors as a whole have done nothing to improve managements that require correction. Such improvement as does occur from time to time comes about for special reasons which reflect no credit upon the intelligence of the public owners—who seem to have abdicated all claim to control over the paid superintendents of their property.

Viewed in a broader sense, the best opportunity for demonstrating investor intelligence is in the field of stockholder-management relationships; for here investors can act as a class and not as individuals. We shall devote some final chapters to that novel but important branch of the science of investment.

IMPORTANT RULES RE TAXABILITY OF INVESTMENT INCOME AND SECURITY TRANSACTIONS (1948 Law)

Rule 1—Interest and Dividends

Interest and dividends are taxable as ordinary income, except income received from state, municipal, and similar obligations, which are tax-free. (There are also certain limited exemptions applicable to United States Government securities.)

Rule 2—Capital Gains

Profits on security sales are taxable as ordinary income if the security was held less than six months ("short term"). If held longer ("long term") the profits are taken into account at 50 per cent and are subject to a maximum tax of 25 per cent of the full amount.

Rule 3—Capital Losses (losses on security sales)

(a) Long-term losses are accounted for at 50 per cent.

(b) A loss in any year can be offset against capital gains in the same year.

(c) A net capital loss (the amount exceeding capital gains) is deductible from ordinary income to a maximum of $1,000 in the current year and in each of the next five years. Alternatively, unused losses may be applied at any time to offset capital gains.

Note re "Regulated Investment Companies"

Most investment funds ("investment companies") take advantage of special provisions of the tax law, by complying with which they are taxed substantially as partnerships. Thus if they make long-term security profits they can distribute these as "capital-gain dividends," which are reported by their stockholders in the same way as long-term gains. These carry a lower tax rate than ordinary dividends.

11

—◆◇◆—

The Investor and
Stock-Market
Fluctuations

THIS CHAPTER will be devoted to an effort to delineate the proper attitude which investors should take in the matter of price fluctuations in common stocks. It is becoming increasingly difficult to attain that peculiar combination of alertness and detachment which characterizes the successful investor as distinguished from the speculator. Intelligent investment is more a matter of mental approach than it is of technique. A sound mental approach toward stock fluctuations is the touchstone of all successful investment under present-day conditions.

If the investor follows the pattern of conduct suggested in our first chapter, his portfolio will consist of (a) United States Savings Bonds, which have no price fluctuations, and (b) common stocks, which are likely to fluctuate widely in their market price.

Such changes in quoted prices may be significant to the investor in two possible directions:

(A) As a measure of the success of his investment program.

(B) As a guide to the selection of his securities and the timing of his transactions.

These two aspects are interrelated, but we shall try to separate them for purposes of orderly discussion.

(A) Price Changes as Measuring Investment Results

Does the investor become richer or poorer as his stocks advance and decline in the market? In the old days the answer was emphatically "No." Only speculators and traders were concerned by the ups and downs of prices. The bona fide investor, who bought for income plus an incidental long-term increase in value, was supposed to be immune to the stock ticker and the market reports. Perhaps this was never entirely true, but it was approximately possible because of the nature of investment-grade common stocks before the First World War. Their dividends were well maintained even in depression years, their prices did not soar to absurd heights in bull markets, and consequently they did not fall into the abyss even in panic times. Thus it was possible for the "permanent holder" of Pennsylvania Railroad or General Electric or American Telephone & Telegraph stocks to ignore their price fluctuations as irrelevant to his own purposes and philosophy.

Nowadays the situation is different. No one believes seriously that the common-stock investor can remain indifferent to price fluctuations. The reason for this about-face is found in a change in the stock market itself. Before the First World War common stocks could be divided into a small number of investment issues and a much larger number of speculative issues. The price movements of the investment issues were relatively narrow, even when the market as a whole was fluctuating widely. Thus the holder of these quality stocks was under no real psychological pressure to pay attention to the market.

Beginning with the bull market of the 1920's this condition has changed. Because the high-grade issues have risen to excessive heights in periods of speculative enthusiasm, they have tended to swing far downward in the ensuing bear markets. The difference between the two periods is illustrated in Table II, which gives the range of price fluctuations of the Dow-Jones Railroad Stock Average and of Pennsylvania Railroad stock in the pre-1914 period and in later market swings. (In the earlier years most of the investment-grade common stocks were found among the railroads.) We add the figures for General Electric, which in the earlier years had somewhat wider fluctuations than the leading rails.

Note that in the twelve months from March, 1937, to March, 1938—a period of mere "recession"—the price variations in these railroad stocks were far wider than in the entire fourteen years 1901–14, which included the famous panic of 1907. (The prices of General Electric in 1929–47 should be multiplied by about 35 for comparison with those of 1901–14.)

Confronted with price variations of the kind experienced since 1929, it is impossible for the modern investor to ignore these phenomena. Clearly the success of his investment program in common stocks must depend in great part on what happens ultimately to their prices. But how far must he commit himself to concern with the market's conduct? By what market tests should he consider that he has been successful or not? Certainly not by short-term or minor fluctuations, for this attitude would make him indistinguishable from the stock trader.

TABLE II

| | RANGE OF PRICES | | | | | |
| | Dow-Jones R.R Average | | Pennsylvania R.R. Common | | General Electric | |
Period	High	Low	High	Low	High	Low
1901–14	129.9	81.4	85.5	52	242	90
1929–32	189.1	13.2	110.0	6.5	110	8½
1937–38	64.6	19.0	50.3	14.1	65	27
1946–47	68.3	41.2	47.5	15.5	52	32

The current practice among experienced investors leans toward using a combination of dividend return and market-price change over a suitable period of time as the measure of investment success. These calculations are made preferably between dates, several years apart, on which the general market level has not changed appreciably. Let us apply this test to a few characteristic investment issues and groups, for an illustrative period.

The figures in Table III argue eloquently that Abbott Laboratories was a successful investment over the eleven-year period, whereas Pennsylvania

Railroad was an unsuccessful one. The use of "neutral" terminal dates and the inclusion of the dividend income make this method a highly satisfactory one for testing investment results. It may be employed to measure the over-all performance of an investor's portfolio, or to compare one investment fund with another, or to assess the merits of alternative principles of investment—for example, buying "growth stocks" versus buying undervalued securities—as we shall do in a later chapter. Table IV presents an example of the use of this technique to compare the management results of three investment funds.

TABLE III. Method of Calculating Results from an Investment

EXAMPLES BASED ON THE ELEVEN-YEAR PERIOD—
DECEMBER, 1936, TO DECEMBER, 1947

Market Price:	Dow-Jones Industrial Average	Standard-Poor's 90 Stocks	U.S. Steel	Penna. R.R.	Abbott Lab.
Dec. 31, 1947	177.7	121.5	78.5	18.5	179.0 (adj.)
Dec. 31, 1936	179.7	136.4	78.5	40.5	51.0
Change in Price	—2.2	—14.9	....	—22.0	128.0
Dividends Received	77.2	53.7	33.0	18.3	30.7
Total Gain, 11 years	75.0	38.8	33.0	—3.7	158.7
Per Cent Gain	41.7%	28.5%	42.1%	def.	311.2%
Per Cent Gain per year	3.8%	2.6%	3.8%	def.	28.3%

When the general market declines or advances substantially, nearly all investors will have somewhat similar changes in their portfolio values. We do not believe that the investor should pay serious attention to such price developments unless they fit into a previously established program of buying at low levels and selling at high levels. He is neither a smart investor nor a richer one when he buys in an advancing market and the market continues to rise. That is true even when he cashes in a goodly profit, unless either (a) he is definitely through with buying stocks—an unlikely story—or

(b) he is determined to reinvest only at considerably lower levels. In a continuous program no market profit is fully realized until the later reinvestment has actually taken place, and the true measure of the trading profit is the difference between the previous selling level and the new buying level.

TABLE IV. METHOD OF CALCULATING PERFORMANCE OF INVESTMENT FUNDS

EXAMPLES BASED ON THE ELEVEN-YEAR PERIOD—
DECEMBER, 1936, TO DECEMBER, 1947

	Lehman Corp.	Niagara Share Corp.	Overseas Securities Co.
Net Asset Value per Share:			
December 31, 1947	$49.03	$16.70	$11.03
December 31, 1936	45.73	22.59	15.65
Change in Value	3.30	−5.89	−4.62
Dividends Paid	25.72	3.10	16.90
Total Gain, 11 Years	$30.02	def.—$2.79	$11.28
Per Cent Gain	61.2%	def.—12.3%	102.3%
Per Cent Gain per Year	5.6%	def.—1.1%	9.1%

Let us repeat, however, that investment success may be judged by a long-term or secular rise in market price, without the necessity of sale. The proof of that achievement lies in the price advances made between successive points of equality in the general market level. In most cases this favorable price performance will be accompanied by a well-defined improvement in the average earnings, in the dividend, and the balance-sheet position. Thus in the long run the market test and the ordinary business test of a successful equity commitment tend to be largely identical.

We have the converse situation in the case of market declines and unsuccessful stock investments. There is a vital difference here between temporary and permanent influences. A price decline is of no real importance to the bona fide investor unless it is either very substantial—say, more than a third from cost—or unless it reflects a known deterioration of consequence in the company's position. In a well-defined bear market many sound common stocks sell temporarily at extraordinarily low prices. It is possible that the investor may then have a paper loss of fully 50 per cent on some of his holdings, without any convincing indication that the underlying values have been permanently affected. Let us illustrate this point with the case of Great Atlantic & Pacific Tea Company common stock in 1937–38.

A. & P. shares were introduced to trading on the New York Curb in 1929 and sold as high as 494. By 1932 they had declined to 104, although the company's earnings were nearly as large in that generally catastrophic year as previously. In 1936 the range was between 111 and 131. In the business recession and bear market of 1938 the shares fell to a new low of 36.

That price was extraordinary. It meant that the preferred and common were together selling for $126 million, although the company had just reported that it held $85 million in cash alone and a working capital (or net current assets) of $134 million. A. & P. was the largest retail enterprise in America, if not in the world, with an uninterrupted record of large earnings for many years. Yet in 1938 this outstanding business was considered in Wall Street to be worth less than its current assets alone—which means less as a going concern than if it were liquidated. Why? First, because there were threats of special taxes on chain stores; second, because net profits had fallen off in the previous year; and, third, because the general market was depressed. The first of these reasons was an exaggerated and eventually groundless fear; the other two were typical of temporary influences.

Let us assume that the investor had bought A. & P. common in 1937 at, say, twelve times its five-year average earnings, or about 80. We are far from asserting that the decline to 36 was of no importance to him. He would have been well advised to scrutinize the picture with some care, to see whether he had made any miscalculations. But if the results of his study were reassuring—as they should have been—he was entitled then to disregard the market decline as a temporary vagary of finance, unless he had the funds and the courage to take advantage of it by buying more on the bargain basis offered.

(B) Market Fluctuations as a Guide to Investment Decisions

Since common stocks, even of investment grade, are subject to recurrent and wide fluctuations in their prices, the intelligent investor should be interested in the possibilities of profiting from these pendulum swings. There are two possible ways by which he may try to do this: the way of *timing* and the way of *pricing*. By timing we mean the endeavor to anticipate the action of the stock market—to buy or hold when the future course is deemed to be upward, to sell or refrain from buying when the course is downward. By pricing we mean the endeavor to buy stocks when they are quoted below their fair value and to sell them when they rise above such value. A less ambitious form of pricing is the simple effort to make sure that when you buy you do not pay too much for your stocks. This may suffice for the defensive investor, whose emphasis is on long-pull holding; but as such it represents an essential minimum of attention to market levels.

We are convinced that the intelligent investor can derive satisfactory results from *pricing* of either type. We are equally sure that if he places his emphasis on *timing*, in the sense of forecasting, he will end up as a speculator and with a speculator's financial results. This distinction may seem rather tenuous to the layman, and it is not commonly accepted in Wall Street. Something of a controversy has raged in the financial press during recent years over the validity of market forecasting on the one hand and the concept of "intrinsic value" on the other. As a matter of business practice, or perhaps of thorough-going conviction, the stock brokers and the investment services seem wedded to the principle that both investors and speculators in common stocks should devote careful attention to market forecasts.

The farther one gets from Wall Street the more scepticism one will find, we believe, as to the pretensions of stock-market forecasting or timing. The investor can scarcely take seriously the innumerable predictions which appear almost daily and are his for the asking. Yet in many cases he pays attention to them and even acts upon them. Why? Because he has been persuaded that it is important for him to form some opinion of the future course of the stock market, and because he feels that the brokerage or service forecast is at least more dependable than his own.

This attitude will bring the typical investor nothing but regrets. Without realizing it, he is likely to find himself transformed into a market trader. During a sustained bull movement, when it is easy to make money by simply swimming with the speculative tide, he will gradually lose interest in the quality and the value of the securities he is buying and become more and more engrossed in the fascinating game of beating the market. But "beating the market" really means beating himself—for he and his fellows constitute the market. Thus he begins by studying market movements as a "common-sense investment precaution" or a "desirable supplement to his study of security values"; he ends as a stock-market speculator, indistinguishable from all the rest.

We lack space here to discuss in detail the pros and cons of market forecasting. A great deal of brain power goes into this field, and undoubtedly *some people* can make money by being good stock-market analysts. But it is absurd to think that the *general public* can ever make money out of market forecasts. For who will buy when the general public, at a given signal, rushes to sell out at a profit? If you, the reader, expect to get rich over the years by following some system or leadership in market forecasting, you must be expecting (a) to try to do what countless others are aiming at and (b) to be able to do it better than your numerous competitors in the market. There is no basis either in logic or in experience for assuming that any typical or average investor can anticipate market movements more successfully than the general public, of which he is himself a part.

There is one aspect of the "timing" philosophy which has escaped everyone's notice. Timing is of great psychological importance to the speculator because he wants to make his profit in a hurry. The idea of waiting a year before his stock moves up is repugnant to him. But a waiting period, as such, is of no consequence to the investor. What advantage is there to him in having his money uninvested until he receives some (presumably) trustworthy signal that the time has come to buy? He enjoys an advantage only if by waiting he succeeds in buying later at a sufficiently *lower price* to offset his loss of dividend income. What this means is that timing is of no real value to the investor unless it coincides with pricing—that is, unless it enables him to repurchase his shares at substantially under his previous selling price.

TABLE V. Indicated Results from Dow Theory Applied to the Dow-Jones Industrial Average 1897–1948

PERIOD I 1897–1937

Buy Points		Sell Points		Diff. between Sell Point and:	
				(a) Previous Buy	(b) Next Buy
Date	Price Level	Date	Price Level	Point	Point
6/28/97	44.6	12/16/99	63.8	19.2	4.4
10/20/00	59.4	6/1/03	59.6	.2	8.2
7/12/04	51.4	4/26/03	92.4	41.0	22.4
4/24/08	70.0	5/3/10	84.7	14.7	2.8
10/10/10	81.9	1/14/13	85.0	3.0	20.0
4/9/15	65.0	8/28/17	86.1	21.1	3.9
5/13/18	82.2	2/3/20	100.0	17.8	16.3
2/6/22	83.7	6/20/23	90.8	7.1	−3.0
12/7/23	93.8	10/23/29	305.9	212.1	221.6
5/24/33	84.3	9/7/37	164.4	80.1	37.0

PERIOD II 1938–1948

Date	Price Level	Date	Price Level	Point	Point
6/23/38	127.4	3/31/39	131.8	4.4	−10.8
7/17/39	142.6	1/13/40	145.2	2.6	−.7
6/15/44	145.9	9/3/46	178.7	32.8	−9.9
5/14/48	188.6	. . . .	. . . .	. . . .	. . . .

Note: The buying and selling points have been taken from Barbour's Dow Theory Service, except the 5/14/48 buying point. Commissions and other similar factors are not allowed for.

In this respect the famous Dow Theory for timing purchases and sales has had an unusual history. Briefly, this technique takes its signal to buy from a special kind of "break-through" of the stock averages on the up side, and its selling signal from a similar break-through on the down side. The calculated—not necessarily actual—results of using this method show an unbroken series of profits in operations from 1897 to 1946. On the basis of this presentation the practical value of the Dow Theory would appear firmly established; the doubt, if any, would apply to the dependability of this published "record" as a picture of what a Dow theorist would actually have done in the market. But let us examine the schedule afresh, from the standpoint of our "repurchase test." Did the Dow Theory, as set forth in Table V, permit the practitioner to buy back his stocks at a price lower than those of his previous sale? The answer is curious and a bit disturbing. In the first forty years covered—between 1899 and 1938—this genuine advantage would have been realized in nine repurchases out of a total of ten. But in the three repurchases indicated since 1938 the trader would in each case have paid more than his previous sales price. Thus he would have been better off financially if he had just held on to his position. By so doing he would have gained both in principal value and, what is more important, in having a continuous dividend return throughout the period.

In our view, based on much study of this problem, the recent change in the Dow Theory results is not accidental. It demonstrates an inherent characteristic of forecasting and trading formulas in the fields of business and finance. Those formulas which gain adherents and importance do so because they have worked well over a period, or sometimes merely because they have been plausibly adapted to the statistical record of the past. But as their acceptance increases their reliability tends to diminish. This happens for two reasons: First, the passage of time brings new conditions which the old formula no longer fits. Second, in stock market affairs the popularity of a trading theory has itself an influence on the market's behavior which detracts in the long run from its profit-making possibilities. (The popularity of the Dow Theory may seem to create its own vindication, since it would make the market advance or decline by the very action of its followers when a buying or selling signal is given. A "stampede" of this kind is, of course, much more of a danger than an advantage to the public trader.)

As a check on the reported results produced by the Dow Theory, we have applied a similar resistance-point technique to *monthly* figures for the Dow-Jones Industrial Average alone, covering the period 1897–1948. The indicated results are on the whole similar to those claimed for the orthodox Dow Theory. Up to June, 1933, this alternative method proved highly successful, registering an over-all gain of 234 points against a possible increase of only 58 points if the unit had been held throughout with no trading. But between

June, 1933, and June, 1948, the situation has been reversed, four out of the five sales and repurchases having proved unprofitable. Thus the gain through merely holding would have been 55 points, whereas the gain to the resistance-point trader would have been only 24 points.

Value Approach

By shifting his emphasis from price movements as such to their effect on the level of *values* the investor can retain his original and proper status as the buyer of sound securities and at the same time react intelligently to the recurrent fluctuations of the stock market. If we study these fluctuations over a period of half a century, they seem at first to be made to order for the investor's profit. According to the Dow-Jones Industrial Average, as shown in Chart I, the upswings and downswings appear to have followed each other with sufficient regularity to make possible an easy application of the copybook maxim: "Buy during periods of pessimism and low prices; sell during periods of optimism and high prices."

Why could the typical investor expect any better success in trying to buy at low levels and sell at high levels than in trying to forecast what the market is going to do? Because if he does the former he acts only after the market has moved down into buying levels or up into selling levels. His role is not that of a prophet but of a businessman seizing clearly evident investment opportunities. He is not trying to be smarter than his fellow investors but simply trying to be less irrational than the mass of speculators who insist on buying after the market advances and selling after it goes down. If the market persists in behaving foolishly, all he seems to need is ordinary common sense in order to exploit its foolishness.

If the investor is going to buy common stocks at all it is logical for him to ask whether he really can take easy advantage of the cyclical swings of the stock market. Our answer is that such advantage can be taken but it is not so easy as it looks on the chart. There are two types of difficulty in the way— one arising from the market, the other from the investor himself.

The market's swings are not so regular in either their timing or their extent as they appear at first glance. Looking back at the end of the first half period, in 1923, one could have devised various pat formulas that matched the market's historical fluctuations reasonably well. For example, it would

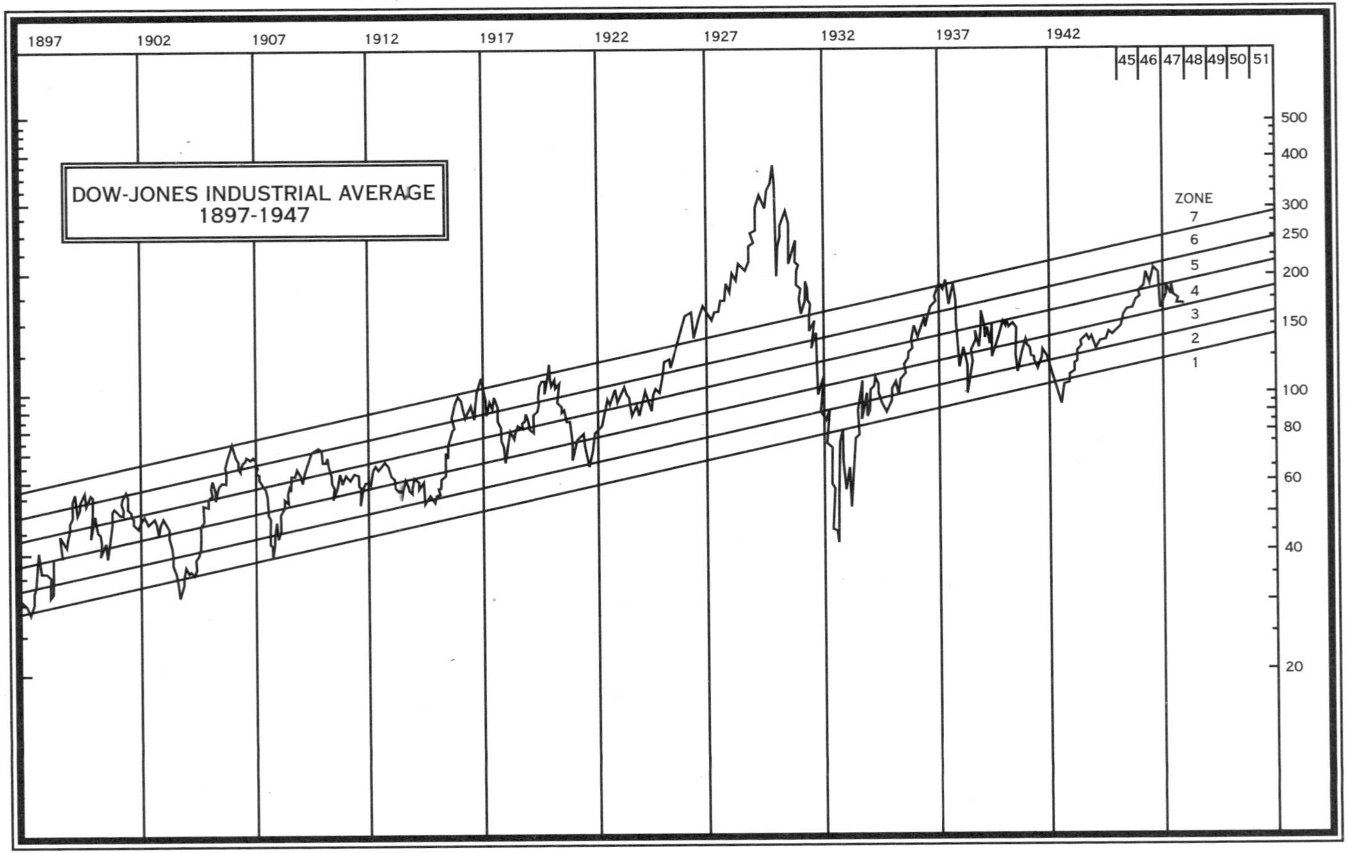

CHART I. (Courtesy of The Keystone Co. of Boston)

have appeared a good idea to buy at, say, 60 per cent of a previous high price and then sell out at 50 per cent profit. Obviously no careful investor would have tried any method like this unless he had seen it work out well several times in the past. Unfortunately, had he waited until 1923 before adopting such a policy, he would have found it entirely unsuitable for the market of the next decade. (He would have sold out his stocks at the 120 level in 1925 and bought them back at 235 right in the 1929 break.)

Other and more respectable techniques might be devised which are based on the idea of a "central value" or "intrinsic value" of the thirty stocks in the Dow-Jones Industrial Average. We could establish this value by using average earnings and a suitable "multiplier" related to going interest rates. When the market goes down we should expect to buy at, say, 80 per cent of the value and then sell out in an upswing at 120 per cent. Our own experiments with this method have yielded interesting results on paper, but we hasten to warn our readers that they are not sufficiently dependable to warrant its use as a pattern for future operations. (The results indicated by the use of this method, as applied during 1924–48, are summarized in the Appendix, p. 251.)

It would be surprising if it were otherwise. The investor has a right to expect good results to flow from a consistent and courageous application of the principle of buying after the market has declined substantially and selling after it had a spectacular rise. But he cannot expect to reduce this principle to a simple and foolproof formula, with profits guaranteed and no anxious periods.

If you look again at our chart you will be struck by the exceptional nature of the market's fluctuations during 1927–32—the period of the "new era" and its aftermath. The boom and collapse of prices during this period were so extreme that former concepts of intrinsic value seemed completely irrelevant. Under our suggested method the investor would have sold out at about 156 in 1925—and then watched the average soar to 381 in 1929. Had he stuck to his guns, he would have bought back at 109 in 1931—and after that the price promptly plummeted to 41.

Many conservative investors actually sold out their stocks in 1925 or 1926, believing the market was too high. Probably the majority of them were later so carried away by the market's insistent advance as to blame themselves for a foolish blunder in selling, and therefore returned to the buying side at much higher levels. Similarly, many of those who bought in the declining market after 1929 were demoralized by its subsequent fall to completely unexpected depths. These fluctuations, of course, were unique in their amplitude; but even in more normal markets the typical investor feels uncomfortable when he buys too soon and unhappy when he sells too soon. Yet to be a true practitioner of the buy-low-sell-high rule he must be entirely ready to do both.

The reader can test his own psychology by asking himself whether he would consider, in retrospect, that selling at 156 in 1925 and buying back at 109 in 1931 was a satisfactory operation. Some may think that an intelligent investor should have been able to sell out much closer to the high of 381 and to buy back nearer to the low of 41. If that is your own view you are probably a speculator at heart and will have trouble keeping to true investment precepts while the market rushes up and down. It is worth pointing out that assuredly not more than one person out of a hundred who stayed in the market *after* 1925 emerged from it with a net profit and that the speculative losses taken were appalling.

A more basic kind of psychological problem, however, is inherent in the simple maxim of buying in low and selling in high markets. That practice might be easy if the market were something impersonal. Actually it is people generally who make high and low markets, because they are optimistic (and greedy) in high markets and pessimistic (and disgusted) in low markets. How can you—the general reader representing the public at large—be expected to act otherwise than the public acts? Does not this mean that you are doomed, by some law of logic, to buy when you should be selling and to sell when you should be buying?

This point is vital. The investor cannot enter the arena of the stock market with any real hope of success unless he is armed with mental weapons that distinguish him in *kind*—not in a fancied superior *degree*—from the trading public. One possible weapon is indifference to market fluctuations; such an investor buys carefully when he has money to place and then lets prices take care of themselves. But, if the investor intends to buy and sell recurrently, his weapons must be a frame of mind and a principle of action which are basically different from those of the trader and speculator. He must deal in values, not in price movements. He must be relatively immune to optimism or pessimism and impervious to business or stock-market forecasts. In a word, he must be psychologically prepared to be a true investor and not a speculator masquerading as an investor. If he can meet this test, he will be a member not of the public at large but of a specialized and self-disciplined group.

Returning to the matter of the market's cyclical swings, we must point out that the duration or frequency of these swings has changed considerably since 1921. This is an added obstacle to the pleasing project of investing regularly in low markets and selling out in high ones. Between 1899 and 1921 the industrial average made five well defined highs and five definite lows, an average cycle of about four years. Since then there have been only two clean-out swings, and the intervals between low points have been eleven years and ten years, respectively. An investor nowadays is likely to grow uneasy and impatient while waiting for his cyclical buying opportunity to reappear. In the meantime, also, his funds will bring him no interest in the bank and only a negligible rate if placed in short-term securities. Thus he can lose more in dividends foregone than he can ever gain from buying at eventual low levels.

Formula Timing Device

In recent years certain compromise methods have been devised by which the investor can take some advantage of the stock market's cycles without running the risk of an unduly long wait or of "missing the market" altogether. These are known as "formula timing plans." The essence of all such plans is that the investor automatically does some selling of common stocks when the market advances substantially. We shall discuss these techniques in some detail in our later chapter on portfolio policy for the enterprising investor. They can be counted on to yield results better than a mere buy-and-hold policy, provided the market does not "run away" permanently on the up side.

Continuity of the Market

These mechanical formulas for varying the proportion of capital invested in common stocks, in a ratio opposite to the movements of prices, are predicated on the theory that sales made at historically high levels can always be replaced later on more advantageous terms. It is interesting to observe from our chart that this simple principle has held true in the market for the past fifty years and possibly much longer. A concrete way of expressing the point is as follows: Whenever the investor sold out in an upswing as soon as the top level of the *previous* well-recognized bull market was reached, he had a chance in the next bear market to buy back at one-third (or better) below his selling price.

This fact means that, up to now at least, the market has never gone into permanently new high ground in one bull movement. The average price level of industrial common stocks is undoubtedly far higher today than it was a generation ago, but the low area of as recently as 1942 was under the high area recorded in 1916. (The low of 1932 was under the average of 1899!) When we consider the extraordinary economic and political developments of the twentieth century, it seems remarkable that stock prices should have proved, at bottom, so unresponsive to the influence of these developments in any permanent way. There is nothing in our chart to distinguish the effect of the two world wars on the stock market from that of any ordinary business cycle; in particular, the well-defined price inflations which were generated in the rest of our economy by these catastrophes are by no means clearly evident in the course of stock prices.

The graph does show one tremendous rise and collapse which stands out starkly from all the other fluctuations. This is commonly called the "new era" stock market of 1927–33. The striking feature of this phenomenon was that the new era existed solely in the minds of the market speculators. The whole episode, in retrospect, now seems to have been one of those rare manifestations of mass financial madness which we used to study in our history books under the titles of "the South Sea Bubble," "the Mississippi Bubble," and so on.

The stock-market insanity of the 1920's was lacking in obvious economic causes, but its economic effects were tremendous and temporarily disastrous. The most permanent result has applied to Wall Street itself—whether it was disastrous or not is a matter of opinion. The creation of the Securities and Exchange Commission (S.E.C.) has virtually revolutionized the conduct of the investment banking and brokerage businesses and has significantly affected the conduct of corporate affairs in relation to stockholders. Manipulation in the stock market has been all but abolished. Marginal trading—a potent cause of financial ruin to many—has been held within strict limits and at times suspended entirely. (This has resulted from new powers granted to the Federal Reserve authorities.) The issuers of new securities have been compelled to supply an almost overwhelming amount of information about all aspects of the enterprise.

Thus the way of doing business in Wall Street is vastly different now from what it was before. Strangely enough, the movement of stock prices does not seem to have changed recognizably. If to the record ending in 1926 we tack on the graph beginning in 1936—thus eliminating 1927–35—the more recent behavior of the market is scarcely distinguishable from that of former days.

The point of all this discussion is that past experience appears to have particular validity and value in dealing with the stock market. The good old rules all seem to be good still. It is conceivable, of course, that the continuity of the market may end some day—perhaps tomorrow—and past experience may really prove a handicap in meeting the new conditions, as it *appeared* to be a handicap for a great many months in 1927–29. But is it not the part of intelligence to run the small risk of being wrong by sticking to the old principles, rather than to run the big risk of being wrong by breaking away from past experience?

Market Fluctuations in Individual Stocks

As indicated above, we are sympathetic to efforts on the part of the enterprising investor to take advantage of the cyclical swings of the general market, by limiting his buying to historically low or neutral levels and by beginning his sales as soon as the market passes into historically high levels. On the whole, however, we believe that the principle of buy-low-sell-high can be applied more satisfactorily with primary reference to individual stocks and with comparatively little regard for the level of the general market.

If the investor is bargain-minded he might as well be on the lookout continuously for individual bargains, instead of seeking to operate in leading stocks at widely spaced intervals or even on a sliding-scale basis as dictated by formula timing plans. Individual security bargains may be located by the processes of security analysis practically at any time. They can be bought with good over-all results at all periods except when the general market itself is clearly in a selling range for investors. They show up to best advantage during the years in which the market remains in a relatively narrow and neutral area. These periods are rather wearying to the alert investor if his method permits him to operate only at definitely low and definitely high general levels, and they seem to run for a longer time now than formerly. In such periods many interesting and profitable opportunities may be found by the study of individual issues.

The purchase of a bargain issue presupposes that the market's current appraisal is wrong, or at least that the buyer's idea of value is more likely to be right than the market's. In this process the investor sets his judgment against that of the market. To some this may seem arrogant or foolhardy. In fact, there is an age-old tradition, still firmly believed in by many, that the current market price always represents a better-informed view of sound value than any individual could arrive at by himself; the knowledge, the expectations, and the judgment of every interested party are said to play their appropriate part in reaching what long ago was termed "the bloodless verdict of the marketplace." Thus it would seem that modesty and plain common sense should restrain the investor from any presumption that he knows better than the market.

As a corollary of this well-established belief we find that forecasting significance is attached by Wall Street generally to the distinctive market movement of individual common stocks or of particular industry groups. If a given performer has moved up "against the market," this is thought to be a dependable sign that great things are in store for the stock. In the old days it was usually sufficient to hint that the famous "they" were engineering a "big move" in the issue. Today, with "they" (the manipulators) abolished, the standard interpretation is that if a stock "acts well" it means that wise people know that the company is going to do better than the average; hence the issue should now be bought. For converse reasons, experienced Wall Street men will counsel you to stay away from and even dispose of issues that have "acted poorly" in the recent past.

It is our firm conviction that investors cannot soundly base their operations on indications afforded by the market action of individual stocks. "Technical studies" of separate issues are essentially the same as technical studies of the general market. The indications they yield are sometimes correct and sometimes wrong; on the whole they are not sufficiently reliable for conservative use. They are a vital part of the apparatus of trading and speculating. Hence it would be strange if they belonged in the investor's arsenal as well. Their most familiar argument is that a stock should be bought because it has advanced and should be sold because it has declined. If true investment has one fundamental principle, it is likely to be the opposite of that one.

In the case of the typical undervalued issue, the previous market action has not been encouraging; the issue is unpopular with stock traders and technical experts and is relatively unknown or neglected. There is no reason at all to expect that its price will advance promptly after the investor decides to buy it. In fact, one might wonder why, if the market undervalues the issue at the time he purchases, it should not continue indefinitely to do so and perhaps even increase the measure of undervaluation. There is no theoretical reason why these unpalatable results could not occur. The comfort and encouragement to the intelligent investor are to be found in practical experience. In the long run, securities tend to reach and sell at a price level not disproportionate to their indicated value. This statement is indefinite as to time; in some cases the day of vindication has actually been deferred for many years. But the investor should base his policy on average experience rather than on the exceptions. Our own records indicate that the interval required for a substantial undervaluation to correct itself averages approximately 1½ to 2½ years.

Some may think this is a long time to wait for one's superior judgment and courage to prove profitable. In truth, if our estimate is reasonably accurate, it means that the stock market is extraordinarily obliging to the bargain-hunting investor. First, it creates a fair number of real undervaluations available to the investor's choice at almost any time. Then, after ignoring or running counter to the investor's valuation for a period long enough generally to test his fortitude, it again conveniently changes its attitude in the majority of instances and proceeds to establish a price for the security roughly corresponding to the indicated value. Surely the intelligent investor has no cause to berate the perversity of the stock market; in this very perversity lie both his opportunities and his ultimate profits.

Business Valuations vs. Stock-Market Valuations

Later on, when we discuss the technique of identifying bargain securities, we shall point out that a fundamental test of the existence of under-or over-valuation consists in comparing the price of the stock with the value of the business as a whole to a private owner or owners. If General Motors is worth $60 a share to an investor it must be because the full common-stock ownership of this gigantic enterprise as a whole is worth 43 million (shares) times $60, or no less than $2,600 million. (This is probably true, despite the enormous total valuation involved.) On the other hand, to return to our Great Atlantic & Pacific Tea Company example, one reason why we could say with confidence that its common stock was greatly undervalued when it sold at 36 in 1938 was because this price meant that the whole enterprise was being appraised by the market at less than the company's working capital alone. Thus no value at all was then ascribed to the store fixtures, the warehouses, and so forth, plus the good will and earning power of what was perhaps the largest retail enterprise in the world. It is absurd to imagine that the business as a whole was not worth a good deal more to a private owner than the pessimistic valuation suggested by the stock market's daily quotations at the time.

What, then, did the individual holder of 10 or 100 or 1,000 shares of A. & P. really own in March, 1938? Did he own a small fraction of the entire enterprise, just as the Hartford family owned a large fraction? Or did he own primarily a stock certificate entitling him only to receive dividends when and if declared and to receive the quoted market price when he sold out? Another way of putting this vital question is as follows: Did the investor who bought A. & P. stock at 80 really lose money when its price dropped to 36? Was he definitely poorer than before? The correct answer to this question is the key to the broader problem of the investor's relationship to the price fluctuations of his common stocks.

As we see it, the investor-stockholder occupies a middle or compromise position between true ownership of part of a business and mere ownership of a stock certificate. He undoubtedly lacks some important powers of control which inhere in individual or partnership-group possession of the enterprise. But in this respect he is in a position no different from that of a minority holder of shares in a private business, when such holder is not part of the controlling group. But he also has what is in truth a tremendous advantage over such a minority holder, in that he can sell his own shares *any time he wants to* at their quoted market price.

But note one important fact: The true investor scarcely ever *has to sell* his shares, and at all other times he is free to disregard the current price quotation. He need pay attention to it and act upon it only to the extent that it suits his book, and no more. Thus the investor who permits himself to be stampeded or unduly worried by unjustified market declines in his holdings is perversely transforming his basic advantage into a basic disadvantage. That man would be better off if his stocks had no market quotation at all, for he would then be spared the mental anguish caused him by *other persons'* mistakes of judgment.

Incidentally, a widespread situation of this kind actually existed during the dark days of the 1931–33 depression. There was then a psychological advantage in owning business interests which had no quoted market. For example, people who owned first mortgages on real estate which continued to pay interest were able to tell themselves that their investments had kept their full value, there being no market quotations to indicate otherwise. On the other hand, many listed corporation bonds of even better quality and greater underlying strength suffered severe shrinkages in their quoted markets, thus making their owners believe they were growing distinctly poorer. In reality the owners were better off with the listed securities, despite the low prices of these. For if they had wanted to, or were compelled to, they could at least have sold the issues—possibly to exchange them for even better bargains. Or they could just as logically have ignored the market's action as temporary and basically meaningless. But it is self-deception to tell yourself that you have suffered no shrinkage in value *merely because* your securities have no quoted market at all.

Returning to the A. & P. stockholder in 1938, we assert that as long as he held on to his shares he suffered no loss in their price decline beyond what his own judgment may have told him was occasioned by a shrinkage in their underlying or intrinsic value. If no such shrinkage had occurred, he had a right to expect that in due course the market quotation would return to his cost price or better—as in fact it did the following year.[1] In this respect his position was the same as if he had owned an interest in a private business with no quoted market for its shares. For in that case, too, he might or might not have been justified in mentally lopping off part of the cost of his holdings because of the impact of the 1938 recession—depending on what had happened to his company.

Critics of the value approach to stock investment argue that listed common stocks cannot properly be regarded or appraised in the same way as an interest in a similar private enterprise, because the presence of an organized security market "injects into equity ownership the new and extremely important attribute of liquidity."[2] But what this liquidity really means is, first, that the investor has the benefit of the stock market's daily and changing ap-

---

[1] In 1939 A. & P. common sold as high as 117½.

[2] Molodovsky and Mindell, "The Scientific Basis of Internal Stock Market Analysis," *Commercial & Financial Chronicle,* December 25, 1947, p. 22.

praisal of his holdings, *for whatever that appraisal may be worth*, and, second, that the investor is able to increase or decrease his investment at the market's daily figure—*if he chooses*. Thus the existence of a quoted market gives the investor *certain options* which he does not have if his security is unquoted. But it does not impose the current quotation on an investor who prefers to take his idea of value from some other source.

Let us close this section with something in the nature of a parable. Imagine that in some private business you own a small share which cost you $1,000. One of your partners, named Mr. Market, is very obliging indeed. Every day he tells you what he thinks your interest is worth and furthermore offers either to buy you out or to sell you an additional interest on that basis. Sometimes his idea of value appears plausible and justified by business developments and prospects as you know them. Often, on the other hand, Mr. Market lets his enthusiasm or his fears run away with him, and the value he proposes seems to you a little short of silly.

If you are a prudent investor or a sensible businessman will you let Mr. Market's daily communication determine your view as the value of your $1,000 interest in the enterprise? Only in case you agree with him, or in case you want to trade with him. You may be happy to sell out to him when he quotes you a ridiculously high price, and equally happy to buy from him when his price is low. But the rest of the time you will be wiser to form your own ideas of the value of your holdings, based on full reports from the company about its operations and financial position.

The true investor is in that very position when he owns a listed common stock. He can take advantage of the daily market price or leave it alone, as dictated by his own judgment and inclination. He must take cognizance of important price movements, for otherwise his judgment will have nothing to work on. Conceivably they may give him a warning signal which he will do well to heed—this in plain English means that he is to sell his shares *because* the price has gone down, foreboding worse things to come. In our view such signals are misleading at least as often as they are helpful. Basically, price fluctuations have only one significant meaning for the true investor. They provide him with an opportunity to buy wisely when prices fall sharply and to sell wisely when they advance a great deal. At other times he will do better if he forgets about the stock market and pays attention to his dividend returns and to the operating results of his companies.

Summary

The most realistic distinction between the investor and the speculator is found in their attitude toward stock-market movements. The speculator's primary interest lies in anticipating and profiting from market fluctuations. The investor's primary interest lies in acquiring and holding suitable securities at suitable prices. Market movements are important to him in a practical sense, because they alternately create low price levels at which he would be wise to buy and high price levels at which he certainly should refrain from buying and probably would be wise to sell.

It is far from certain that the typical investor should regularly hold off buying until low market levels appear, because this may involve a long wait, the loss of considerable dividend income, and the possible missing of investment opportunities. On the whole it may be better for the investor to do his stock buying whenever he has money to put in stocks, except when the general market level is higher than can be justified by well-established standards of value. If he wants to be shrewd he can look for the ever present bargain opportunities in individual securities.

Aside from forecasting the movements of the general market, much effort and ability is directed in Wall Street toward selecting stocks or industrial groups that in the matter of price will "do better" than the rest over a fairly short period in the future. Logical as this endeavor may seem, we do not believe it is suited to the needs or temperament of the true investor— particularly since he would be competing with a large number of stock-market traders who are trying to do the same thing. As in all other activities which emphasize price movements first and underlying values second, the work of many intelligent minds constantly engaged in this field tends to be self-neutralizing and self-defeating over the years.

The investor with a portfolio of sound stocks should expect their prices to fluctuate and should neither be concerned by sizable declines nor become excited by sizable advances. He should always remember that market quotations are there for his convenience, either to be taken advantage of or to be ignored. He should never buy a stock because it has gone up or sell one *because* it has gone down. He would not be far wrong if this motto read more simply: "Never buy a stock immediately after a substantial rise or sell one immediately after a substantial drop."

An Added Consideration

Something should be said about the significance of average market prices as a measure of managerial competence. The stockholder judges whether his own investment has been successful in terms both of dividends received and of the long-range trend of the average market value. The same criteria should logically be applied in testing the effectiveness of a company's management and the soundness of its attitude toward the owners of the business.

This statement may sound like a truism, but it needs to be emphasized. For as yet there is no accepted technique or approach by which management is brought to the bar of market opinion. On the contrary, managements have always insisted that they have no responsibility *of any kind* for what happens to the market value of their shares. It is true, of course, that they are not accountable for those *fluctuations* in price which as we have been insisting, bear no relationship to underlying conditions and values. But it is only the lack of alertness and intelligence among the rank and file of stockholders which permits this immunity to extend to the entire realm of market quotations, including the permanent establishment of a depreciated and unsatisfactory price level. Good managements produce a good average market price, and bad managements produce bad market prices.

III

The Investor and
His Advisers

THE INVESTMENT of money in securities is unique among business operations in that it is almost always based in some degree on advice received from others. The great bulk of investors are amateurs. Naturally they feel that in choosing their securities they can profit by professional guidance. Yet there are peculiarities inherent in the very concept of investment advice.

If the reason people invest is to make money, then in seeking advice they are asking others to tell them how to make money. That idea has some element of naïveté. Businessmen seek professional advice on various elements of their business, but they do not expect to be told how to make a profit. That is their own bailiwick. When they, or non-business people, rely upon others to make *investment* profits for them, they are expecting a kind of result for which there is no counterpart in ordinary business affairs.

If we assume that there are normal or standard *income* results to be obtained from investing money in securities, then the role of the adviser can be more readily established. He will use his superior training and experience to protect his clients against mistakes and to make sure that they obtain the results to which their money is entitled. It is when the investor demands more than an average return on his money, or when his adviser undertakes to do better for him, that the question arises whether more is being asked or promised than is likely to be delivered.

Advice on investments may be obtained from a variety of sources. These include: (a) a relative or friend, presumably knowledgeable in securities; (b) a local (commercial) banker; (c) a brokerage firm or investment banking house; (d) a financial service or periodical; and (e) an investment counselor. The miscellaneous character of this list suggests that no logical or systematic approach in this matter has crystallized, as yet, in the minds of investors.

Certain common-sense considerations relate to the criterion of normal or standard results mentioned above. Our basic thesis is this: If the investor is to rely chiefly on the advice of others in handling his funds, then either (a) he must limit himself and his advisers strictly to standard, conservative, and even unimaginative forms of investment or (b) he must have an unusually intimate and favorable knowledge of the person who is going to direct his funds into other channels; for only to the extent that the investor himself grows in knowledge and competence and therefore becomes qualified to pass independent judgment on the recommendations of others can he be receptive to less conventional suggestions from his advisers. The first type of person is our defensive or unenterprising investor; the second is our aggressive or enterprising investor.

Investment Counsel

The truly professional investment advisers—that is, the well-established investment counsel firms, who charge substantial annual fees—are the most modest in their promises and pretensions. For the most part they place their clients' funds in standard interest- and dividend-paying securities, and they rely mainly on normal investment experience for their over-all results. In the typical case it is doubtful whether more than 10 per cent of the total fund is ever invested in securities other than those of leading companies, plus government bonds; nor do they make a serious effort to take advantage of swings in the general market.

The leading investment counsel firms make no claim to being brilliant; they do pride themselves on being careful, conservative, and competent.

Their primary aim is to conserve the principal value over the years and produce a conservatively acceptable rate of income. Any accomplishment beyond that—and they do strive to better the goal—they regard in the nature of extra service rendered. Perhaps their chief value to their clients lies in shielding them from costly mistakes. They offer as much as the defensive investor has the right to expect from any counselor serving the general public.

Financial Services

The so-called financial services are organizations which send out uniform bulletins (sometimes in the form of telegrams) to their subscribers. The subjects covered may include the state and prospects of business, the behavior and prospects of the securities markets, and information and advice regarding individual issues. There is often an "inquiry department" which will answer questions affecting an individual subscriber. The cost of the service averages much less than the fee which investment counselors charge their individual clients. Some organizations—notably Babson's—operate on separate levels as a financial service and as investment counsel. (Incidentally, other organizations—such as Scudder, Stevens & Clark—operate separately as investment counsel and as an investment fund or "trust.")

The financial services direct themselves, on the whole, to a quite different segment of the public than do the investment counsel firms. The latters' clients generally wish to be relieved of bother and the need for making decisions. The financial services offer information and guidance to those who are directing their own financial affairs or are themselves advising others. Many of these services confine themselves exclusively, or nearly so, to forecasting market movements by various "technical" methods. We shall dismiss these with the observation that their work does not concern "investors" as the term is used in this book.

On the other hand, some of the best known—such as Moody's Investment Service, Standard & Poor's, or Fitch—are identified with statistical organizations which compile the voluminous statistical data that form the basis for all serious security analysis. These services have a varied clientele, ranging from the most conservative-minded investor to the rankest speculator. As a result they must find it difficult to adhere to any clear-cut or fundamental philosophy in arriving at their opinions and recommendations.

An old-established service of the type of Moody's and the others must obviously provide something worth while to a broad class of investors. What is it? Basically they address themselves to the matters in which the average active investor-speculator is interested, and their views on these either command some measure of authority or at least appear more reliable than those of the unaided client.

For years the financial services have been making stock-market forecasts without anyone's taking this activity very seriously. Like everyone else in the field they are sometimes right and sometimes wrong. Wherever possible they hedge their opinions so as to avoid the risk of being proved completely wrong. (There is a well-developed art of Delphic phrasing which adjusts itself successfully to whatever the future brings.) In our view—perhaps a prejudiced one—this segment of their work has no real significance except for the light it throws on human nature in the securities markets. Nearly everyone interested in common stocks wants to be told by someone else what he thinks the market is going to do. The demand being there, it must be supplied.

Their interpretations and forecasts of business conditions, of course, are much more authoritative and informing. These are an important part of the great body of economic intelligence which is spread continuously among buyers and sellers of securities and tends to create fairly rational prices for stocks and bonds under most conditions. Undoubtedly the material published by the financial services adds to the store of information available and fortifies the investment judgment of their clients.

It is difficult to evaluate their recommendations of individual securities. Each service is entitled to be judged separately, and the verdict could properly be based only on an elaborate and inclusive study covering many years. In our own experience we have noted among them a pervasive attitude which we think tends to impair what could otherwise be more useful advisory work. This is their general view that a stock should be bought if the near-term prospects of the business are favorable and should be sold if these are unfavorable—*regardless of the current price.* Such a superficial principle often prevents the services from doing the sound analytical job of which their staffs are capable—namely, to ascertain whether a given stock appears over- or undervalued at the current price in the light of its indicated long-term future earning power.

The intelligent investor will not do his buying and selling solely on the basis of recommendations received from a financial service. Once this point is established, the role of the financial service then becomes the useful one of supplying information and offering suggestions.

Advice from Brokerage Houses

Probably the largest volume of information and advice to the security-owning public comes from stockbrokers. These are members of the New York Stock Exchange, and of other exchanges, who execute buying and selling orders for a standard commission. Practically all the houses that deal with the public maintain a "statistical" or analytical department, which answers inquiries and makes recommendations. A great deal of analytical literature, some of it elaborate and expensive, is distributed gratis to the firms' customers—more impressively referred to as clients.

A great deal is at stake in the innocent-appearing question whether "customers" or "clients" is the more appropriate name. A business has customers; a professional person or organization has clients. The Wall Street brokerage fraternity has probably the highest ethical standards of any *business*, but it is still feeling its way toward the standards and standing of a true profession.

Because Wall Street has thrived mainly on speculation, and because stock-market speculators as a class are almost certain to lose money, it has been logically impossible for brokerage houses to operate on a thoroughly professional basis. To do that would require them to direct their efforts toward reducing rather than increasing their business.

The farthest that brokerage houses have gone in that direction—and could have been expected to go—is to refrain from inducing or encouraging anyone to speculate. Such houses have confined themselves to executing orders given them, to supplying financial information and analyses, and to rendering opinions on the *investment* merits of securities. Thus, in theory at least, they are devoid of all responsibility for either the profits or the losses of their speculative customers.[1]

Most stock-exchange houses, however, still adhere to the old-time slogans that they are in business to make commissions and that the way to succeed in business is to give the customers what they want. Since the most

---

[1] This is the announced policy of Merrill Lynch *et al.*, by far the largest brokerage house.

profitable customers want speculative advice and "suggestions," the thinking and activities of the typical firm are pretty closely geared to day-to-day trading in the market. Thus it tries hard to help its customers make money in a field where they are condemned almost by mathematical law to lose.

The investor obtains advice and information from stock-exchange houses through two types of employees, now known officially as "customers' brokers" and "security analysts."

The customer's broker, also called a "registered representative," formerly bore the less dignified title of "customer's man." Today he is almost invariably an individual of good character and considerable knowledge of securities, who operates under a rigid code of right conduct. Nevertheless, since his business is to earn commissions, he can hardly avoid being speculation-minded. Thus the security buyer who wants to avoid being influenced by speculative considerations will ordinarily have to be careful and explicit in his dealing with his customer's broker; he will have to show clearly, by word and deed, that he is not interested in anything faintly resembling a stock-market "tip." Once the customer's broker understands clearly that he has a real investor on his hands, he will respect this point of view and co-operate with it.

The security analyst is a person of particular concern to the author, who has been one himself for more than a generation and has helped educate countless others. At this stage we refer only to the security analysts employed by brokerage houses. The function of the security analyst is clear enough from his title. It is he who works up the detailed studies of individual securities, develops careful comparisons of various issues in the same field, and forms an expert opinion of the safety or attractiveness or intrinsic value of all the different kinds of stocks and bonds.

By what must seem a quirk to the outsider there are no formal requirements for being a security analyst. Contrast with this fact that a customer's broker must pass an examination, meet the required character tests, and be duly accepted and registered by the New York Stock Exchange. As a practical matter, nearly all the younger analysts have had extensive business-school training, and the oldsters have acquired at least the equivalent in the school of long experience. In the great majority of cases, the employing brokerage house can be counted on to assure itself of the qualifications and competence of its analysts.

The customer of the brokerage firm may deal with the security analysts directly, or his contact may be an indirect one via the customer's broker. In either case the analyst is available to the client for a considerable amount of information and advice. Let us make an emphatic statement here. The value of the security analyst to the investor depends largely on the investor's own attitude. If the investor asks the analyst the right questions, he is likely to get the right—or at least valuable—answers. The analysts hired by brokerage houses, we are convinced, are greatly handicapped by the general feeling that they are supposed to be market analysts as well. When they are asked whether a given common stock is "sound," the question often means, "Is this stock likely to advance during the next few months?" As a result many of them are compelled to analyze with one eye on the stock ticker—a pose not conducive to sound thinking or worth-while conclusions.

In the next section of this book we shall deal with some of the concepts and possible achievements of security analysis. A great many analysts working for stock-exchange firms could be of prime assistance to the bona fide investor who wants to be sure that he gets full value for his money, and possibly a little more. As in the case of the customers' brokers, what is needed at the beginning is a clear understanding by the analyst of the investor's attitude and objectives. Once the analyst is convinced that he is dealing with a man who is value-minded rather than quotation-minded, there is an excellent chance that his recommendations will prove of real over-all benefit.

Investment Bankers

The term "investment banker" is applied to a firm which engages to an important extent in originating, underwriting, and selling new issues of stocks and bonds. (To underwrite means to guarantee to the issuing corporation, or other issuer, that the security will be fully sold.) A number of the brokerage houses carry on a certain amount of underwriting activity. Generally this is confined to participating in underwriting groups formed by leading investment bankers. There is an additional tendency for brokerage firms to originate and sponsor a minor amount of new-issue financing, particularly in the form of smaller issues of common stocks when a bull market is in full swing.

Investment banking is perhaps the most respectable department of the Wall Street community, because it is here that finance plays its constructive role of supplying new capital for the expansion of industry. In fact, much of the theoretical justification for maintaining active stock markets, notwithstanding their frequent speculative excesses, lies in the fact that organized security exchanges facilitate the sale of new issues of bonds and stocks. If investors or speculators could not expect to see a ready market for a new security offered them, they might well refuse to buy it.

The relationship between the investment banker and the investor is basically that of the salesman to the prospective buyer. For many years the great bulk of the new offerings has consisted of bond issues which were purchased in the main by financial institutions such as banks and insurance companies. In this business the security salesmen have been dealing with shrewd and experienced buyers. Hence any recommendations made by the investment bankers to these customers has had to pass careful and skeptical scrutiny. Thus these transactions are almost always effected on a businesslike footing.

But a different situation obtains in the relationship between the *individual* security buyer and the investment banking firms, including the stockbrokers acting as underwriters. Here the purchaser is frequently inexperienced and seldom shrewd. He is easily influenced by what the salesman tells him, especially in the case of common-stock issues, since often his unconfessed desire in buying is chiefly to make a quick profit. The effect of all this is that the public investor's protection lies less in his own critical faculty than in the scruples and ethics of the offering houses.[2]

It is a tribute to the honesty and competence of the underwriting firms that they are able to combine fairly well the discordant roles of adviser and salesman. But it is imprudent for the buyer to trust himself to the judgment of the seller. The bad results of this unsound attitude show themselves recurrently in the underwriting field and with notable effect in the sale of new common-stock issues during periods of active speculation.

The intelligent investor will pay attention to the advice and recommendations received from investment banking houses, especially those known to

---

[2]New offerings may now be sold only by means of a prospectus prepared under the rules of the S.E.C. This document must disclose all the pertinent facts about the issue and issuer, and it is fully adequate to inform the *prudent investor* as to the exact nature of the security offered him. But the very copiousness of the data required usually makes the prospectus of prohibitive length. It is generally agreed that only a small percentage of *individuals* buying new issues read the prospectus with thoroughness. Thus they are still acting mainly not on their own judgment but on that of the house selling them the security.

him to have an excellent reputation; but he will be sure to bring sound and independent judgment to bear upon these suggestions—either his own, if he is competent, or that of some other type of adviser.

Other Advisers

It is a good old custom, especially in the smaller towns, to consult one's local banker about investments. A commercial banker may not be a thoroughgoing expert on security values, but he is experienced and conservative. He is especially useful to the unskilled investor, who is often tempted to stray from the straight and unexciting path of a defensive policy and needs the steadying influence of a prudent mind. The more alert and aggressive investor, seeking counsel in the selection of security bargains, will not ordinarily find the commercial banker's viewpoint to be especially suited to his own objectives.

We take a more critical attitude toward the widespread custom of asking investment advice from relatives or friends. The inquirer always thinks he has good reason for assuming that the person consulted has superior knowledge or experience. Our own observation indicates that it is almost as difficult to select satisfactory lay advisers as it is to select the proper securities unaided. Much bad advice is given free.

Summary

Investors who are prepared to pay a fee for the management of their funds may wisely select some well-established and well-recommended investment counsel firm. Alternatively, they may use the investment department of a large trust company or the supervisory service supplied on a fee basis by a few of the leading New York Stock Exchange houses. The results to be expected are in no wise exceptional, but they are commensurate with those of the *average* well-informed and cautious investor.

Most security buyers obtain advice without paying for it specifically. It stands to reason, therefore, that in the majority of cases they are not entitled to and should not expect better-than-average results. They should be wary of all persons, whether customers' brokers or security salesmen, who promise spectacular income or profits. This applies both to the selection of securities and to guidance in the elusive art of trading in the market.

Defensive investors, as we have defined them, will not ordinarily be equipped to pass independent judgment on the security recommendations made by their advisers. But they can be explicit—and even repetitiously so—in stating the kind of securities they want to buy. If they follow our prescription they will confine themselves to United States Savings Bonds and the common stocks of leading corporations purchased at levels that are not high in the light of experience and analysis. The security analyst of any reputable stock exchange house can make up a suitable list of such common stocks and can certify to the investor whether or not the existing price level is a reasonably conservative one as judged by past experience.

The aggressive investor will ordinarily work in active co-operation with his advisers. He will want their recommendations explained in detail, and he will insist on passing his own judgment upon them. This means that the investor will gear his expectations and the character of his security operations to the development of his own knowledge and experience in the field. Only in the exceptional case, where the integrity and competence of the advisers have been thoroughly demonstrated, should the investor act upon the advice of others without understanding and approving the decision made.

IV

———◆◇◆———

General Portfolio Policy:
The Defensive Investor

THE BASIC CHARACTERISTICS of an investment portfolio will be determined largely by the position of the individual owner. At one extreme we have savings banks, life insurance companies, and so-called "legal" trust funds. Their investments are limited by law in the majority of states to high-grade bonds and, in some cases, high-grade preferred stocks. At the other extreme we have the well-to-do and experienced businessman, who will include any kind of bond or stock in his security list provided he considers it an attractive purchase.

It is an old and sound principle that those who cannot afford to take risks should be content with a low return on their invested funds. From this there has developed the general notion that the rate of return which the investor should aim for is more or less proportionate to the degree of risk he is ready to run. Our view is different. The rate of return sought should be dependent, rather, on the amount of intelligent effort the investor is willing and able to bring to bear on his task. The minimum return goes to our passive investor, who wants both safety and freedom from concern. The maximum return would be realized by the alert and enterprising investor who exercises maximum intelligence and skill. In many cases there may be less real risk associated with buying a "bargain issue" offering the chance of a large profit than with a conventional bond purchase yielding under 3 per cent.

We have already outlined the portfolio policy of the defensive investor. He should divide his funds between high-grade bonds and high-grade common stocks. The bond component will ordinarily run between 25 and 75 per cent, depending largely on subjective considerations—the need he feels for a somewhat higher income, on the one hand, and for price stability on the other. Under the conditions prevailing in 1948 we are positive that all of the bond money should be placed in United States obligations. For the vast majority of investors the complete answer will be found in United States Savings Bonds, Series E or Series G. These will be discussed in detail in a later chapter.

What we are recommending here is by no means the standard practice in the administration of conservatively slanted funds. From all indications it would seem that the typical list still includes a fair proportion of corporate bonds and preferred stocks.[1] Careful reflection will support the view that under present conditions corporate senior securities are not sufficiently attractive for the individual investor.

At the present time corporate bonds of the highest grade yield about 2.75 per cent, as against 2.90 and 2.50 per cent, respectively, on United States Savings Bonds E and G, and about 2.50 per cent also on listed long-term United States issues. Government bonds are exempt from state income tax, and they are undoubtedly safer than any corporate bonds. The difference in yield between the one and the other is negligible in amount and much less

---

[1]One of the large Philadelphia trust companies operates a "commingled trust fund" of $36 millions, representing no less than 1,800 different accounts. At the end of 1947 the investments of the funds were divided in the following proportions:

U.S. Government Bonds and Cash	31.3%
Other Bonds and Guaranteed Stocks	5.5
Preferred Stocks	33.6
Common Stocks	29.6
	100.0%

The preferred-stock component here is unusually large because of Pennsylvania tax considerations. A similar New York fund showed 25% in U.S. bonds, 30% in corporate bonds, 17% in preferred stocks and 28% in common stocks.

than the historical range, as shown in Table VI. The present relationship has been created by the enormous supply of United States bonds resulting from the Second World War and also, we believe, by the fact that there has been a special demand for corporation bonds from our gigantic life insurance companies and other financial institutions, which have been reluctant to appear as engaged solely in the purchase of government bonds.

TABLE VI. COMPARATIVE YIELDS ON VARIOUS TYPES OF INVESTMENTS

Date	U.S. Savings Bonds Series E	U.S. Treasury Bonds (Long Term)	Corporate Issues AAA Bonds[1]	BAA Bonds	High Grade Pfd. Stocks[2]	Savings Bank Deposits[3]
1919 (av.)	. . . . .	4.73%	5.49%	7.25%	6.31%	4.00%
1928 (av.)	. . . . .	3.33	4.55	5.48	5.12	4.39
1932 (av.)	. . . . .	3.68	5.01	9.30	6.13	3.71
Mar. 1935	2.90%[4]	2.69	3.67	6.20	4.70	2.23
1940 (av.)	2.90	2.21	2.84	4.75	4.14	1.94
Apr. 1946	2.90	2.08	2.46	2.96	3.42	1.66
Jan. 1948	2.90	2.45	2.86	3.52	4.10	1.69[5]

[1]From Moody's.
[2]From Standard & Poor's.
[3]N.Y. State average for full years.
[4]Series A bonds; similar to Series E. This was the first issue of U.S. Savings Bonds.
[5]Year 1947.

These reasons have no bearing on the basic truth that government bonds are better for the private investor than corporation issues which yield very slightly more. The financial history of 1946–48 affords an important object lesson on this point. Private investors who in 1946 bought Atchison Railroad General 4s, due 1995—one of our premier long-term issues—paid as high as 141 for them. Within two years the price had declined to 114, a loss of six and one-half years' interest. In the meantime there would have been no loss in the value of United States Savings Bonds yielding about the same return.

It is true that a somewhat higher income could have been obtained by purchasing corporate bonds with somewhat lower ratings. For example, in April, 1946, the average yield on Moody's list of BAA bonds was 2.96 per cent, as against 2.46 per cent for the AAA group. But past experience indicates that this was an extraordinarily small advantage in yield in exchange for the sacrifice in quality. The record appears in Table VI. It shows not only that the investor buying BAA bonds in 1946 acted in defiance of past experience—and has already sustained a substantial loss in consequence[2]— but also that even at the more favorable differential existing in 1948 the second-quality bonds are still much less attractive than United States governments.

The price history of high-grade preferred stocks carries the same implications. For an unimportant gain in annual income the buyer of these instead of United States Savings Bonds in 1946 found himself paying unheard-of prices, and he also found himself faced soon afterwards with price declines running to as much as 25 per cent and more.

Preferred Stocks

Certain additional observations should be made here on the subject of preferred stocks. Really good preferred stocks can and do exist, but they are good in spite of their investment form, which is an inherently bad one. The typical preferred stockholder is dependent for his safety on the ability and desire of the company to pay dividends on its *common stock*. Once the common dividends are omitted, or even in danger, his own position becomes precarious, for the directors are under no obligation to continue paying him unless they also pay on the common. On the other hand, the typical preferred stock carries no share in the company's profits beyond the fixed dividend rate. Thus the preferred holder lacks both the legal claim of the bondholder (or creditor) and the profit possibilities of a common stockholder (or partner).

These weaknesses in the legal position of preferred stocks tend to come to the fore recurrently in periods of depression. Only a small percentage of

---

[2] An increase of ½ per cent in the yield of a typical BAA bond in 1946 meant a *decline* of more than 10 per cent in the price.

all preferred issues are so strongly entrenched as to maintain an unquestioned investment status through all vicissitudes. Experience teaches that the time to buy preferred stocks is when their price is unduly depressed by temporary adversity. In other words, they should be bought on a bargain basis or not at all. We shall refer later to convertible and similarly privileged issues, which carry some special possibilities of profits. These are not ordinarily selected for a conservative portfolio.

Another peculiarity in the general position of preferred stocks deserves mention. They have a much better tax status for corporation buyers than for individual investors. Corporations pay income tax on only 15 per cent of the income they receive in dividends, but on the full amount of their ordinary interest income. Since the 1948 corporate rate is 38 per cent, this means that $100 received as preferred stock dividends is taxed only $5.70, whereas $100 received as bond interest is taxed $38. On the other hand, individual investors pay exactly the same tax on preferred stock investments as on bond interest. Thus, in strict logic, all investment-grade preferred stocks should be bought by corporations, just as all tax-exempt bonds should be bought by investors in high income-tax brackets.

Security Forms

The bond form and the preferred stock form, as hitherto discussed, are well-understood and relatively simple matters. A bondholder is entitled to receive fixed interest and payment of principal on a definite date. The owner of a preferred stock is entitled to a fixed dividend, and no more, which must be paid before any common dividend. His principal value does not come due on any specified date. (The dividend may be cumulative or non-cumulative. He may or may not have a vote.)

The above describes the standard provisions, and no doubt the majority of bond and preferred issues, but there are innumerable departures from these forms. The best-known types are (a) convertible and similar issues and (b) income bonds. Besides these there are many issues which display individual vagaries in matters of their claim to principal, interest or dividends; voting rights; rights in dissolution; and so forth.

A hybrid or otherwise irregular security form must be regarded as a prima facie argument against inclusion of the issue in a standard investment portfolio. It is often difficult to appraise the true effect or value of these special provisions. The terms of the issue may, in fact, be unusually attractive, and it may thus constitute the exceptional case where the irregular form is a reason for rather than against a purchase. But it is almost invariably true that such issues should be acquired by the enterprising investor only and that the defensive investor should leave them alone.

Investment Merits of Common Stocks

Our argument against the purchase of corporate bonds and preferred stocks by the defensive investor needs now to be balanced by an argument in favor of placing some part of his funds in high-grade common stocks. In the old days such a proposal was little short of heresy. All common stocks were considered more or less risky and therefore unsuited for a conservative portfolio. This concept was and remains embedded in state laws governing the investments of trust funds (unless the instrument provides to the contrary) and also those of savings banks and life insurance companies, which in many states may not hold common stocks.

It is interesting to observe that the prohibitions expressed in the laws are matched in good part by the prejudices of the man in the street. The Federal Reserve Board published a *Survey of Consumer Finances* in July, 1948, which included answers by the public to questions about their investment preferences. The vote on common stocks was in the proportion of only 5 in favor and 62 against. Of those opposed, about half gave the reason "Not safe, a gamble," and about half the reason "Not familiar with."

Experienced and informed investors, however, have become increasingly receptive to the idea that an investment portfolio of substantial size should include some component of better-grade common stocks. Many have expressed this conviction in their wills by specifically empowering their executors and trustees to invest funds in so-called "non-legal" securities, including common stocks. Most lawyers will now advise their clients to follow this course, in order to avoid the limitations otherwise imposed by the statutes. This change in viewpoint has grown out of the investment experience of the past generation. It reflects certain weaknesses inherent in an all-bond program which challenge the validity of the old generalization that bonds as a class are sounder investments than common stocks as a class. Let us devote a little space to these factors.

(A) Inflation Angle. Good bonds carry no protection against inflation. The bondholder suffers the full effect of any loss in purchasing power of the dollars that he lent. Since the two world wars have each had pronounced inflationary effects in this country—and incomparably larger ones abroad—intelligent investors are conscious of the need of doing whatever is possible to escape this erosion of the value of their capital. If in the course of the years their $1,000 remains intact in money but becomes worth only $500 in goods, they realize they are no better off than if they were getting back only $500 in money with the same purchasing power as before.

Good common stocks provide a better degree of protection against inflation than do high-grade bonds. A number of investment authorities have insisted that common stocks are by no means a perfect hedge against inflation, and they are right. Nevertheless, there is a sound theoretical basis for expecting their dividends and their average market value to be pushed upward by the forces of inflation. Past experience shows that this has in fact occurred and that the careful common-stock buyer has gained somewhat in income and principal value to offset the inroads of inflation. Chart II presents comparative data on the "real income" received from bonds and from common stocks since 1913.

(B) Call Provision. High-grade bonds have a second drawback in their almost universal "call provision." This feature permits the issuing company, *at its option*, to pay off the bonds long before maturity, generally with the addition of a modest premium to the face value. Comparatively little attention has been paid to the unsatisfactory position in which the call provision has placed bondholders as a class. It has meant that, during a period of wide fluctuations in the underlying interest rates, the bond investor has had to bear the full brunt of unfavorable changes and has been deprived of all but a meager participation in favorable ones. Let us try to make this point clear by an example, for it is both important and widely overlooked.

In 1928, the American Gas & Electric Company sold an issue of 100-year 5 per cent debentures to the public at 101, yielding 4.95 per cent. Four years later, in the depth of the depression, the bonds sold as low as 62½, with a yield of 8 per cent. This reflects the impact of unusually unfavorable economic and market conditions on a good-quality investment bond. Conversely, in later years and under favorable circumstances, the interest rate applicable to bonds of this quality fell to under 3 per cent. This *should* have meant an advance in the price of this 5 per cent issue to more than 160. But

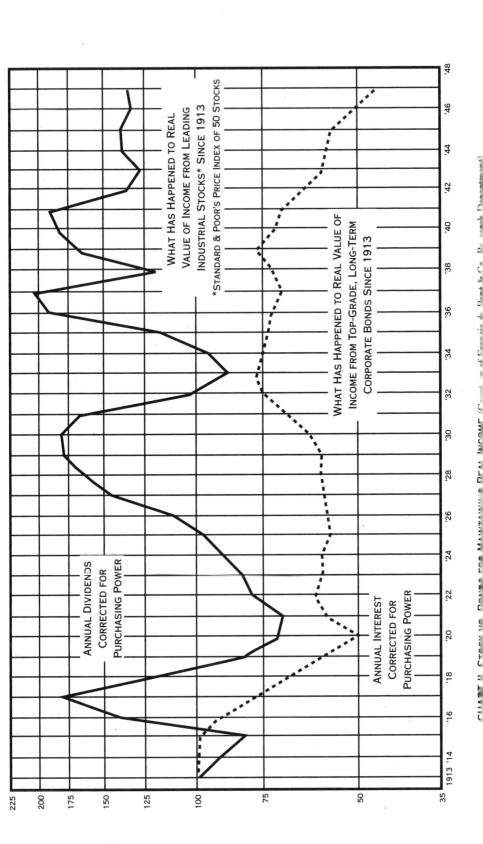

CHART II. STOCK VS. BONDS FOR MAINTAINING REAL INCOME (Courtesy of Economics Dept., Brett & Co. Research Department)

at this point, in March, 1946, the call feature became effective and the issue was redeemed at only 106.

The call feature in the typical bond contract is a thinly disguised instance of "heads I win, tails you lose." In the twelve years of declining interest rates, 1934–46, most investors had their long-term, high-coupon bonds called and were compelled to accept a lower and lower rate of return. Without the call feature their income would have remained unimpaired and the principal value of their bonds would have advanced tremendously. Now that interest rates have turned upward and may conceivably continue in that direction for some years, the investor who bought *low-coupon* bonds in recent years is faced with a substantial decline in their principal value. In sum: When interest rates go down, the call feature forces the investor to lose income; when the rate goes up, the investor loses principal.

This arrangement is so unsound from the investor's standpoint that it would not be stretching the point unduly to call it unsafe.

(C) Comparative Income Return. A third reason to question whether first-grade bond investments are sounder than common-stock investments is found in the higher income return of the latter over the years. The comparative soundness of two types of investment should be judged by the performance of representative-samples of both types during several extended periods of time. In such a comparison the honors will go to a diversified list of high-quality common stocks, *provided* they were purchased at price levels no higher than those justified by established standards of value.

The history of stock-versus-bond comparisons is an interesting one and in itself illustrates the dangers that lurk in all financial generalizations— including essentially accurate ones. In 1924 Edgar Lawrence Smith published a small book entitled *Common Stocks as Long-Term Investments.* This study consisted mainly of a careful comparison of the investment performance of representative common-stock lists with that of representative bond lists over various periods during the preceding sixty-five years. The results were measured both in terms of income realized and in terms of changes in market prices. They showed uniform and impressive superiorities on the side of common stocks.

On the thinking of the financial community, which rarely pays much attention to works of scholarship, E. L. Smith's book made a deep impression. The probable reason for this is that the book's appearance coincided with some psychological groundswell in the direction of the exploiting of common stocks and the study was seized upon as an academic justification for what the public was eager to do. Thus it happened that the sound research and reasoning in favor of common-stock investment were so twisted as to seem to sponsor a fatally overblown speculative bubble.

The factual research of Smith had shown that the advantage of common-stock investment lay in the ability of the typical successful company to earn appreciably better than bond interest on its capital. In that way it could both pay an average dividend in excess of bond interest and build up the value of its common stock through the reinvestment of undistributed earnings.[3] This meant that, *on the average*, if $100 invested in bonds for ten years would return the owner 4 per cent per annum, then $100 invested in leading common stocks in that period might return the owner, say, 7 per cent per annum.

All this was true *provided* the common-stock buyer paid no more for his shares than the amount invested in the business. If, acting with more enthusiasm than prudence, he paid several times the amount of the actual investment, then earnings of 7 per cent on the latter figure would result in a very small return on his purchase price. In other words, by bidding up the market quotations for common stocks to unprecedented heights the self-styled common-stock investor destroyed the very arithmetical advantage which was supposed to justify *prudent* commitments in stocks rather than in bonds.

Put concretely, there was a good statistical or analytical basis for buying the stocks represented in the Dow-Jones Industrial Average at a price of about 100 in 1924, when Smith's book was published. At that time they might have been termed sounder or at least shrewder investments than a corresponding list of bonds. But by the time the "Dow Average" had risen to 300 or more in 1928–29, not only had the stock buyer lost all the inherent advantages of a *normal* stock investment over a bond investment, but he was making commitments that could not possibly be supported by any reasonably expectable future earnings.

The extreme depth of the depression of the early 1930's was accounted for in good part, this writer believes, by the insane height of the preceding stock-market boom. Naturally there was a great revulsion of feeling toward

[3]This would be true even if the value increased by only a *part* of the reinvested profits. The studies of the Cowles Commission, covering the period 1871–1937, indicated, first, that common stocks failed to get *full* benefit from such reinvestment, but, second, that the partial benefit obtained was sufficient to give them an important advantage over representative bonds. (See *Common Stock Indexes*, Monograph 3 of the Cowles Commission on Research in Economics, published in 1938.)

the investment merits of common stocks. One eminent authority—whose field had always been bonds—went so far as to deny the possibility of any sort of "investment" in stocks. In other words, if you bought a common stock you were a speculator—and that was that.[4]

We have a sufficient perspective now to permit us to view investments in bonds and in common stocks in their proper proportions. Individual common stocks, however impressive their record, carry greater risks than do high-grade bonds. Common-stock investment *as a whole* presents a psychological hazard, because stock buyers are subject to human weakness and are prone to talk like investors and to act like speculators. But assuming that the common-stock investor can hold himself rigidly to a true investment pattern—which means that he will stick to high-grade stocks bought at reasonable prices—then the experience of the past fifty years supports the view that he will fare appreciably better than the bond investor. The conclusions of Edgar Lawrence Smith remain sound, as long as the investor does not depart from the fundamental relationships of *price* to earnings and to the assets upon which those conclusions were founded.

Rules re the Common-Stock Component

The selection of common stocks for the portfolio of the defensive investor is a relatively simple matter. Here we would suggest four rules to be followed:

(1) There should be adequate though not excessive diversification. This might mean a minimum of ten different issues and a maximum of about thirty.

(2) Each company selected should be large, prominent, and conservatively financed. Indefinite as these adjectives must be, their general sense is clear. Observations on this point are added at the end of the chapter.

(3) Each company should have a long record of continuous dividend payments. The acid test is the payment of dividends during the great depression years, 1931–33. We are reluctant, however, to include 1931–33 dividend payments as a positive requirement here. It would mean carrying the test of investment quality too far backward into the past and thus into circumstances

[4]This was the categorical assertion of Lawrence Chamberlain in *Investment & Speculation*, 1931, p. 8.

that may no longer be sufficiently relevant to future probabilities. As a logical compromise we would suggest the requirement of continuous dividend payments beginning at least in 1936. This would cover the period now generally referred to as "pre-war."

(4) The price paid for each should be reasonable in relation to its *average* earnings for the last five years or longer. We would recommend a price not to exceed twenty times such earnings. (Until a record of post-war earnings has been established, we suggest also a price not to exceed twenty-five times the 1936–40 earnings.) This would protect the investor against the common error of buying good stocks at high levels of the general market. It would also bar the purchase, even in normal markets, of a number of fine issues which sell at unduly high prices in anticipation of greatly increased *future* earnings. We feel that such common stocks are not appropriate for the defensive investor, who should not be called upon to use the judgment and foresight necessary to avoid errors in this field.

Investment Company Shares

The investor with a common-stock fund of under $5,000 would be well advised to acquire his list indirectly, through the medium of investment company shares.[5] Most of the shares now being purchased are issued by so-called "open end" companies, which sell their securities continuously through distributing organizations. The price charged includes a mark-up for selling costs, which tend to run about 8 per cent of the value of the underlying assets. The shares may be sold back to the company at any time at the then asset value. The investor receives dividends equivalent to those paid on the underlying securities, minus an operating-expense charge, which averages about 0.7 per cent on the net assets and possibly 15 per cent of the company's income.[6]

The well-established open-end companies are competently managed; they certainly make fewer serious mistakes than the typical small investor. For the latter the expense items involved in buying these shares are little, if any, in ex-

---

[5]These were originally known as "investment trusts," now a misnomer. They may properly be called "investment funds." Open-end companies are often called Mutual Funds.
[6]The larger funds show much lower expense ratios.

cess of the commissions on very small lots of many different common stocks. Undoubtedly, therefore, the open-end companies are performing a sound function on behalf of the average investor of small means who wishes to obtain an interest in an adequately diversified list of common stocks.

Whether the defensive investor with substantial means should buy open-end company shares rather than select his own common-stock portfolio is a more controversial question. There are good arguments on both sides; the investor may follow his own leanings in the matter.

The investment-company question is complicated by the existence of another type of fund, known as the closed-end company. Such enterprises do not buy and sell their own shares continuously, as do the open-end funds; hence the price of closed-end shares, like that of U.S. Steel common, is determined by buyers and sellers in the open market. Most of them sell regularly at substantial *discounts* from their asset value. In other words, when the market value of the typical company's assets is equal to, say, $20 per share of its stock, the latter can often be bought for only $14.

Practically all these "trusts" were originally floated in the lush days of the 1920's, which proved to be precisely the wrong time for the buyers. They suffered large losses in asset value and popularity after 1929; nor was their record free from the taint of mismanagement. They are run differently now, under strict supervision of the Securities and Exchange Commission. In spite of exemplary behavior and creditable over-all results for more than a decade, the closed-end companies have not regained public favor. There are complex reasons for this, to which we shall return later. Our summary judgment is that these shares are not unsuitable for purchase by the defensive investor. He should ask his adviser to select one or more companies which (a) have a better-than-average ten-year record and (b) can be bought at a discount of 25 per cent or better.

Investment in a "Common Trust Fund"

An alternative to the purchase of investment-fund shares is participation in a "common trust fund" operated by a bank or trust company. The salient provisions of one such common trust fund—"Diversified Trust Fund A," maintained by the Girard Trust Company of Philadelphia—may be summarized as follows:

To participate in the Fund it is necessary to establish an individual trust of which the Girard Trust Company is a trustee. There may be individual co-trustees. Participation in the Fund on the part of a single trust may not exceed $50,000—in order to limit the Fund to "trusts of modest size." There are no management fees, or charges for entering the Fund ("loading charges"), or charges for withdrawing money, but the Trust Company is compensated by receiving the standard fee for acting as a trustee of the "trust estate." Entries or withdrawals may be made at the beginning of each quarter, and the Fund's income is computed and distributed quarterly.

The Fund is invested in United States government securities, corporate bonds, preferred stocks, and common stocks. The proportions at the end of 1947 are given in the footnote on page 56. The return for 1947, based on the November, 1947, value, was 4.08 per cent—subject to the trustee's fee.

Let us assume that the Fund just described is typical of "common trust funds" generally—except, perhaps for its unusually large investment in preferred stocks. An investor could submit his ordinary capital to such administration by setting up a (revocable) trust fund for his own benefit. This would differ from buying shares in the usual open-end investment fund in one important respect. The latter concentrates almost entirely on a common-stock portfolio, and its shares would therefore represent only that portion of the investor's capital which he elects to place in common stocks. He would buy his United States Savings Bonds directly. The bank-administered trust fund, however, includes all the components of the investment portfolio, of which common stocks will ordinarily be less than half.

Portfolio Changes

It is now standard practice to submit all security lists for periodic inspection in order to see whether their quality can be improved. This, of course, is a major part of the service provided for clients by investment counselors. Nearly all brokerage houses are ready to make corresponding suggestions, without special fee, in return for the commission business involved.

Presumably our defensive investor should obtain—at least once a year—the same kind of advice regarding changes in his portfolio as he sought when his funds were first committed. Since he will have little expertness of his own on which to rely, it is important that he entrust himself only to firms of the highest reputation; otherwise he may easily fall into incompetent or unscrupulous hands. It is important, in any case, that at every such consultation he make clear to his adviser that he wishes to adhere closely to the four rules of common-stock selection given earlier in this chapter. Incidentally, if his list has been competently selected in the first instance, there should be no need for frequent or large-scale changes.

Formula Timing for the Defensive Investor

Aside from switches to improve quality, the defensive investor must consider whether he is going to sell when the market shows a substantial advance. An argument may be made here on either side. Some will contend that any endeavor to take advantage of market fluctuations must be thought of as taking the investor out of the category of the defensive and into the ranks of the enterprising. Others will say that, if the intelligent investor must not buy stocks at demonstrably high prices, the same minimum of prudence should lead him to sell at least part of his holdings when such levels are reached.

The reader must choose which of these semantic applications he will follow. If he elects to become a seller in high markets, then his best course undoubtedly is to adopt some formula timing plan, such as that already referred to in Chapter II. A scheme of that sort will relieve him of the necessity of making difficult decisions and at the same time protect him from the psychological danger of joining the crowd of enthusiastic buyers just when his principles should make him at least a partial seller. Important, too, is the fact that it will exempt him from having to hear and consider a vast lot of stock-market predictions and advice.

Dollar Averaging

An increasing amount of favorable attention in recent years has been directed toward the comparatively simple idea of placing the same amount of money in the same stock, or group of stocks, in successive months, quarters, or years. The statistical results shown by this method are quite satisfactory. As an example, let us summarize some figures presented by C. R. Sanderson in an article in the July, 1947, issue of *Exchange*, the monthly publication of the New York Stock Exchange.

In this article the consequences of investing $1,000 each year in Atchison, Topeka & Santa Fe Railroad common, beginning in 1927 and ending in 1946, are traced. The number of shares acquired each year ranged from 4 bought at 247 in 1929 to 52 bought at 19 in 1940. The annual average was 18.2 shares at 55, which is a much better result than is obtained by taking the straight average of the high and low prices during the period. Hence, although the price of 80 in June, 1947, was far lower than that in the early purchases, it indicated an appreciation of 44 per cent on the entire holding. In the meantime the dividends received averaged 6.3 per cent per annum on cost. Similar results were shown for ten other prominent common stocks assumed to have been purchased in the same manner.

In a period of wide fluctuations in stock prices, dollar averaging will show better results than the method of purchasing a fixed number of shares each year regardless of price. Either type of calculation, however, appears to us to be somewhat unrealistic. Scarcely anyone is so situated that he will normally have available for investment the same amount of money each year for twenty years—or, alternatively, enough to buy, say, 50 shares of a given stock each year at varying prices. Nor is it possible to plan such a procedure in advance, since the investor's financial position changes in important and unpredictable ways during so long a period.

For most investors, we think, the real meaning of dollar averaging indicates that they should be wary of putting more money in stocks at higher prices than they did at lower prices—which is a common failing—and that they should never let a lower price level scare them away from buying.

The Investor's Personal Situation

At the beginning of this chapter we referred briefly to the position of the individual portfolio owner. Let us return to this matter, in the light of our subsequent discussion of general policy. To what extent should the type of securities selected by the investor vary with his circumstances? As concrete examples representing widely different conditions, we shall take (a) a widow left $100,000 with which to support herself and her children; (b) a successful doctor in mid-career, with savings of $100,000 and yearly accretions of $5,000; and (c) a young man earning $100 per week and saving $500 a year.

For the widow, the problem of living on her income is a very difficult one. On the other hand the need for conservatism in her investments is paramount. A division of her fund about equally between United States bonds and first-grade common stocks is a compromise between these objectives and corresponds to our general prescription for the defensive investor. (The stock component may be placed as high as 75 per cent if the investor is psychologically prepared for this decision.)

We do not preclude the possibility that the widow may qualify as an enterprising investor, in which case her objectives and methods will be quite different. For that purpose she would need a temperament and preparation that are unusual in women; hence she should be very sure of her ground before departing from a defensive portfolio.

The one thing the widow must *not* do is to take speculative chances in order to "make some extra income." By this we mean trying for profits or high income without the necessary equipment to warrant full confidence in overall success. It would be far better for her to draw $1,000 per year out of her principal, in order to make both ends meet, than to risk half of it in poorly grounded, and therefore speculative, ventures.

The prosperous doctor has none of the widow's pressures and compulsions, yet we believe that his choices are pretty much the same. Is he willing to take a serious interest in the business of investment? If he lacks the impulse or the flair, he will do best to accept the easy role of the defensive investor. The division of his portfolio should then be no different from that of the "typical" widow, and there would be the same area of personal choice in fixing the size of the stock component. The annual savings should be invested in about the same proportions as the total fund.

The average doctor may be more likely than the average widow to elect to become an enterprising investor, and he is perhaps more likely to succeed in the undertaking. He has one important handicap, however—the fact that he has less time available to give to his investment education and to the administration of his funds. In fact, medical men are notoriously unsuccessful in their security dealings. The reason for this is that they usually have a strong desire to make a good return on their money, without the realization that to do so successfully requires both ample attention to the matter and something of a professional approach to security values.

Finally, the young man who saves $500 a year—and expects to do better gradually—finds himself with the same choices, though for still different reasons. Some of his savings should go automatically into Series E bonds. The balance is so modest that it seems hardly worth while for him to undergo a tough educational and temperamental discipline in order to qualify as an aggressive investor. Thus a simple resort to our standard program for the defensive investor would be at once the easiest and the most logical policy.

Let us not ignore human nature at this point. Finance has a fascination for many bright young people with limited means. They would like to be both intelligent and enterprising in the placement of their savings, even though investment income is much less important to them than their salaries. This attitude is all to the good. There is a great advantage for the young capitalist to begin his financial education and experience early. If he is going to operate as an aggressive investor he is certain to make some mistakes and to take some losses. Youth can stand these disappointments and profit by them. We urge the beginner in security buying not to waste his efforts and his money in trying to beat the market. Let him study security values and test out his judgment on price vs. value with the smallest possible sums initially.

Thus we return to the statement, made at the outset, that the kind of securities to be purchased and the rate of return to be sought depend not on the investor's financial resources but on his financial equipment in terms of knowledge, experience, and temperament.

Note on the Concept of "Risk"

It is conventional to speak of good bonds as less risky than good preferred stocks and of the latter as less risky than good common stocks. From this is derived the popular prejudice against common stocks because they are not "safe," which was demonstrated in the Federal Reserve Board's survey. We should like to point out that the words "risk" and "safety" are applied to securities in two different senses, with a resultant confusion in thought.

A bond is clearly proved unsafe when it defaults its interest or principal payments. Similarly, if a preferred stock or even a common stock is bought with the expectation that a given rate of dividend will be continued, then a reduction or passing of the dividend means that it is unsafe. It is also true that an investment contains a risk if there is a fair possibility that the holder may have to sell at a time when the price is well below cost.

Nevertheless, the idea of risk is often extended to apply to a possible decline in the price of a security, even though the decline may be of a cyclical and temporary nature and even though the holder is unlikely to be forced to sell at such times. These chances are present in all securities, other than United States Savings Bonds, and to a greater extent in the general run of common stocks than in senior issues generally. But we believe that what is here involved is not a true risk in the useful sense of the term. The man who holds a mortgage on a building might have to take a loss if he were forced to sell it at an unfavorable time. That element is not taken into account in judging the safety or risk of ordinary real-estate mortgages, the only criterion being the certainty of punctual payments. In the same way the risk attached to an ordinary commercial business is measured by the chance of its losing money, not by what would happen if the owner, were forced to sell.

In line with our discussion in Chapter II we would emphasize our conviction that the bona fide investor does not lose money merely because the market price of his holdings declines; the fact that a decline may occur does not mean that he is running a true risk of loss. If a group of well-selected common-stock investments shows a satisfactory over-all return, as measured through a fair number of years, then this group investment has proved to be "safe." During that period its market value is bound to fluctuate, and as likely as not it will sell for a while under the buyer's cost. If that fact makes the investment "risky" it would then have to be called both risky and safe at the same time. This confusion may be avoided if we apply the concept of risk solely to a loss of value which either (a) is realized through actual sale or (b) is ascertained to be caused by a significant deterioration in the company's position.

Many common stocks do involve risks of such deterioration. But it is our thesis that a properly executed group investment in common stocks does not carry any substantial risk of this sort and that therefore it should not be termed "risky" merely because of the element of price fluctuation.

Note on the Category of "Large, Prominent, and Conservatively Financed Corporations"

The quoted phrase in our caption was used earlier in the chapter to describe the kind of common stocks to which defensive investors should limit their purchases—provided also that they had paid continuous dividends for a considerable number of years. A criterion based on adjectives is always ambiguous. Where is the dividing line for size, for prominence, and for conservatism of financial structure? On the last point we can suggest a specific standard which, though arbitrary, is in line with accepted thinking. An industrial company's finances are not conservative unless the common stock (at book value) represents at least half of the total capitalization, including all bank debt. For a railroad or public utility the figure should be 30 per cent.

The words "large" and "prominent" carry the notion of substantial size combined with a leading position in the industry. Such companies are often referred to as "primary"; all other common stocks are then called "secondary," except that growth stocks are ordinarily placed in a separate class by those who buy them as such. To supply an element of concreteness here, let us suggest that to be "large" in present-day terms a company should have $50 million of assets or do $50 million of business. Again, to be "prominent" a company should rank among the first quarter or first third in size within its industry group.

It would be foolish, however, to insist upon such arbitrary criteria. They are offered merely as guides to those who may ask for guidance. But any rule which the investor may set for himself and which does no violence to the common-sense meanings of "large" and "prominent" should be acceptable. By the very nature of the case there must be a large group of marginal companies which some will and others will not include among those suitable for defensive investment. There is no harm in such diversity of opinion and action. In fact, it has a salutary effect upon stock-market conditions, because it permits a gradual differentiation or transition between the categories of primary and secondary stock issues.

V

Portfolio Policy for the Aggressive Investor: Negative Approach

THE ENTERPRISING INVESTOR should start from the same base as the defensive investor, namely, a division of his funds between United States Savings Bonds and high-grade common stocks bought at reasonable prices. He will be prepared to branch out into other kinds of security commitments, but in each case he will want a well-reasoned justification for the departure. There is a difficulty in discussing this topic in orderly fashion, because there is no single or ideal pattern for aggressive operations. The field of choice is wide; the selection should depend not only upon the individual's competence and equipment but perhaps equally well upon his interests and preferences.

The most useful generalizations for the enterprising investor are of a negative sort. Let him avoid ordinary corporate bonds as long as the best-grade issues yield little more than his United States Savings Bonds. Let him leave high-grade preferred stocks to corporate buyers. Let him also avoid inferior types of bonds and preferred stocks unless they can be bought at bargain levels—which means ordinarily at prices at least 30 per cent under par. He will let someone else buy foreign government bond issues, even though the yield may be attractive. He will also be wary of all kinds of new issues, including convertible bonds and preferreds that seem quite tempting and common stocks with excellent earnings confined to the recent past.

Second-Grade Bonds and Preferreds

We have already given our reasons for advising against high-grade corporate senior issues when their yields are as close to those obtainable on United States Savings Bonds as they are at present. Something should be said now about investing in second-grade issues, which can readily be found to yield any specified return up to 8 per cent or more. The main difference between first- and second-grade bonds is usually found in the number of times the interest charges have been covered by earnings. Many investors buy securities of this kind because they "need income" and cannot get along with the meager return offered by top-grade issues. Experience clearly shows that it is unwise to buy a bond or a preferred which lacks adequate safety merely because the yield is attractive. (Here the word "merely" implies that the issue is not selling at a large discount and thus does not offer an opportunity for a substantial gain in principal value.) Where such securities are bought at full prices—that is, not many points under 100—the chances are very great that at some future time the holder will see much lower quotations. For when bad business comes, or just a bad market, issues of this kind prove highly susceptible to severe sinking spells; often interest or dividends are suspended or at least endangered, and frequently there is a pronounced price weakness even though the operating results are not at all bad.

As a specific illustration of this characteristic of second-quality senior issues, let us summarize the price behavior of a group of ten railroad *income bonds* in 1946–47. These comprise all of those which sold at 96 or more in 1946, their high prices averaging 102½. By the following year the group had registered low prices averaging only 68, a loss of one-third of the market value in a very short time. Peculiarly enough, the railroads of the country were showing much better earnings in 1947 than in 1946; hence the drastic price decline ran counter to the business picture and was a reflection of the sell-off in the general market. But it should be pointed out that the shrinkage in these income bonds was proportionately larger than that in the *common stocks* in the Dow-Jones Industrial List (about 23 per cent). Obviously the purchaser of these bonds at a cost above 100 could not have expected to participate to any extent in a further rise in the securities market. The only attractive feature was the income yield, averaging about 4¼ per cent. Yet the sequel showed all too soon and too plainly that for that slight advantage in annual income the buyer of these second-grade bonds was risking the loss of a substantial part of his principal.

The above example permits us to pay our respects to the popular fallacy that goes under the sobriquet of a "businessman's investment." That involves the purchase of a security showing a larger yield than is obtainable on a high-grade issue and carrying a correspondingly greater risk. It is bad business to accept an acknowledged possibility of a loss of principal in exchange for a mere 1 or 2 per cent of additional yearly income. If you are willing to assume some risk you should be certain that you can realize a really substantial gain in principal value if things go well. Hence a second-grade 4½ per cent bond selling at par is almost always a bad purchase. The same issue at 70 might make more sense—and if you are patient you will probably be able to buy it at that level.

Second-grade bonds and preferred stocks possess two contradictory attributes which the intelligent investor must bear clearly in mind. Nearly all of them suffer severe sinking spells in bad markets. On the other hand, a large proportion of them recover their position when favorable conditions return, and these ultimately "work out all right." This is true even of (cumulative) preferred stocks which fail to pay dividends for many years. During the boom period of 1945–47 many of these large accumulations were paid off either in cash or in new securities, and the principal was often discharged as well. As a result, large profits were made by people who, a few years previously, had bought these issues when they were friendless and sold at low prices.[1]

It may well be true that, in an over-all accounting, the higher yields obtainable on second-grade senior issues will prove to have offset those principal losses which were irrecoverable. In other words, an investor who bought all such issues at their offering prices might conceivably fare as well, *in the long run*, as one who limited himself to first-quality securities. Only an elab-

---

[1] For example: Cities Service $6 First Preferred, not paying dividends, sold at as low as 15 in 1937 and at 27 in 1943. In 1947 it was retired by exchange for $196.50 of 3 per cent debentures for each share, and it sold as high as 186.

orate statistical study, covering many years and innumerable issues, could prove whether this is so.[2]

But for practical purposes the question is largely irrelevant. Regardless of the outcome, the buyer of second-grade issues at full prices will be worried and discommoded when their price declines precipitately. Furthermore, he cannot buy enough issues to assure an "average" result, nor is he in a position to set aside a portion of his larger income to offset or "amortize" those principal losses which prove to be permanent. Finally, it is mere common sense to abstain from buying securities at around 100 if long experience indicates that they can probably be bought at 70 or less in the next weak market.

Foreign Government Bonds

All investors with even small experience know that foreign bonds, as a whole, have had a bad investment history since 1914. This was inevitable in the light of two world wars and an intervening world depression of unexampled depth. Yet every few years market conditions are sufficiently favorable to permit the sale of some new foreign issues at a price of about par. This phenomenon tells us a good deal about the working of the average investor's mind.

Why does he buy these bonds at their offering prices? Is it possible that he feels it his duty to help balance our international accounts by lending to other countries? We doubt that any such altruistic consideration enters his thoughts or that he is willing to risk or lose his money to maintain our export trade. The fact is, simply, that he would like more interest on his money than he can obtain from good domestic bonds. In the 1920's he was attracted by the 7 per cent and the 8 per cent promised on Latin-American flotations. These high interest rates themselves helped to make default inevitable. Most of these issues have paid no interest, or only small amounts, for nearly twenty years. Their prices have declined, for the most part, to less than 10 cents on the dollar. In spite of great economic advantages accruing to the neutral South American countries during the Second World War, the in-

---

[2]Such a study is now being carried on under the direction of the National Bureau of Economic Research.

vestors in these issues have since obtained comparatively small recoveries of principal or interest.

After 1945 it was again possible to sell a few foreign issues in this market—as, for example, the Australian 3¼s, which were offered at 100 in August, 1946. At that time the buyer was obtaining just three-quarters of one per cent more on his money than the yield on AAA corporate bonds— hardly enough to warrant the assumption of a recognized risk. The purchasers of the Australian issue must have told themselves that the bonds were practically riskless, presumably on the ground that Australia was a far different kind of debtor than Italy or Brazil.

By what process of calculation could the buyers of the Australian bonds assure themselves that at no time before their maturity in 1956 would that commonwealth suffer severe economic, or internal political, or international problems? Were they certain that the low price of 38 registered for the 5 per cent bonds of Australia in 1942 had no bearing on future possibilities—or were they perhaps ignorant of this market record? We doubt that the purchasers did much thinking along these lines. They wanted "just a little more income." Australia seemed like a good risk—and that was enough.[3]

In writing thus critically of the wisdom of buying these issues, we are conscious of the broad problem of international financial relationships that underlies foreign-bond investment. It is normal for rich, creditor nations to lend abroad. A free-enterprise country like ours should do its lending on a private rather than on a governmental basis. The private lenders must accept a moderate interest rate. All this justifies the Australian flotations— from every standpoint except that of the investor who seeks a thoroughly satisfactory security. It is not our function here to reconcile the conflicting objectives just noted. Perhaps they will be reconciled in the future, as they have been in the past, by the fortunate presence of enough not-too-careful investors.

---

[3] By the end of 1947 the Australian 3¼s had declined to 87½. Note also the following vicissitudes of Czechoslovak 8s, originally sold in 1922 at 96½. They advanced to 112 in 1928, declined to 67¾ in 1932, recovered to 106 in 1936, collapsed to 6 in 1939, recovered to 117 in 1946, and fell to 35 in 1948.

New Issues Generally

It might seem ill-advised to attempt any broad statements about new is-sues as a class, since they cover the widest possible range of quality and at-tractiveness. Certainly there will be exceptions to any suggested rule. Our one recommendation is that all investors should be wary of new issues—which means, simply, that these should be subjected to careful examination and unusually severe tests before they are purchased.

There are two reasons for this double caveat. The first is that new issues have special salesmanship behind them, which calls therefore for a special de-gree of sales resistance. The second is that most new issues are sold under "favorable market conditions"—which means favorable for the seller and consequently less favorable for the buyer. The 1946–47 offerings of Aus-tralian bonds just discussed are a particular example of this general thesis.

The effect of these considerations becomes steadily more important as we go down the scale from the highest-quality bonds through second-grade se-nior issues to common-stock flotations at the bottom. A tremendous amount of refinancing, consisting of the repayment of existing bonds at call price and their replacement by new issues with lower coupons, was done in recent years. Most of this was in the category of high-grade bonds and preferred stocks. The buyers were largely financial institutions, amply qualified to pro-tect their interests. Hence these offerings were carefully priced to meet the going rate for comparable issues, and high-powered salesmanship had little effect on the outcome. As interest rates fell lower and lower the buyers fi-nally came to pay too high a price for these issues, and some of them have since declined appreciably in the market. This is one aspect of the general tendency to sell new securities of all types when conditions are most favor-able to the issuer; but in the case of first-quality issues the ill effects to the purchaser are likely to be unpleasant rather than serious.

The situation proves somewhat different when we study the lower-grade bonds and preferred stocks sold during the 1945–46 period. Here the effect of the selling effort is more apparent, because most of these issues were probably placed with individual and inexpert investors. It was characteristic of these offerings that they did not make an adequate showing when judged by the performance of the companies in the pre-war period. They did look safe enough, for the most part, if it could be assumed that war-time and post-war earnings would continue without a serious setback. The investment bankers who brought out these issues presumably accepted this assumption, and their salesman had little difficulty in persuading themselves and their customers to a like effect. Nevertheless it was an unsound approach to investment, and one likely to prove costly.

Like all bull-market periods, the years 1944–46 were characterized by the transformation of a large number of privately owned businesses into companies with quoted shares. The most frequent procedure was to sell an issue of preferred stock to the public—usually to raise money for the expanded needs of the enterprise—and also to sell about 25 per cent of the common stock for the account of the old owners. Thus the latter would retain about 75 per cent of the common and would cash in on the remainder at attractive terms. In the majority of cases the preferred stock was made convertible into the common stock at a price somewhat higher than the offering price of the common.

This device, now standard in corporate finance, deserves consideration here. For convenience we shall deal not only with new offerings of convertible issues but also with the form in general. Many investors have undoubtedly been introduced to convertibles through security salesmen who have had new issues to distribute.

Convertible Issues

Securities of this type are claimed to be especially advantageous to both the investor and the issuing corporation. The investor receives the superior protection of a bond or preferred stock, plus the opportunity to participate in any substantial rise in the value of the common stock. The issuer is able to raise capital at a moderate interest or preferred-dividend cost, and if the expected prosperity materializes the issuer will get rid of the senior obligation by having it exchanged into common stock. Thus both sides to the bargain will fare unusually well.

Obviously the foregoing paragraph must overstate the case somewhere, for you cannot by a mere ingenious device make a bargain much better for both sides. In exchange for the conversion privilege the investor usually gives up something important in quality or yield, or both. Conversely, if the company gets its money at lower cost because of the conversion feature, it is surrendering in return part of the common stockholders' claim to future enhancement. On this subject there are a number of tricky arguments to be advanced both pro and con. The safest conclusion that can be reached is that convertible issues are like any other *form* of security, in that their form itself guarantees neither attractiveness nor unattractiveness. That question will depend on all the facts surrounding the individual issue.

We do know, however, that the *typical* convertible issue floated in 1945–46 proved to be unattractive. In fact, the market behavior of this whole group turned out to be far more disappointing than that of the preferred stocks offered without conversion features. The compilation in Table VII will summarize the picture.

The conclusion to be drawn from these figures is not that convertible issues are in themselves less desirable than non-convertible or "straight" securities. Other things being equal, the opposite is true. But we clearly see that other things are *not* equal in practice and that the addition of the conversion privilege often—perhaps generally—betrays an absence of genuine investment quality for the issue.

It is true, of course, that a convertible preferred is safer than the common stock of the same company—that is to say, it carries smaller risk of eventual loss of principal. Consequently those who buy new convertibles instead of the corresponding common stock are logical to that extent. But in most cases the common would not have been an intelligent purchase to begin with, and the substitution of the convertible preferred did not improve the picture sufficiently. Furthermore, a good deal of the buying of convertibles was done by investors who had no special interest or confidence in the common stock—that is, they would never have thought of buying the common at the time—but who were tempted by what seemed an ideal combination of a prior claim plus a conversion privilege close to the current market. In a number of instances this combination has worked out well, but the statistics seem to show that it is more likely to prove a pitfall.

TABLE VII. PRICE RECORD OF NEW PREFERRED
STOCK ISSUES OFFERED IN 1946

Price Change from Issue Price to Low up to July, 1947:	"Straight" Issues	Convertible and Participating Issues
No decline	7 issues	0 issues
Declined 0–10%	16 "	2 "
10–20%	11 "	6 "
20–40%	3 "	22 "
40% or more	0 "	12 "
Average Decline	37 issues	42 issues
	About 9%	About 30%

In connection with the ownership of convertibles there is a special problem which most investors fail to realize. Even when a profit appears it brings
a dilemma with it. Should the holder sell on a small rise; should he hold for a
much bigger advance; if the issue is called—as often happens when the common has gone up considerably—should he sell out then or convert into and
retain the common stock?

Let us talk in concrete terms. You buy a 3½ per cent bond at 100, convertible into stock at 25—that is, at the rate of 40 shares for each $1,000
bond. The stock goes to 30, which makes the bond worth at least 120, and so
it sells at 125. You either sell or hold. If you hold, hoping for a higher price,
you are pretty much in the position of a common stockholder, since if the
stock goes down your bond will go down too. Your income return is likely to
be much less than that on the common. A conservative person is likely to say
that beyond 125 his position has become too speculative, and therefore he
sells and makes a gratifying 25 per cent profit.

So far, so good. But pursue the matter a bit. In many cases where the
holder sells at 125 the common stock continues to advance, carrying the
convertible with it, and the investor experiences that peculiar pain that
comes to the man who has sold out much too soon. The next time he decides to hold for 150 or 200. The issue goes up to 140 and he does not sell.

Then the market breaks and his bond slides down to 80. Again he has done the wrong thing.

Aside from the mental anguish involved in making these bad guesses—and they seem to be almost inevitable—there is a real arithmetical drawback to operations in convertible issues. It may be assumed that a stern and uniform policy of selling at 25 or 30 per cent profit will work out best as applied to many holdings. This would then mark the upper limit of profit and would be realized only on the issues that worked out well. But, if—as appears to be true—these issues lack adequate underlying security and tend to be floated and purchased in the latter stages of a bull market, then a goodly proportion of them will fail to rise to 125 but will not fail to collapse when the market turns downward. Thus the spectacular opportunities in convertibles prove to be illusory in practice, and the over-all experience is marked by fully as many substantial losses—at least of a temporary kind—as there are gains of similar magnitude.

The following history of the Eversharp convertible issues during the 1945–48 period is interesting in itself; it also serves to point up our thesis that most convertibles present a peculiar combination of opportunity and risk which is likely to prove tantalizing and disappointing to the investor.

During 1945 Eversharp sold at 103 two issues, each for $3,000,000, of income debenture 4½s, convertible into common stock at $40 per share. The stock advanced rapidly to 65½, and then (after a three for two split-up) to the equivalent of 88. The latter price made the convertible debentures worth no less than 220. During this period the two issues were called at a small premium; hence they were practically all converted into common stock, which was retained by many of the original buyers of the debentures. The price promptly began a severe decline and in March, 1948, the stock sold as low as 7¾. This represented a value of only 27 for the debenture issues, or a loss of 75 per cent of the original price instead of a profit of over 100 per cent.

Our general attitude toward new convertible issues is thus a mistrustful one. We mean here, as in other similar observations, that the investor should look more than twice before he buys them. After such hostile scrutiny he may find some exceptional offerings that are too good to refuse. The ideal combination, of course, is a strongly secured convertible, exchangeable for a common stock which itself is attractive, and at a price only slightly higher than the current market. Every now and then a new offering appears that meets these requirements. By the nature of the securities markets, however, you are more likely to find such an opportunity in some older issue which has developed into a favorable position rather than in a new flotation. (If a new issue is a really strong one, it is not likely to have a good conversion privilege.)

The fine balance between what is given and what is withheld in a standard-type convertible issue is well illustrated by the extensive use of this type of security in the financing of American Telephone & Telegraph Company. Since 1913 the company has sold at least seven separate issues of convertible bonds, most of them through subscription rights to stockholders. The convertible bonds had the important advantage to the company of bringing in a much wider class of buyers than would have been available for a stock offering, since the bonds are popular with many financial institutions which possess huge resources but some of which are not permitted to buy stocks. The interest return on the bonds has generally been less than half the corresponding dividend yield on the stock—a factor which was calculated to offset the prior claim of the bondholders. Since the company has been able to maintain its dividend without change for many years, the result has been the eventual conversion of all the older convertible issues into stock. Thus the buyers of these convertibles have fared well through the years—but not quite so well as if they had bought the capital stock in the first place. This example establishes the soundness of American Telephone & Telegraph, but not the intrinsic attractiveness of convertible bonds. To prove them sound in practice we should need to have a number of instances in which the convertible worked out well even though the common stock proved disappointing. Such instances are not easy to find.

New Common-Stock Offerings

Common-stock financing takes two different forms. In the case of companies already listed, additional shares are offered pro rata to the existing stockholders. The subscription price is set below the current market, and the "rights" to subscribe have an initial money value. The sale of the new shares is almost always underwritten by one or more investment-banking houses, but it is the general hope and expectation that all the new shares will be taken by the exercise of the subscription rights. Thus the sale of additional common stock of listed companies does not ordinarily call for active selling effort on the part of distributing firms.

The second type is the placement with the public of common stock of what were formerly privately owned enterprises. Most of this stock is sold for the account of the controlling interests to enable them to cash in on a favorable market and to diversify their own finances. (When new money is raised for the business it comes most frequently via the sale of preferred stock, as previously noted.) This activity follows a well-defined pattern, which by the nature of the security markets must bring many losses and disappointments to the public. The dangers arise both from the character of the businesses that are thus financed and from the market conditions that make the financing possible.

In the early part of the century a large proportion of our leading companies were introduced to public trading. As time went on, the number of enterprises of first rank which remained closely held steadily diminished; hence original common-stock flotations have tended to be concentrated more and more on relatively small concerns. By an unfortunate correlation, during the same period the stock-buying public has been developing an ingrained preference for the major companies and a similar prejudice against the minor ones. This prejudice, like many others, tends to become weaker as bull markets are built up; the large and quick profits shown by common stocks as a whole are sufficient to dull the public's critical faculty, just as they sharpen its acquisitive instinct. During these periods, also, quite a number of privately owned concerns can be found that are enjoying excellent results—although most of these would not present too impressive a record if the figures were carried back, say, ten years or more.

When these factors are put together the following consequences emerge: Somewhere in the middle of the bull market the first common-stock flotations make their appearance. These are priced not unattractively, and some large profits are made by the buyers of the early issues. As the market rise continues, this brand of financing grows more frequent; the quality of the companies becomes steadily poorer; the prices asked and obtained verge on the exorbitant. One fairly dependable sign of the approaching end of a bull swing is the fact that new common stocks of small and nondescript companies are offered at prices somewhat higher than the current level for many medium-sized companies with a long market history. (It should be added that very little of this common-stock financing is ordinarily done by banking houses of prime size and reputation.)

The heedlessness of the public and the willingness of selling organizations to sell whatever may be profitably sold can have only one result—price collapse. In many cases the new issues lose 75 per cent and more of their offering price. The situation is worsened by the aforementioned fact that, at bottom, the public has a real aversion to the very kind of small issue that it bought so readily in its careless moments. Many of these issues fall, proportionately, as much below their true value as they formerly sold about it.

An elementary requirement for the intelligent investor is an ability to resist the blandishments of salesmen offering new common-stock issues during bull markets. Even if one or two can be found that can pass severe tests of quality and value, it is probably bad policy to get mixed up in this sort of business. Of course the salesman will point to many such issues which have had good-sized market advances—including some that go up spectacularly the very day they are sold. But all this is part of the speculative atmosphere. It is easy money. For every dollar you make in this way you will be lucky if you end up by losing only two.

Some of these issues may prove excellent buys—a few years later, when nobody wants them and they can be had at a small fraction of their true worth.

VI

—◆◆◆—

Portfolio Policy for the
Enterprising Investor:
The Positive Side

THE ACTIVITIES characteristic of the enterprising investor may be classified under four heads:

(1) Buying in low markets and selling in high markets
(2) Buying carefully chosen "growth stocks"
(3) Buying bargain issues of various types
(4) Buying into "special situations"

1. General Market Policy—Formula Timing

In Chapter II we discussed briefly the possibilities and limitations of a policy of entering the market when it is depressed and selling out in the advanced stages of a boom. This bright idea appeared feasible from a first inspection of the market chart covering the gyrations of the past fifty years. But closer study indicated that no simple and fool-proof formula could be counted upon to work out in the future. For example, the history of the Dow-Jones Industrial Average suggests that it *should* be possible to buy at 140 during the next few years and sell out at 280 later. But this is only an indication and not a true prediction. Nor can we tell whether the probability of its working out is good enough to justify the basing of an investment policy upon it.

The various formula timing plans, which have come into prominence in recent years, all represent a compromise attempt to deal with this probability. Instead of planning to do all the buying at 140—or some similar price— and all the selling at 280, the formula user buys at various stages on the downside and sells in installments on the upside. By this means he can obtain some benefit from market fluctuations, even if they do not fall precisely within the range suggested by the chart. Thus his formula assures him at least *some* profit if the future performance of the market is only reasonably close to that of the past.

A simple application of this idea would be to sell 10 per cent of your holdings when the market advances 10 per cent above a chosen base or central level; then to sell 20 per cent of the remainder when it advances another 10 per cent; and so on. Repurchases would be made after the market had declined to the central level, and on some similar schedule. Following this plan, you would have sold all your stocks if and when the market level reached double the base figure, and you would then have realized a profit of 37 per cent above the base.

For a full and illuminating discussion of the ins and outs of formula timing plans the reader is referred to two books: *Investment Timing by Formula Plans*, by H. T. Carpenter[1] and *Successful Investing Formulas*, by Lucile Tomlinson.[2] These supply many examples of different types of plans, with calculations of their results—in a few cases taken from the record of actual operations, but more often as applied to hypothetical or imaginary funds.

There is some danger here for both writers and investors to lose themselves in a maze of alternative procedures. It is well to bear certain basic facts in mind. No one plan has an *a priori* or guaranteed advantage over any other. The relative results of various plans will depend on how well each happens to fit the market fluctuations of the future.

The more certain the investor is that the range of future fluctuations will

---

[1] New York: Harper & Brothers, 1943.
[2] Boston: Barron's, 1947.

duplicate the past, the more justified he is in concentrating his buying close to the bottom line of the Dow-Jones performance chart and his selling not much below the top line. But, since we lack any proof that the past range must determine that of the future, most of us will prefer a compromise formula by which buying and selling is done in various stages below and above the indicated median level. So, too, there is no assured advantage as between a plan to sell 100 per cent of our stock holdings by the time a designated high point is reached and a plan that assures retention of some stocks under all circumstances. The latter in some measure protects against an inflationary breakout of a permanent character into a much higher band of fluctuation than we have experienced hitherto. But like all the other choices in formula timing plans the wisdom of this one depends not on reasoning but on results.

The sovereign virtue of all formula plans lies in the compulsion they bring upon the investor to sell when the crowd is buying and to buy when the crowd lacks confidence. If the reader adopts a formula plan today and it happens to turn out badly—because the market chances to soar upwards to unexpected heights and does not return—it will still prove to have been worth while. For the principle and the psychology will remain sound and applicable to the markets of the future, however far removed their middle range may be from the line of the past.

Since all the rest is a matter of detail or of guesswork, we strongly underscore Lucile Tomlinson's sage advice to "formula investors" that they select a plan that is simple and convenient in their circumstances.

2. Growth-Stock Approach

Every investor would like to select a list of securities that will do better than the average over a period of years. A growth stock may be defined as one which has done this in the past and is expected to do so in the future.[3] Thus it seems only logical that the intelligent investor should concentrate upon the selection of growth stocks. Actually the matter is more complicated, as we shall try to show.

---

[3] A company with an ordinary record cannot, without confusing the term, be called a growth company or a "growth stock" merely because its proponent expects it to do better than the average in the future. It is just a "promising company."

It is a mere statistical chore to identify companies that have "outperformed the averages" in the past. The investor can obtain a list of fifty or a hundred such enterprises from his broker. Why, then, should he not merely pick out the fifteen or twenty most likely-looking issues of this group—and lo! he has a guaranteed-successful stock portfolio?

There are two catches to this simple idea. The first is that common stocks with good records and apparently good prospects sell at correspondingly high prices. The investor may be right in his judgment of their prospects and still not fare particularly well, merely because he has paid in full (and perhaps overpaid) for the expected prosperity. The second is that his judgment as to the future may prove wrong. Unusually rapid growth cannot keep up forever; when a company has already registered a brilliant expansion, its very increase in size makes a repetition of its achievement more difficult. At some point the growth curve flattens out, and in many cases it turns downward.

An interesting sidelight on the results of investing in the most popular issues appeared in the *Commercial & Financial Chronicle* of June 16, 1948. In a contest, run by another magazine, on how to invest $100,000 for a widow, specific suggestions were made by 801 entrants. The five most popular common-stock suggestions were: Du Pont, American Telephone & Telegraph, General Electric, International Nickel, and General Motors. From August, 1939, to June, 1948, these five issues appreciated only 11 per cent on the average, although the Dow-Jones Industrial List—which included these and twenty-five other issues—advanced 45 per cent.

Note that the five stocks most frequently suggested were the favorite selections of well-informed students of securities. The trouble with them was that they were too obvious a choice: Their future was already being paid for in the 1939 price. In Chapter XII we shall supply examples of popular growth stocks which in recent years have failed to continue their progress and have even reported downright disappointing results. Naturally their purchase at a time when they were most favored and active in the market would have had disastrous consequences.

Presumably it is the function of intelligent investment to overcome these hazards by the exercise of sound judgment and skillful selection. This is a natural and appropriate endeavor for our aggressive investor. We regret that we have little concrete guidance to offer him in this field. The exercise of specialized foresight, the weighing of future probabilities and possibilities,

are not to be learned out of books—nor can they be aided much by suggested rules and techniques.

Investors who may wish to pursue this aspect of investment policy in detail are referred to an elaborate study of the life cycle of industries, entitled
The Ebb and Flow of Investment Values, by Mead and Grodinsky.[4] The book
discusses a number of "symptoms of decay," by the noticing of which the
alert investor may escape out of a once expanding industry before it is too
late. In our view the suggested techniques require more ability and application than most investors can bring to bear on the problem. (Furthermore, we
are in complete disagreement with the underlying thesis of the book that
once an industry has turned downward it will never recover and that all securities within it must be permanently avoided.)

The stock of a growing company, if purchasable at a suitable price, is obviously preferable to others. No matter how enthusiastic the investor may
feel about the prospects of a particular company, however, he should set a
limit upon the price that he is willing to pay for such prospects. Let us anticipate for a moment the technique of stock valuation which we shall sketch
out in the next section of the book. Assume that the investor is willing to pay
fourteen times the estimated per-share earnings—projecting the average of
the next five or seven years—for a sound and large company of merely
medium quality and prospects. In the case of a growth company we should
recommend payment of a premium for the growth potential not to exceed
about 50 per cent of the value determined without it. This would mean that
our investor would pay *not more* than, say, twenty times the estimated average future earnings for a growth stock, as against fourteen times for an "ordinary" stock.[5]

Such a rule would result at times in the missing of an unusually good opportunity. More often, we think, it would mean the investor's saving himself
from "going overboard" on an issue that looked especially good to him and
everyone else and consequently was selling much too high. The two types of
experiences may be illustrated by the example of Abbott Laboratories on the
one hand and Parke Davis on the other in 1939.

Both Abbott Laboratories and Parke Davis were popular issues in 1939.

[4]New York: D. Appleton-Century Co., 1939.

[5]Note that by this procedure the growth factor receives double recognition— first, in the optimistic
estimate of future earnings, and then in the liberal multiplier.

They represented two highly successful enterprises in the field of "ethical drugs" and were considered to have excellent prospects of long-term growth. The average price of Parke Davis in 1939 was 42, or 22 times that year's earnings. The price of Abbott was 62, which also was 22 times the current earnings. The ordinary investor was as likely to buy one issue as the other.

If we proceed now to April, 1948, we find that Abbott's earnings had risen from $2.90 per share in 1939 to $10.90 in 1947. Its price, allowing for a split-up, was equivalent to 150, or much more than double its 1939 average. In the same years the profits of Parke Davis had moved only from $1.89 to $2.13, in spite of the record prosperity of 1947. And its price had fallen from 42 to 29.

Thus the choice between the attractive issue that turns out well and the one that does poorly is by no means easy to make in the growth-stock field. It might be interesting here to add some figures on Sharp & Dohme common, a third pharmaceutical stock which was by no means well regarded in 1939—for its average price was only 6 (as against 28 in 1929) and it paid no dividend. On its past record it could not qualify at all as a growth issue. Yet in 1947 its earnings were $3.14 per share as against only 13 cents in 1939, and its April price in 1948 had risen to 26—a much better percentage gain than Abbott's. The best opportunity in the field of drug stocks turned out to be where it was least expected—an all-too-frequent happening.

It is perhaps superfluous to warn the reader that he should never consider any investment principle proved by the mere citing of a few examples. Single experiences may be adduced in favor of any speculative or investment rule, however silly. Thus, strictly speaking, our own quoted examples demonstrate nothing except that certain events can happen. If we say that they are typical and illustrate general experience, the reader must take our statement on trust. Some special validity attaches, however, to examples which comprise group experiences and are taken without the benefit of hindsight.

In this connection we present in Table VIII a calculation showing how a carefully selected list of thirty-two growth stocks would have fared from their date of purchase in December, 1939, to December, 1947. The list is the early 1940 portfolio of National Investors Company, an investment fund which concentrates on the selection of growth companies.

The dividend return is not allowed for in the figures given; it would not materially affect the indicated results. This selection of 32 growth stocks shows up better than the two other lists of 30 and 354 stocks respectively. It demonstrates that superior results may be obtained in this field if the choices are competently made. Even with careful selection, some of the individual issues may fare relatively poorly. Among the thirty-two growth stocks there were six that actually declined and four others that had only slight advances. (Incidentally, these ten issues include the best-known names in the list, such as American Airlines, Du Pont, and Montgomery Ward.) Thus for good results in the growth-stock field there is need not only for skillful analysis but for ample diversification as well.

To summarize this section: The enterprising investor may properly buy growth stocks. He should beware of paying excessively for them, and he might well limit the price by some practical rule. A growth-stock program will not be automatically successful; its outcome will depend on the foresight and judgment of the investor or his advisers rather than on any clear-cut methods of analysis. (Some additional material on this subject appears in Chapter XIII.)

TABLE VIII. PERFORMANCE OF A GROUP OF GROWTH STOCKS
SELECTED EARLY IN 1940

(PORTFOLIO OF NATIONAL INVESTORS COMPANY)

	Price Dec. 31, 1939	Price Dec. 31, 1947 (adjusted for split-ups)
Addressograph-Multigraph	17¾	35½
Allied Laboratories, Inc.	19	26
Aluminum Co. of America	141½	181½
American Airlines, Inc.	46¼	36¼
American Home Products	59½	72¾
Bendix Aviation Corp.	31¼	30⅛
Bond Stores, Inc.	23½	53
Chrysler Corp.	89½	127½
Copperweld Steel Co.	16½	14½
Cuneo Press, Inc.	26½	32½
Decca Records, Inc.	7½	23½
Du Pont	182½	187
Eastern Airlines	30⅝	74½
Fruehauf Trailer Co.	28	48

(Continued)

TABLE VIII. PERFORMANCE OF A GROUP OF GROWTH STOCKS
SELECTED EARLY IN 1940 *(Continued)*

(PORTFOLIO OF NATIONAL INVESTORS COMPANY)

	Price Dec. 31, 1939	Price Dec. 31, 1947 (adjusted for split-ups)
Heyden Chemical Corp.	71½	232½
International Business Machines	185½	300
International Nickel Co. of Canada	36¾	26¾
Le Tourneau, Inc.	35	18
Libbey Owens Ford Glass	52¼	53¼
Master Electric Co.	23½	47
Mead Johnson & Co.	165	245
Minnesota Mining & Manufacturing Co.	58	140
Montgomery Ward & Co.	55	53⅜
Mueller Brass Co.	25⅝	39
Novadel Agene Corp.	36¾	21⅝ .
Owens Illinois Glass Co.	61	73¼
J. C. Penney Co.	94¼	138
Pittsburgh Plate Glass Co.	101	141⅜
Sangamo Electric Co.	27¼	31½
U.S. Gypsum Co.	83¼	105½
U.S. Plywood Corp.	21½	136
Western Auto Supply Co.	36¼	39
Total	1,890	2,784

	Aggregate Price of 1 share each of 32 Growth Stocks	Dow-Jones Industrial Index (30 stocks)	Standard-Poor's Industrial Index (354 stocks)
December 31, 1939	1,890	150.2	98.7
December 31, 1947	2,784	181.2	130.6
Gain in Value	47.0%	20.6%	32.5%

3. Purchase of Bargain Issues

We define a bargain issue as one which, on the basis of facts established by analysis, appears to be worth considerably more than it is selling for. The genus includes bonds and preferred stocks selling well under par, as well as common stocks. To be as concrete as possible, let us suggest that an issue is not a true "bargain" unless the indicated value is at least 50 per cent more than the price. What kind of facts would warrant the conclusion that so great a discrepancy exists? How do bargains come into existence, and how does the investor profit from them?

There are two tests by which a bargain common stock is detected. The first is by our method of appraisal, which we elaborate in Chapter X. As already noted, this relies largely on estimating future earnings and then multiplying these by a factor appropriate to the particular issue. If the resultant value is sufficiently above the market price—and if the investor has confidence in the technique employed—he can tag the stock as a bargain. The second test is the value of the business to a private owner. This value also is often determined chiefly by expected future earnings—in which case the result may be identical with the first. But in the second test more attention is likely to be paid to the realizable value of the assets, with particular emphasis on the net current assets or working capital.

At low points in the general market a large proportion of common stocks are bargain issues, as measured by these standards. (A typical example would be General Motors when it sold at less than 30 in 1941. It had been earning in excess of $4 and paying $3.50, or more, in dividends.) It is true that current earnings and the immediate prospects may both be poor, but a level-headed appraisal of average future conditions would indicate values far above ruling prices. Thus the wisdom of having courage in depressed markets is vindicated not only by the voice of experience but also by application of plausible techniques of value analysis.

The same vagaries of the marketplace which recurrently establish a bargain condition in the general list account for the existence of many individual bargains at almost all market levels. The market is always making mountains out of molehills and exaggerating ordinary vicissitudes into major setbacks. Even a mere lack of interest or enthusiasm may impel a price decline to absurdly low levels. Thus we have two major sources of undervaluation: (a) currently disappointing results, and (b) protracted neglect or unpopularity.

Lee Rubber & Tire Company supplies us with a current example of the first type. In 1946, aided by the bull market and by steadily rising earnings, the stock sold at 72. In the second half of 1947 the reported profits fell off moderately from the previous year's figures. This minor development apparently generated enough pessimism to drive the shares down to 35 in early 1948. That price was much less than the working capital alone (about $50 per share) and no greater than the amount actually earned in the previous five years.

Example of the second type: During the 1946–47 period the price of Northern Pacific Railway declined from 36 to 13½. As we shall demonstrate in Chapter XI, the true earnings of Northern Pacific in 1947 were close to $10 per share. The price of the stock was held down, in great part, by its $1 dividend. It was neglected, also, because much of its earning power was concealed by conventional accounting methods.

Value-to-a-Private-Owner Test. The private-owner test would ordinarily start with the net worth as shown in the balance sheet. The question then arises as to whether the indicated earning power is sufficient to validate the net worth as a measure of what a private buyer would be justified in paying for the business as a whole. If the answer is definitely yes, we suggest that an *ordinary* investor should find the common stock attractive *at a price one-third or more below* such a figure. If instead of using all the net worth as a starting point the investor considered only the working capital and applied his test to that, he would have a more convincing demonstration of the existence of a bargain opportunity. For it is something of an axiom that a business is worth to any private owner *at least* the amount of its working capital, since it could ordinarily be sold or liquidated for more than this figure.

Hence, if a common stock can be bought at no more than two-thirds of the working-capital value alone—disregarding all the other assets—and if the earnings record and prospects are reasonably satisfactory, there is strong reason to believe that the investor is getting substantially more than his money's worth. Peculiarly enough, many such opportunities present themselves in ordinary markets.

As an example let us supply some figures on National Department Stores as of January 31, 1948, the close of its fiscal year. The price of the stock was 16½. The working capital was no less than $26.60 per share, after deducting all the (small) liabilities ahead of the common stock. The total asset value was $33.30. If contingency reserves were deducted—mainly to mark down the inventory to a "LIFO" (last-in-first-out) basis—these figures would be reduced by about $2.20 per share. The company had earned $4.12 per share in the year just closed. The seven-year average was $3.43; the twelve-year average was $2.29. The year's dividend had been $1.50. As compared with a decade before, the working-capital value had risen from $7.40 per share to $26.60, the sales had doubled, and the net after taxes had risen from $654,000 to $3,224,000.

Thus we had a business selling for $13 million, with $25 million of assets, mostly current. Its sales were $88 million. A fair estimate of average future earnings might be $2 million.

The average earnings prior to 1941 had been unimpressive, and the company was regarded as a "marginal" one in its field—that is, it could earn a reasonably good return only under favorable business conditions. In the past eight years, however, it has improved both in financial strength and in the quality of its management. Let us grant that Wall Street would still consider the company as belonging in the second rank of department-store enterprises. Even after proper allowance is made for such an unfavorable factor, we may still conclude that on the basis of the figures the stock is intrinsically worth well above its market price.

This conclusion seems to follow in the case of National Department Stores, considered at 16½, whether we apply the appraisal test or the test of value to a private owner.

Bargain-Issue Pattern in Secondary Companies. We have defined a secondary company as one which is not a leader in a fairly important industry. Thus it is usually one of the smaller concerns in its field, but it may equally well be the chief unit in an unimportant line. By way of exception, any company that has established itself as a growth stock is not ordinarily considered as "secondary."

In the 1920's relatively little distinction was drawn between industry leaders and other listed issues, provided the latter were of respectable size. The public felt that a middle-sized company was strong enough to weather storms and that it had a better chance for really spectacular expansion than one which was already of major dimensions. The 1931–33 depression, however, had a particularly devastating impact on companies below the first rank either in size or in inherent stability. As a result of that experience investors have since developed a pronounced preference for industry leaders and a corresponding lack of interest in the ordinary company of secondary importance. This has meant that the latter group has usually sold at much lower prices in relation to earnings and assets than have the former. It has meant further that in many instances the price has fallen so low as to establish the issue in the bargain class.

When investors rejected the stocks of secondary companies, even though these sold at relatively low prices, they were expressing a belief or fear that such companies faced a dismal future. In fact, at least subconsciously, they calculated that *any* price was too high for them because they were heading for extinction—just as in 1929 the companion theory for the "blue chips" was that no price was too high for them because their future possibilities were limitless. Both of these views were exaggerations and were productive of serious investment errors. Actually, the typical middle-sized listed company is a large one when compared with the average privately-owned business. There is no sound reason why such companies should not continue indefinitely in operation, undergoing the vicissitudes characteristic of our economy but earning on the whole a fair return on their invested capital.

This brief review indicates that the stock market's attitude toward secondary companies tends to be unrealistic and consequently to create in normal times innumerable instances of major undervaluation. As it happens, the war period and the post-war boom were more beneficial to the smaller concerns than to the larger ones, because then the normal competition for sales was suspended and the former could expand sales and profit margins more spectacularly. Thus by 1946 the market's pattern had completely reversed itself. Whereas the leading stocks in the Dow-Jones Industrial Average had advanced only 40 per cent from the end of 1938 to the 1946 high, Standard & Poor's Index of low-priced stocks had shot up no less than 280 per cent in the same period. Speculators and many self-styled investors—with the proverbial short memories of people in the stock market—were eager to buy both old and new issues of unimportant companies at inflated levels. Thus the pendulum had swung clear to the opposite extreme. The very class of secondary issues which had formerly supplied by far the largest proportion of bargain opportunities was now presenting the greatest number of examples of overenthusiasm and overvaluation.

If past experience can be relied upon, the post-war bull market will itself prove to have created an enlarged crop of bargain opportunities. For in all probability a large proportion of the new common stock offerings of that period will fall into disfavor, and they will join many secondary companies of older vintage in entering the limbo of chronic undervaluation.[6]

If secondary issues tend *normally* to be undervalued, what reason has the investor to hope that he can profit by such a situation? For if it persists indefinitely, will he not always be in the same position market wise as when he bought the issue? The answer here is somewhat complicated. Substantial profits from the purchase of secondary companies at bargain prices arise in a variety of ways. First, the dividend return is high. Second, the reinvested earnings are substantial in relation to the price paid and will ultimately affect the price. In a five- to seven-year period these advantages can bulk quite large in a well-selected list. Third, when a bull market appears it is most generous to low-priced issues; thus it tends to raise the typical bargain issue to at least a reasonable level. Fourth, even during relatively featureless market periods a continuous process of price adjustment goes on, under which secondary issues that were undervalued may rise at least to the normal level for their type of security.

As a parallel to the performance record of a list of growth stocks, as set forth in the preceding section, we submit the corresponding record of two groups of bargain issues from December, 1939, to December, 1947. These are also taken without benefit of hindsight. They appeared in the 1940 edition of Graham & Dodd's *Security Analysis* (pp. 689–690) and represented opportunities current at the time of the book's publication.

[6]It should be pointed out that some part of the war-derived advantage of secondary and lower-grade stocks appears to be permanent. For example, at the bottom points of 1947 the Dow-Jones list was only 8% above the December 1938 level, while the low-priced group remained 48% above its corresponding figure.

TABLE IX. PERFORMANCE OF TWO GROUPS OF UNDERVALUED SECURITIES
SELECTED AT THE BEGINNING OF 1940

(EXCLUDING DIVIDENDS RECEIVED)

	Market Price Dec. 31, 1939	Market Price Dec. 31, 1947
Group A:		
J. D. Adams Mfg.	10	$14\frac{3}{4}$
American Seating	$10\frac{1}{8}$	19
Bunte Bros.	$14\frac{1}{4}$	80
Grand Union	$9\frac{7}{8}$	33
International Silver	$27\frac{1}{2}$	227^2
I. B. Kleinert	10	$14\frac{1}{4}$
New Idea	$12\frac{1}{8}$	30^3
New York Merchandise	8	$15\frac{1}{2}$
Pacific Commercial	$11\frac{1}{2}{}^1$	. . .[4]
Seton Leather	$7\frac{1}{4}$	$15\frac{1}{2}$
Total	$120\frac{5}{8}$	449
Group B:		
Butler Bros.	7	$12\frac{1}{2}$
Ely & Walker Dry Goods	19	138^2
Gilchrist	$4\frac{7}{8}$	$11\frac{1}{2}$
Hale Bros. Stores	$13\frac{1}{2}$	18
Intertype	$8\frac{1}{4}$	25
Lee & Cady	6	$10\frac{1}{2}$
H. D. Lee Mercantile	19	44
Manhattan Shirt	$15\frac{1}{8}$	$24\frac{1}{8}$
Reliance Mfg.	$12\frac{1}{4}$	22^2
S. Stroock	10	$62\frac{1}{4}{}^2$
Total	115	$367\frac{7}{8}$
Total of Both Groups	236	817 Increase 246%

[1]December 31, 1938 price.   [2]Adjusted for split-ups.   [3]Based on cash offer in acquisition.   [4]No quotation available.

Note: These lists appear on pp. 689 and 690 of *Security Analysis*, by Graham and Dodd, 1940 edition.

This performance is superior not only to that of the Dow-Jones list but to that of the growth-stock list as well. Allowance should be made for the fact, as previously noted, that nearly all the smaller companies benefited more from the war than did the bigger ones. The figures prove without a doubt that under favorable conditions bargain issues can yield a handsome profit.

Our experience over many years leads us to assert that the average results from this area of activity are satisfactory.

The field of bargain issues extends to bonds and preferred stocks which sell at large discounts from the amount of their claim. It is far from true that every low-priced senior issue is a bargain. No doubt the inexpert investor is well advised to eschew these completely, for they can easily burn his fingers. But there is an underlying tendency for market declines in this field to be overdone; consequently the group as a whole offers an especially rewarding invitation to careful and courageous analysis. In the decade ending in 1948 the billion-dollar group of defaulted railroad bonds presented numerous and spectacular opportunities in this area.

4. Special Situations

A particular kind of undervalued security in which the profit is expected to be realized from a definite corporate event rather than from a mere change in the market's attitude is known as a "special situation." Such events include sale of the business, merger, recapitalization, reorganization, and liquidation.

A great deal of money has been made by shrewd investors in recent years through the purchase of bonds of railroads in bankruptcy—bonds which they knew would be worth much more than their cost when the railroads were finally reorganized. Similar large profits have been made in the preferred and common stocks of public-utility holding companies which either were being broken up under the so-called death-sentence clause of the 1935 legislation or were subject to recapitalization plans.

The underlying factor here is the tendency of the security markets to undervalue issues which are involved in any sort of complicated legal proceedings. An old Wall Street motto has been: "Never buy into a lawsuit." This may be sound advice to the speculator seeking quick action on his holdings. But the adoption of this attitude by the general public is bound to create bargain opportunities in the securities affected by it, since the prejudice against them holds their price down to unduly low levels.

The exploitation of special situations is a technical branch of investment which requires a somewhat unusual mentality and equipment. Probably only a small percentage of our enterprising investors are likely to engage in it, and this book is not the appropriate medium for expounding its complications. Our readers may be interested, however, in following through some typical examples of special situations. The material which follows is taken from the author's article on "Special Situations" published in the *Analysts' Journal* for the fourth quarter of 1946. A brief description of the situations covered in the article and current at the time of its publication, together with the sequel, is presented below:

(1) Metropolitan West Side Elevated 5s (Chicago), then selling at 23. A purchase deal for the property was pending which, if consummated, was expected to make the bonds worth about 35 in cash.

The purchase was effected, and the bondholders have since received 33½ in cash, retaining also "stubs" currently worth about 5.

(2) Central & South West Utilities Second Preferred, selling at 185. Under a pending recapitalization plan the holders were to have the right to receive either 220 in cash or the same amount in new common stock.

The plan was carried out, and the preferred holders who asked for cash received 223 in February, 1947.

(3) A comparison between Cities Service First Preferred, selling at 132, and American Power & Light $6 Preferred, selling at 117. Our conclusion was: "If continued weakness in the stock market should result in the indefinite postponement of the American Power & Light plan, the purchaser of Cities Service Preferred will undoubtedly fare the better of the two."

The pending plan for paying off the American Power & Light Preferred was withdrawn, and the $6 issue sold at 91 at the end of 1947. Conversely, a plan was proposed and carried out for paying off the Cities Service Preferred issues. As a consequence the First Preferred was exchanged for bonds, making it worth 157 per share at the end of 1947.

(4) A reference to a bid for the purchase of stock of Luther Manufacturing Company, at $365 per share, contingent on acceptance by not less than 95 per cent of the stock. A week before the purchase offer was made public, the stock was quoted at only $150 bid.

The purchase at $365 was consummated.

(5) Brewster Corporation shares, selling at 4¼. The Company was in liquidation, and the current "expert" estimate of ultimate realization ranged between 5½ and 6.

The stockholders have since received $5.75 per share in cash, and are expected to realize something additional.

(6) In a list of "litigated matters" two (of the same type) were referred to which were current at the end of 1946. These were the appeals of the stockholders of New Haven Railway and St. Louis Southwestern Railway from reorganization plans which would wipe them out completely. At the end of 1946 New Haven common was quoted at about 1½, and St. Louis Southwestern common at about 20. Our comment on this section was: "In general, the market undervalues a litigated claim as an asset and overvalues it as a liability. Hence students of these situations often have an opportunity to buy into them at less than their true value, and to realize attractive profits—on the average—when the litigation is disposed of."

In the sequel, the New Haven stockholders lost their appeal and were actually wiped out. However, the St. Louis Southwestern stockholders managed to have the receivership lifted, and their stock advanced to 139 in 1948. (See p. 185.)

Broader Implications of our Rules for Investment

Investment policy, as it has been developed here, depends in the first place upon a choice by the investor of either the defensive (passive) or aggressive (enterprising) role. The aggressive investor must have a considerable knowledge of security values—enough, in fact, to warrant viewing his security operations as equivalent to a business enterprise. There is no room in this philosophy for a middle ground, or a series of gradations, between the passive and aggressive status. Many, perhaps most, investors seek to place themselves in such an intermediate category; in our opinion that is a compromise that is more likely to produce disappointment than achievement.

As an investor you cannot soundly become "half a businessman," expecting thereby to achieve half the normal rate of business profits on your funds.

It follows from this reasoning that the majority of security owners should elect the defensive classification. They do not have the time, or the determination, or the mental equipment to embark upon investing as a quasi business. They should therefore be satisfied with the reasonably good return obtainable from a defensive portfolio, and they should stoutly resist the recurrent temptation to increase this return by deviating into other paths.

The enterprising investor may properly embark upon any security operation for which his training and judgment are adequate and which appears sufficiently promising *when measured by established business standards.* In our recommendations and caveats for this group of investors we have attempted to apply such business standards. In those for the defensive investor we have been guided largely by the three requirements of (a) underlying safety, (b) simplicity of choice, and (c) promise of satisfactory results, in terms of psychology as well as arithmetic. The use of these criteria has led us to exclude from the field of recommended investment a number of security classes which are normally regarded as suitable for various kinds of investors. These prohibitions were listed in our first chapter, on pages 16–17.

Let us consider a little more fully than before what is implied in these exclusions. We have advised against the purchase at "full prices" of three important categories of securities: (a) foreign bonds; (b) ordinary corporate bonds and preferred stocks, under present conditions of relative yield; and (c) secondary common stocks, including, of course, original offerings of such issues. By "full prices" we mean prices close to par for bonds or preferred stocks, and prices that represent about the fair business value of the enterprise in the case of common stocks. The greater number of defensive investors are to avoid these categories regardless of price; the enterprising investor is to buy them only when obtainable at bargain prices—which we define as prices not more than two-thirds of the appraisal value of the securities.

What would happen if all investors were guided by our advice in these matters? That question was considered in regard to foreign bonds, on page 78, and we have nothing to add at this point. Corporate bonds and preferred stocks would either have to increase their yields so as to offer a reasonable alternative to United States Savings Bonds for the individual investor or else would be bought solely by financial institutions—insurance companies, savings banks, commercial banks, and the like. Such institutions have their own justification for buying corporate securities at current yields; in this book we are not concerned with their policies.

The most troublesome consequence of our policy of exclusion is in the field of secondary common stocks. If the majority of investors, being in the defensive class, are not to buy them at all, the field of possible buyers becomes seriously restricted. Furthermore, if aggressive investors are to buy them only at bargain levels, then these issues would be doomed to sell for less than their fair value, except to the extent that they were purchased unintelligently.

This may sound severe and even vaguely unethical. Yet in truth we are merely recognizing what has actually happened in this area for the past twenty years. Secondary issues, for the most part, do fluctuate about a central level which is well below their fair value. They reach and even surpass that value at times; but this occurs in the upper reaches of bull markets, when the lessons of practical experience would argue against the soundness of paying the prevailing prices for common stocks.

Thus we are suggesting only that the aggressive investor recognize the facts of life as it is lived by secondary issues and that they accept the central market levels which are normal for that class as their guide in fixing their own levels for purchase.

There is a paradox here, nevertheless. The average well-selected secondary company may be fully as promising as the average industrial leader. What the smaller concern lacks in inherent stability it may readily make up in superior possibilities of growth. Consequently it may appear illogical to many readers to term "unintelligent" the purchase of such secondary issues at their full "enterprise value." We think that the strongest logic is that of experience. Financial history says clearly that the investor may expect satisfactory results, on the average, from secondary common stocks only if he buys them for less than their value to a private owner, that is, on a bargain basis.

The last sentence indicates that this principle relates to the ordinary *outside* investor. Anyone who can control a secondary company, or who is part of a cohesive group with such *control*, is fully justified in buying the shares on the same basis as if he were investing in a "close corporation" or other private business. The distinction between the position, and consequent investment policy, of insiders and of outsiders becomes more important as the enterprise itself becomes *less* important. It is a basic characteristic of a primary or leading company that a single detached share is ordinarily worth as much as a share in a controlling block. In secondary companies—even one as substantial and as prosperous as National Department Stores, described earlier in this chapter—the average market value of a detached share is substantially less than its worth to a controlling owner. Because of this fact, the matter of stockholder-management relations and of those between inside and outside stockholders tends to be much more important and controversial in the case of secondary than in that of primary companies. This point will be developed in later chapters. At the end of Chapter IV we commented upon the difficulty of making any hard-and-fast distinction between primary and secondary companies. The many common stocks in the boundary area may properly exhibit an intermediate price behavior. It would not be illogical for an investor to buy such an issue at a *small* discount from its indicated or appraisal value, on the theory that it is only a small distance away from a primary classification and that it may acquire such a rating unqualifiedly in the not-too-distant future.

Thus the distinction between primary and secondary issues need not be made too precise; for, if it were, then a small difference in quality must produce a large differential in justified purchase price. In saying this we are admitting a middle ground in the classification of common stocks, although we counseled against such a middle ground in the classification of investors. Our reason for this apparent inconsistency is as follows: No great harm comes from some uncertainty of viewpoint regarding a single security, because such cases are exceptional and not a great deal is at stake in the matter. But the investor's choice as between the defensive or the aggressive status is of major consequence to him, and he should not allow himself to be confused or compromised in this basic decision.

PART II

---◆◇◆---

Principles of
Security Selection

VII

——◆◇◆——

United States

Savings Bonds:

A Boon to Investors

UNITED STATES SAVINGS BONDS are by far the most important security ever issued in this country—or anywhere else, for that matter. The total amount sold to March, 1938, exceeds $77 billion, two-thirds of which were in Series E. On that date $53 billion were still outstanding, of which $31½ billion were in Series E. The United States Treasury estimates that these bonds are owned by some 80 million separate investors. A survey conducted for the Federal Reserve Board in July, 1948, concludes that they are owned by about half the families or "spending units" in the country.

The United States Treasury Department is to be congratulated on its success in distributing these savings issues in such enormous quantities and among so large a proportion of the population. Nevertheless we believe that the merits of United States Savings Bonds are by no means fully understood and that many investors fail to accord an appropriate position to them in their portfolios.

In the philosophy of investment here expounded United States Savings Bonds play the primary and, in the aggregate, the most important role.

Every non-professional investor should have a substantial portion of his funds in these issues; the small investors, who preponderate in terms of numbers, should own as many Series E bonds as they possibly can, even though they buy nothing else. As it happens, the space we shall devote to a discussion of United States Savings Bonds is far less than would be justified by their overshadowing importance. The reason for this, of course, is that investment in these bonds is a simple matter, whereas common-stock investment—constituting the remainder of our total program—is full of possible complexities and dangers. (We say "possible" because investment in common stocks can also be made comparatively simple for the defensive investor if he will adhere to a few guiding principles.)

In the present chapter we should like to present a reasonably complete picture of the investment characteristics of United States Savings Bonds.

It will perhaps be appropriate to begin by appending, in smaller type, the official summary of the provisions of the three series of United States Savings Bonds that are currently being offered. This should constitute an adequate though brief description of the securities.

Series E
10-Year Appreciation Bonds. The interest yield on Series E bonds is the highest offered by the Treasury—2.9 per cent, compounded semiannually, when held to maturity. Series E bonds are issued only in the name of individuals, in their own right. Redeemable after 60 days from issue date.

Series F
12-Year Appreciation Bonds. Yield is 2.53 per cent, interest compounded semi-annually, when held to maturity. Redeemable after 6 months from issue date. Issued in the names of corporations, unincorporated associations, partnerships, trustees, executors, and administrators, as well as individuals in their own right.

Series G
12-Year Current-Income Bonds. Two and five-tenths per cent is paid semi-annually to the registered owner by United States Treasury check. Redeemable after 6 months from issue date, but at par only if held to maturity or in the event of death as set forth in the official circular. Series G Bonds, like Series F, are issued to individuals and other non-bank investors.

LIMITATION ON HOLDINGS

Series E

There is an annual limit of $10,000 maturity value, or $7,500 cost price, for each calendar year, of bonds originally issued during that year to any one person. However, for the purpose of computing the limitation, bonds issued to co-owners may be applied to the holdings of either or apportioned between them.

Series F and G

$100,000 issue price of Series F and G Bonds or a combination of both may be issued to any one holder in any calendar year.

TAXABLE STATUS

Income from the bonds is exempt from income taxes imposed by any state, possession of the United States, or other local taxing authority, but is subject to Federal income tax. Value of the bonds as such is not exempt from estate, inheritance, or gift taxes, Federal or state.

United States Savings Bonds possess three sovereign merits: (1) they are the safest bond investment in the world; (2) their holders are guaranteed against effective loss, no matter when they sell; and (3) their yield is remarkably generous under current market conditions.

Savings Bonds have other advantages, of less significance than those just mentioned, which we shall comment on below. Let us deal first, however, with certain supposed disadvantages which many investors, and some authorities, believe are attached to these issues.

Objection 1: "The investor is not allowed to buy enough of them to meet his needs."

This objection does not apply to Series F and G bonds, since anyone can buy up to $100,000 of these, combined, in any year. The Series E bonds, however, have until recently been limited to $3,750 cost price per person per year, which figure has just been increased to $7,500. Few people have more than that amount to invest out of income; but the restriction may seem to offer some difficulties to the conversion of the entire bond component of existing portfolios into Series E's.

The $7,500 annual figure may be substantially increased by the provision for co-ownership. In effect this means that as many times $7,500 can be invested in E bonds each year as there are members of the family. The actual purchaser, by retaining physical control of the bonds, is in the same practical position as if he were the sole owner.

Clearly there is no problem in setting up an investment fund of any ordinary size so that the bond portion will consist of Series E bonds, or of E's combined with F's and G's.

Objection 2: "The Series E bonds do not yield an annual cash income."

Many people do not like the idea of waiting ten years to receive interest on their money, even though the amount is large when finally cashed in. Others insist that they need the interest money to live on. An obvious answer to such objections is the purchase of the Series G bonds, which pay 2½ per cent interest semi-annually like ordinary bonds.

The Series E bonds, however, are well suited to every normal investment program. So long as a person is saving more than his interest accrual he does not need that income in the form of cash. Assume that a man now owns $5,000 of Series E bonds, on which interest accrues at the rate of $145 per annum. If his current year's savings, over all, are $200, they will take the form of $145 added to the value of his Series E bonds—that is, reinvested at compound interest—and $55 of cash surplus available to buy more Series E bonds.

Most bondholders save regularly for a number of years, and during that period they do not use the cash income on their investments except to reinvest. In a continuous Series E program the first purchase matures in ten years, and each subsequent investment matures serially thereafter. At that time the investor is free to spend all or part of each ten-year accumulation of interest, or to reinvest it, or to draw on the principal.

A standard Series E program might call for putting $75 each month in that security. This means saving $900 a year. Ten years after the first purchase a steady annual income in cash becomes available. This takes the form of a $100 bond maturing each month, of which $75 can be used to replace the original investment and $25 per month remains as realized interest. Thus $900 per year saved for ten years will produce thereafter a continuous annual income of $300, while the principal is constantly renewed. Furthermore, the $9,000 saved will then have an immediate cashable value of about $10,400. This will also remain intact thereafter, as long as the investor continues to reinvest the $75 portion and spend the $25 monthly.

The fact is that very few investors would need to draw upon their Series E holdings for the purpose of cashing in interest income—as distinct from emergency needs for *principal*, which are quite another matter. It is possible, however, to arrange to cash in a small portion of the bonds held, at designated intervals, for the purpose of obtaining such cash income. This would involve a slight reduction in the projected 2.90 per cent yield, since the small fractions cashed in will receive somewhat less than that rate.

The following computation will show how the investor will fare who makes a single purchase of $3,750 of Series E bonds in one year only, and then draws down regular interest income by cashing in a $75 bond in the middle of each year. His annual cash income will range from $75 the first year to $98 the tenth year—because the bond he cashes in becomes worth more as time goes on. Thus his realized annual income grows from 2 per cent to 2.61 per cent. In addition, the bonds remaining uncashed ($3,000 at cost) become worth $4,000 at the end of the tenth year, representing an additional interest return of $250 above the $3,750 paid in. This is equivalent to about 0.6 per cent more of annual income. Taking these various amounts together, it is clear that he realizes close to the 2.90 per cent promised, and he has received the greater part of his yield in the form of *current income.*

Objection 3: "Those cashing in their bonds lose most of their interest."

A large portion of the Series E bonds have been cashed in before maturity—the figure is running at some 40 per cent—and all such owners realize a smaller interest rate than the 2.90 per cent, compounded, obtainable at the end of ten years. We doubt, however, if any considerable fraction of true investors—the people for whom this book is written—have found it necessary to cash in their bonds. An enormous amount of this issue was placed by energetic sales methods under the stress of war, and the bonds were bought by millions of people who had no serious interest in an investment program. Many of these cashed in their bonds for a variety of reasons, running from the necessitous to the frivolous.

The reader should appreciate why the government does not pay the full 2.90 per cent on bonds held for less than ten years. The going rate of interest on short-term issues is much less than for longer-term issues. For example, the Treasury is at present borrowing for one year at 1.25 per cent, whereas the open-market yield on its regular ten-year bonds is about 1.70 per cent. Obviously it would be unfair to let the public obtain 2.90 per cent on a one- or two-year loan to the government by buying E bonds and then cashing them in. In addition, there is a large expense attached to setting up an investor's account with the government—not only in the engraving of the bond but also in the elaborate records required to keep track of ownership. If a purchaser puts the government to all these costs and then promptly demands his money back, he is hardly entitled to a generous interest rate on the refund.

Actually, the interest rates allowed on bonds cashed in are quite satisfactory to the holder after the first few years. In five years a $75 bond can be cashed in for $82. This is equivalent to interest of $1.40 per year, or 1.87 per cent. That rate is better than the average now allowed by savings banks in New York State, as shown by the table on page 57.

If the investor wants to commit his money for only a year or two, it is unwise for him and unfair to the Treasury to buy Series E bonds. A savings bank is the place for such money, as well as for funds that he thinks he will *probably* need to draw on in the reasonably near future, even though he is not sure of it. But if such withdrawal is merely a possibility—say, less than one chance in two—he should have no hesitation in carrying through a Series E program without regard to his future need for money. The redemption privilege of the Series E bond is there precisely to take care of unexpected needs for money. In the last analysis, also, the actual loss of interest by cashing in a bond after one year, as against a choice of a savings account, is so small in dollars as to be scarcely worth arguing about.

As will be pointed out, instead of constituting a handicap the redemption terms of all series of United States Savings Bonds provide the owners with a valuable option which is not duplicated in any other investment.

Objection 4: "There may be difficulty in getting your money, when you want it."

During the war years many people who should have known better seemed to harbor some mental reservations about the certainty of repayment on United States Savings Bonds, particularly if presented before their maturity. For that reason some investors preferred the open-market bonds, on the theory that they could always be sold to someone else even if the government was not honoring its contract in the United States Savings Bonds.

This apprehension betrays a misunderstanding of the realities of modern finance as they apply to governments. Aside from the question of the financial strength of the United States Treasury—which rests on a taxing power now producing over $40 billion in annual revenue—it is now out of the question for our government, or any other, to fail to meet its obligations to its own citizens. A maturing debt of any government is always as good as its paper money, because it always can and will pay it in paper money. All governments now have unlimited access first to the credit of their banking systems and then to the printing press. Internal default is now an anachronism.

The point of this argument is that the danger, if any, to investors in United States securities lies exclusively in the area of inflation. That is where the effect of a future war, or any other catastrophe, would show itself. Thus, if the owner of United States Savings Bonds has anything to worry about, it is not whether he will get his money but what his money will be worth when he gets it. This hazard—which we pointed out was an important reason for holding some portion of one's investments in common stocks—is in no sense confined to United States Savings Bonds. It applies equally well to all corporate investment-grade bonds and preferred stocks, to commercial and savings-bank deposits, and to currency under the mattress.

Since the United States will always have the power to meet its debt by one means or another, it is equally certain that it will have the desire and the determination to do so. Nothing would be more fatal to the elaborate and delicate fiscal operations of the United States Treasury than any action on its part which is contrary to the terms of its obligations. Thus any fear that the Treasury may arbitrarily refuse to cash in United States Savings Bonds before maturity, because the amounts demanded may run very high, is unrealistic. The obligation to pay these bonds whenever turned in is as precise and as binding as that to pay at maturity. Default on the former contract is just as unlikely—or rather as impossible—as default on the latter.

Let us turn now to the array of advantages which these bonds possess, as compared with any other conventional form of investment.

1. *Combined Safety and Yield*

We have already pointed out that the Series E bonds yield more than high-grade corporation bonds, although their unequaled safety would entitle them to return considerably less. One way of measuring the "yield bonus" given to buyers of Series E bonds is to compare them with open-market government bonds also maturing in ten years. The latter return only about 1.70 per cent. The 12-year Series G bonds also have a distinct yield advantage over listed government bonds, and they are undoubtedly still more attractive—in the safety, yield, and maturity combination—than high-grade corporate securities.

2. *Option to Redeem before Maturity*

This is the opposite of the ordinary call feature in corporate bonds. As was shown in Chapter IV, the latter has operated to deprive investors of any capital profit from a later fall in interest rates and to compel them to receive less income than they had originally expected. The government has no right to redeem United States Savings Bonds before their maturity, no matter how low interest rates may fall. But the investor has this right—which he may potentially exercise to take advantage of a *rise* in interest rates, if the latter produce attractive buying opportunities in other securities.

By way of actual illustration let us assume that a holder of Atchison Topeka & Santa Fe Railroad General 4s, due 1995, had sold them out in 1946 at their high price of 141 and had put the proceeds in Series G bonds. Because of a rise in interest rates, the price of Santa Fe bonds fell to 114 in the very next year. If our investor considered them to be worth buying at that price, he could have redeemed his Series G bonds—receiving a small interest return for the period they were held[1]—and repurchased his Santa Fe bonds at a large profit.

Stated technically, the redemption privilege of United States Savings Bonds is an option vested in the holder to commute his investment at any time from its original ten- or twelve-year term to a nearer date, with a down-

---

[1]He would have received from the Treasury somewhat less than 100 for his G bonds, but the interest income would have more than made up the difference.

ward adjustment of the interest received to correspond to the shorter maturity. (Thus if the buyer of a Series E bond finds later that he would have been better off if he had loaned his money for three years instead of ten, he can change over into a three-year investment without effective penalty.) In the writer's view the value of this unique option is equivalent to adding at least ½ per cent per annum to the yield of all series of United States Savings Bonds.

3. Tax Features

United States Savings Bonds are subject to Federal income tax, but they are exempt from all state and municipal levies. The latter exemption adds something to the yield of these bonds when compared with corporate issues. Holders of Series E and Series F bonds have the option of paying taxes currently on the income as it accrues or of waiting until the accumulated interest is received on redemption or maturity. The delay in paying taxes has several advantages: First, during the war period it permitted buyers to wait for the lower tax rates that were to be expected in peace time and have already been realized to some extent—especially in the income-splitting provision. Second, it gives the holder the right to pick out a year in which to take his interest when his other income, and the resultant tax rate, may be smaller than usual. Third, in the calculation of yield the interest is compounded but the taxes are not; this means that the investor gains a little interest income by deferring his tax liability.

4. Compounding Feature

For the small investor the automatic compounding of the annual interest accrual on Series E bonds is a real advantage. Though he has the same arrangement in a savings account, he would not ordinarily be able to work it out in his security investments. Note that an investment on which the interest is not compounded would have to yield 3.33 per cent annually to equal the return on Series E bonds—since these give you back $4 for $3 in ten years.

5. Co-ownership and Beneficiary Features

These are conveniences for making various kinds of inter-family arrangements. They are especially useful in the event of death. The co-ownership provision also operates to permit the head of a family to buy many more Series E bonds than the $7,500 present annual limitation.

6. Special Feature of Series G Bonds

Series G bonds are payable in full to the estate in the event of the death of an owner or co-owner. In effect, this is equivalent to a small insurance policy, free of cost, which may add as much as 5 per cent to the value of the G bonds in an estate.

7. Registration and Replacement

An investment in Series E bonds cannot be jeopardized by fire, theft, or other similar loss. The bonds are of no value except to the owner. If lost or destroyed they will be replaced by the Treasury at very small expense to the owner. Thus small investors are saved the cost of a safe-deposit vault and perhaps a considerable amount of day-to-day worry over the physical safety of their holdings.

8. Ease of Purchase

The bonds are purchasable without payment of commission. The banks are offering every facility, free of charge, to encourage the systematic purchase of this prime investment.

Conclusion

The creation of United States Savings Bonds in 1935 revolutionized the position of the individual investor. They afford a satisfactory answer to every problem of investment except those which require a commitment in common stocks. All the rest of the investment program may now be carried out without risk or bother or even temporary discomfiture. The investors of the country owe a great debt of gratitude to former Secretary Morgenthau for initiating the United States Savings Bond idea and to the Treasury Department for maintaining it in full effect to this day.

VIII

---◆◇◆---

Security Analysis for the
Lay Investor:
General Approach

SECURITY ANALYSIS is now a well-established and flourishing profession, or semi-profession. The various societies of analysts which make up the National Federation have well over fifteen hundred members, most of whom make their living out of this branch of mental activity. Security analysts have textbooks, a code of ethics, and a quarterly journal. They also have their share of unresolved problems.

The security analyst deals with the past, the present, and the future of any given security issue. He describes the business; he summarizes its operating results and financial position; he sets forth its strong and weak points, its possibilities and risks; he estimates its future earning power under various assumptions, or as a "best guess." He makes elaborate comparisons of various companies, or of the same company at various times. Finally, he expresses an opinion as to the safety of the issue, if it is a bond or investment-grade preferred stock, or as to its attractiveness as a purchase, if it is a common stock.

In doing all these things the security analyst avails himself of a number of techniques, ranging from the elementary to the most abstruse. He may modify substantially the figures in the company's annual statements, even though they bear the sacred imprint of the certified public accountant. He is on the lookout particularly for items in these reports which may mean a good deal more or less than they say.

The security analyst develops and applies standards of safety by which he can conclude whether a given bond or preferred stock may be termed sound enough to justify purchase for investment. These standards relate primarily to past average earnings, but they are concerned also with capital structure, working capital, asset values, and other matters.

In dealing with common stocks the security analyst only rarely applies standards of value which are as well defined as are his standards of safety for bonds and preferred stocks. Most of the time he contents himself with a summary of past performances, a more or less general forecast of the future—with particular emphasis on the next twelve months—and a rather arbitrary conclusion. The latter is often drawn with one eye on the stock ticker or the market charts. So far it is only in the area of public-utility common stocks that security analysts have developed a well-considered and comprehensive approach to what should be their central problem—the valuation or appraisal of the security before them.

In this chapter we shall discuss briefly and in general terms the more important elements and techniques of security analysis. The present highly condensed treatment is directed to the needs of the non-professional investor. At the minimum he should understand what the security analyst is talking about and driving at; beyond that, he should be equipped, if possible, to distinguish between superficial and sound analysis.

Security analysis for the lay investor is thought of as beginning with the interpretation of a company's annual financial report. This is a subject which has been covered for laymen in a separate book, entitled *The Interpretation of Financial Statements*, by Graham and Meredith.[1] We do not consider it necessary or appropriate to traverse the same ground in this chapter, especially since the emphasis in the present book is on principles and attitudes rather than on information and description. Let us pass on to two basic questions

[1] New York: Harper & Brothers, 1937. A nicely written treatment of these matters may be found in "How to Read a Financial Report," an article by Stuart Chase in the March, 1948, issue of *The Lamp*, the house organ of the Standard Oil Company (New Jersey).

underlying the selection of investments: What are the primary tests of safety of a corporate bond or preferred stock? What are the chief factors entering into the valuation of a common stock?

Bond Analysis

The most dependable and hence the most respectable branch of security analysis concerns itself with the safety, or quality, of bond issues and investment-grade preferred stocks. The chief criterion used for corporate bonds is the number of times that total interest charges have been covered by available earnings for some years in the past. In the case of preferred stocks, it is the number of times that bond interest and preferred dividends combined have been covered.

The exact standards applied will vary with different authorities. Since the tests are at bottom arbitrary, there is no way to determine the most suitable criteria. In the forthcoming revision of our textbook, *Security Analysis*, we shall recommend certain "coverage" standards, which appear at the end of this chapter.

Our test is applied only to the *average* results for a period of years. Other authorities require also that a *minimum* coverage be shown for every year considered.

In addition to the earnings-coverage test, a number of others are generally applied. These include the following:

1. *Size of Enterprise.* There is a minimum standard in terms of volume of business for a corporation—varying as between industrials, utilities, and railroads—and of population for a municipality.

2. *"Stock-Equity Ratio."* This is the ratio of the market price of the junior stock issues to the total face amount of the debt, or the debt plus preferred stock. It is a rough measure of the protection, or "cushion," afforded by the presence of a junior investment which must first bear the brunt of unfavorable developments. This factor includes the market's appraisal of the future prospects of the enterprise.

3. *Property Value.* The asset values, as shown on the balance sheet or as appraised, were formerly considered the chief security and protection for a bond issue. Experience has shown that in most cases safety resides in the earning power, and if this is deficient the assets lose most of their reputed

value. Asset values, however, retain importance as a separate test of ample security for bonds and preferred stocks in three enterprise groups: (a) public utilities (because rates may depend largely on the property investment); (b) real-estate concerns; and (c) investment companies.

At this point the alert investor should ask, "How dependable are tests of safety which are measured by past and present performance, in view of the fact that payment of interest and principal depends upon what the future will bring forth?" The answer can be found only on experience. Investment history shows that bonds and preferred stocks which have met stringent tests of safety, based on the past, have in the great majority of cases been able to face the vicissitudes of the future successfully. This has been strikingly demonstrated in the major field of railroad bonds—a field that has been marked by a calamitous frequency of bankruptcies and serious losses. In nearly every case the roads that got into trouble had long been over-bonded, had shown an inadequate coverage of fixed charges in periods of average prosperity, and would thus have been ruled out by investors who applied strict tests of safety. Conversely, practically every road which has met such tests has escaped financial embarrassment.

The same has been true, and to an even greater degree, of the public utilities, which supply the second principal area of bond investment. Receivership of a soundly capitalized (non-traction) utility company or system is virtually unknown. The financial troubles of electric and gas utilities are traceable almost 100 per cent to financial excesses and mismanagement, which left their imprint clearly on the companies' capitalization structures. Simple but stringent tests of safety, therefore, would have warned the investor away from the issues that were later to default.

Among industrial bond issues the record has been different. Although the industrial group as a whole has shown a better growth of earning power than either the railroads or the utilities, it has revealed a lesser degree of inherent stability for individual companies and lines of business. Thus there are persuasive reasons for confining the purchase of industrial bonds and preferred stocks to companies which not only are of major size but also have shown an ability in the past to withstand a serious depression.

Before leaving the field of investment bonds and preferred stocks, we should perhaps point out that here time has played an ironical trick on the security analysts. In the past twenty years we have made our best technical progress in devising good tests of the safety of corporate senior securities. But, now that we have attained real competence in this work, we find that the typical non-institutional investor has supplanted, or should supplant, these securities with United States Savings Bonds—which need no critical analysis. Nevertheless, these tests remain important for banks and insurance companies, and also for the large number of individual investors who persist in buying corporate senior issues. Should a normal differential in yield again be established between the latter and United States Savings Bonds, our intelligent investor will give due consideration to corporate issues and apply the appropriate tests of safety.

Common-Stock Analysis

The ideal form of common-stock analysis leads to a valuation of the issue which can be compared with the current price to determine whether or not the security is an attractive purchase. This valuation, in turn, would ordinarily be found by estimating the average earnings over a period of years in the *future* and then multiplying that estimate by an appropriate "capitalization factor." As a concrete example, the analyst might estimate the average future earnings of General Motors common at $5 per share; multiplying this figure by 15—about a 6.7 per cent rate—to reach a value of $75 per share. If he had confidence in his method he would definitely have favored the purchase of the issue when it sold in the low fifties early in 1948.

But what are the processes by which the security analyst determines both the average future earnings and the suitable capitalization rate? In both cases he is turning himself into a prophet, without the benefit of divine inspiration. As a poor substitute he turns for guidance to a threefold source—the past record of the company, the known or generally accepted factors bearing on the future, and something referred to by the courts as "the informed judgment of the expert."

The fact of the matter is that he almost always rests heavily upon the past record. In so doing he has a fair degree of logical justification. If average recorded earnings can be relied upon fairly well to measure the safety of a bond issue, they must in the typical case supply a useful clue to the normal earnings expectancy of a common stock. Even the rather crude assumption that *past average* earnings will be repeated in the future may be found a more reliable basis of valuation than some other figure plucked out of the air of either optimism or pessimism.

The reason why the analyst devotes himself so diligently to studying and arranging the past figures is largely because they are there to work upon. With them he is on solid ground—ground that responds to his skillful cultivation. He can work out ratios; he can point out trends; he can even throw out items which the accountants properly put in the income account but which the analyst asserts are not part of the "normal earning power." He has a whole armory of statistical data to draw upon. Sometimes he reminds us a bit of the erudite major general in "The Pirates of Penzance," with his "many cheerful facts about the square of the hypotenuse." It follows that a prime test of the competent analyst is his power to distinguish between important and unimportant factors and figures in a given situation.

Earning-Power Estimates

The now standard procedure for estimating future earning power starts with average *past* data for physical volume, prices received, and operating margin. Future sales in dollars are then projected on the basis of assumptions as to the amount of increase in volume and price level over the pre-war base. These estimates, in turn, are grounded first on general economic forecasts of gross national product, and then on special calculations applicable to the industry and company in question. The profit margin is usually taken at somewhat lower than the pre-war rate—to allow for the developing wage pattern—and federal income taxes are placed at 38 per cent or 35 per cent. Since in the typical case the dollar volume is expected to run 200 per cent or more of the 1936–40 average, the present-day analyst is bound to end up with an optimistic conclusion as to future earning power. The usual figure will run about 50 per cent higher than the pre-war rate.

Two illustrations of this method of approach may be summarized at this point. One is an estimate made by C. J. Collins, in 1945, of the earning power of each of the thirty stocks in the Dow-Jones Industrial Average in an active post-war year. (The figures were published in the July, 1945, issue of the *Analysts' Journal*.) The other is a calculation of the earning power of the public-utility industry as a whole for the years 1948–51, made by Charles Tatham in the February 26, 1948, issue of the *Public Utilities Fortnightly*. The conclusions in both cases are set forth in Tables X and XI.

Factors Affecting the Capitalization Rate

Though average future earnings are supposed to be the chief determinant of value, the security analyst takes into account a number of other factors of a more or less definite nature. Most of these will enter into his capitalization rate, which can vary over a wide range, depending upon the "quality" of the stock issue. Thus, although two companies may have the same figure of expected earnings per share in 1948–52—say $4—the analyst may value one as low as 40 and the other as high as 80. Let us deal briefly with some of the considerations that enter into these divergent multipliers.

TABLE X. A 1945 ESTIMATE OF POST-WAR EARNINGS OF COMPANIES
INCLUDED IN THE DOW-JONES INDUSTRIAL AVERAGE COMPARED WITH
ACTUAL FIGURES IN VARIOUS YEARS

AMOUNTS PER SHARE, ADJUSTED FOR
SPLIT-UPS TO END OF 1948

Post-War Estimate		Actual Figures		
		Pre-War (av. 1936–40)	War (1945)	Post-War (1947)
11.50–12.50	Allied Chemical	9.46	8.54	18.07
8.60– 9.75	American Can	5.67	4.23	7.65
7.92	American Smelting & Refining	4.20	3.03	12.65
10.40–10.60	American Tel. & Tel.	9.88	8.51	7.28
5.60– 6.00	American Tobacco B	4.87	3.69	5.70
6.00– 7.33	Bethlehem Steel	1.94	3.17	4.98
8.75– 9.00	Chrysler	4.74	4.31	7.72
3.40– 3.65	Corn Products	3.20	2.74	6.07
9.00–12.00	Du Pont	6.69	6.29	9.83
2.94	Eastman Kodak	1.68	3.27	3.46
2.95	General Electric	1.61	1.96	3.30
3.10– 3.20	General Foods	2.51	2.36	3.19
7.75– 8.50	General Motors	4.06	4.07	6.25
8.35– 8.85	Goodyear	3.04	6.07	14.59

(Continued)

TABLE X. A 1945 ESTIMATE OF POST-WAR EARNINGS OF COMPANIES
INCLUDED IN THE DOW-JONES INDUSTRIAL AVERAGE COMPARED WITH
ACTUAL FIGURES IN VARIOUS YEARS *(Continued)*

AMOUNTS PER SHARE, ADJUSTED FOR
SPLIT-UPS TO END OF 1948

Post-War Estimate		Actual Figures		
		Pre-War (av. 1936–40)	War (1945)	Post-War (1947)
2.33– 2.83	International Harvester	1.39	1.44	3.36
3.45– 3.65	International Nickel	2.56	1.58	2.37
4.92	Johns Manville	1.52	1.91	3.18
3.12– 3.33	Loews, Inc.	2.14	2.61	2.26
1.03– 1.18	National Distillers	1.22	1.72	4.57
9.75	National Steel	5.92	5.04	12.03
4.30	Procter & Gamble	3.45	3.29	10.18
2.30– 2.90	Sears, Roebuck	1.41	1.52	4.56
2.50	Standard Oil of Calif.	2.06	4.27	8.25
6.40– 7.00	Standard Oil of N.J.	4.01	5.64	9.83
4.65– 5.10	Texas Co.	3.61	4.97	10.05
6.00– 8.50	Union Carbide & Carbon	4.03	4.08	7.98
6.40– 6.70	United Aircraft	2.73	4.35	3.21
11.50–14.50	U.S. Steel	3.68	3.77	11.71
3.19– 3.25	Westinghouse Elec.	1.44	2.31	4.21
2.60– 2.65	Woolworth	3.05	2.43	4.32
15.96–17.58	Average for 30-Stock Unit	9.80	10.30	19.30

Note: Because of historical adjustments the "average" price and earnings are now computed by dividing the total figures by 11.

1. *General Long-Term Prospects.* No one really knows anything about what will happen in the distant future, but analysts and investors have strong views on the subject just the same. The pharmaceutical companies are currently supposed to have much better long-term prospects than coal mines, air transports better than railroads, crude oil producers better than

oil refiners, and so on. In some cases these distinctions are founded on basic operating conditions and are entirely valid if not carried too far. In other cases they stem from a superficial projection of past trends into the distant future and are just as likely to be wrong as right.

TABLE XI. PROJECTIONS OF THE PUBLIC UTILITIES INDUSTRY
BY CHARLES TATHAM

(CONDENSED)

		Actual Figures Year Ended Sept. 30, 1947	Projected Figures Year Ended Dec. 31 1948	1951
Kilowatt hours sold (billions)		223	246	302
Long-Term Debt	(millions)	$6,400	$6,742	$7,630
Preferred Stock	(")	2,100	2,330	2,780
Common Stock and Surplus	(")	5,300	5,469	5,916
Operating Revenue (Elec.)	(")	3,574	3,850	4,530
Available for Charges	(")	888	907	1,165
Charges	(")	240	263	298
Net Income	(")	648	644	867
Preferred Dividends	(")	99	114	136
Balance for Common	(")	549	530	731
Times Charges and Preferred Dividends Earned		2.62	2.41	2.69
Return on Common Stock and Surplus		10.3%	9.7%	12.4%

Note: The projections are built up out of separate calculations for the following constituent items, in addition to those shown above: wages, fuel cost, other costs, operating taxes, depreciation, "other income."

2. *Management.* In Wall Street a great deal is constantly said on this subject, but little that is really helpful. Until objective, quantitative, and reasonably reliable tests of managerial competence are devised and applied, this factor will continue to be looked at through a fog. It is fair to assume that an outstandingly successful company has unusually good management. This will have shown itself already in the past record; it will show up again in the estimates for the next five years, and once more in the previously discussed factor of long-term prospects. The tendency to count it still another time as a separate bullish consideration can easily lead to expensive overvaluations.

3. *Financial Strength and Capital Structure.* Stock of a company with a lot of surplus cash and nothing ahead of the common is clearly a better purchase than another one with the same per-share earnings but large bank loans and senior securities. Such factors are properly and carefully taken into account by security analysts. A modest amount of bonds or preferred stock, however, is not necessarily a disadvantage to the common, nor is the moderate use of seasonal bank credit. (Incidentally, a topheavy structure—too little common stock in relation to bonds and preferred—may under favorable conditions make for a huge *speculative* profit in the common. This is the factor known as "leverage.")

4. *Dividend Record.* One of the most persuasive tests of high quality is an uninterrupted record of dividend payments going back over many years and including the period of deep depression in 1931–33. Even though relative conditions may well have changed since then, or may be about to change in the future, a company meeting this test is properly regarded as entitled to a higher multiplier[2]—that is, a lower "capitalization rate"—than the average enterprise.

5. *Current Dividend Rate.* This, our last additional factor, is the most difficult one to deal with in satisfactory fashion. Fortunately, the majority of companies have come to follow what may be called a standard dividend policy. This has meant the distribution of about two-thirds of their average earnings, except that in the recent period of high profits and inflationary demands for more capital the figure has tended to be considerably lower.

---

[2] A multiplier of 16⅔ is the same as a capitalization rate of 6 per cent; a multiplier of 25 means a rate of 4 per cent, etc. The reader should keep clearly in mind that a low capitalization rate means a high value, and vice versa.

Where the dividend bears a normal relationship to the earnings, the valuation may be made on either basis without substantially affecting the result. For example, a typical secondary company with expected average earnings of $3 and an expected dividend of $2 may be valued at either 12 times its earnings or 18 times its dividend, to yield a value of 36 in both cases.[3]

There are some dynamically successful and expanding companies which have paid comparatively low dividends and have ploughed back nearly all their profits into enlarged operations. The low dividend has not been considered an adverse factor in the market, because those interested—whether as investors or speculators—have been thinking mainly in terms of the anticipated expansion of earning power. An example of this group is Amerada Petroleum. In 1945 this company earned $6.84 per share, paid $3, and sold as high as 161. In 1947 the comparable earnings were $18.92, the dividend $6, and the high price 214. (The 1947 figures are adjusted for a two-for-one split-up.)

But where the dynamic quality is lacking and a low dividend policy has been dictated by more-than-average conservatism, the stock tends regularly to sell well below the price justified by earnings and other factors outside of the dividend. Should the analyst's valuation be influenced by the low dividend? The answer is "yes and no." He should establish his value based on earnings and other *non*-dividend considerations; but then he should look to the low dividend for an opportunity to purchase the shares at considerably *below* his indicated appraisal. In other words, a low dividend rate creates a bargain issue. In the majority of cases the dividend policy is corrected with the passage of time, and the investor gains substantially both in income return and market appreciation.

Some Other Aspects of Security Analysis

We have previously alluded, with a touch of levity, to the many different ways in which the security analyst can operate with and upon the financial data furnished him by corporations. This work has serious value, however. For, granted that the past record has a bearing on the future, it is important to present the record in such a way as to bring out the true performance of

---

[3]Note that an estimate of average future earnings is likely to be substantially lower than the extraordinarily high figures shown under the boom conditions of 1947–48.

the business. Some of our readers will be interested in a brief cataloguing of these elements of security analysis.

In studying the report for a single year it is important to separate out non-recurrent profits and losses from the operating results proper. These non-recurrent items are of many different kinds, including the following:

1. Profit or loss on sale of fixed assets
2. Profit or loss on sale of marketable securities
3. Discount or premium on retirement of capital obligations
4. Proceeds of life insurance policies
5. Tax refunds and interest thereon
6. Gain or loss as result of litigation
7. Extraordinary write-downs of inventory
8. Extraordinary write-downs of receivables
9. Cost of maintaining non-operating properties

When items such as the above are included by the company in its income account, the analyst should calculate the indicated "normal" or ordinary earnings exclusive of the non-recurrent transactions. But, conversely, he will add into the year's results any important figures—such as the earnings of affiliates or subsidiaries—which the company has not taken into its accounts.

There is a wide field for study, and for possible adjustment of the reported earnings, in the matter of depreciation and depletion charges. The same applies to methods of valuing the inventory, especially since we now have two different bases—the old "lower of cost of market," and the new "LIFO" (last-in-first-out). The financial results shown in recent years may differ widely between companies according to whether one or the other inventory method has been followed. Comparative studies must take this factor carefully into account.

Of great importance also is the matter of contingency reserves, which are usually arbitrary amounts deducted from earnings to allow for future discomfitures. Since Pearl Harbor they have appeared in income accounts with increasing frequency, and they present a number of complications for the security analyst. Allied to this question is the reconciliation of the deduction for income taxes with the reported earnings.

A good analysis of the results for a number of years will include a comparison of balance-sheet figures at the beginning and at the end of the period. This will not only supply a valuable check on the reported earnings but also throw light on significant changes that may have occurred in the company's position, with a consequent bearing on the future earning power. The matter of excess or insufficient working capital is important in many cases. The analyst will also make allowance in his calculations for the presence and effect of conversion privileges attaching to senior securities, since these may diminish or "dilute" the earning power of the common stock.

Industry Analysis

Because the general prospects of the enterprise carry major weight in the establishment of market prices, it is natural for the security analyst to devote a great deal of attention to the economic position of the industry and of the individual company in its industry. Studies of this kind can go into unlimited detail. They are sometimes productive of valuable insights into important factors that will be operative in the future and are insufficiently appreciated by the current market. Where a conclusion of that kind can be drawn with a fair degree of confidence, it affords a sound basis for investment decisions.

Our own observation, however, leads us to minimize somewhat the practical value of most of the industry studies which are made available to investors. The material developed is ordinarily of a kind with which the public is already fairly familiar and which has already exerted its full influence on market quotations. Rarely does one find a brokerage-house study which points out, with a convincing array of facts, that a popular industry is heading for a fall or that an unpopular one is due to prosper. Wall Street's view of the longer future is notoriously fallible, and this necessarily applies to that important part of its investigations which is directed toward the forecasting of the course of profits in various industries.

Applications of Security Analysis

In subsequent chapters we shall supply concrete examples of the application of analytical techniques. But they will only be illustrations. If the reader finds the subject interesting he should pursue it systematically and thoroughly before he considers himself qualified to pass a final buy-or-sell judgment of his own on a security issue.

TABLE XII. RECOMMENDED MINIMUM "COVERAGE" FOR BONDS AND PREFERRED STOCKS

A. FOR INVESTMENT-GRADE BONDS

Minimum ratio of Earnings *before* Income Taxes to total Fixed Charges:

	Earning Period	
	1936–40	*1947 to date*
Type of Enterprise:	*Average*	*Average*
Public-utility operating company	2 times	2¼ times
Railroad	2½ "	3 "
Industrial	3½ "	4 "

Notes:
(1) Present charges may be used instead of past charges, if the current figure is lower.
(2) Requirements should be met in *both* the 1936–40 and the recent period. After 1951, the period 1947–51, 1947–52, etc., may be used alone.

B. FOR INVESTMENT-GRADE PREFERRED STOCKS

The same minimum figures as above are required to be shown by the ratio of Earnings *before* Income Taxes to the sum of Fixed Charges plus 1⅔ Preferred Dividends.

Note: The addition of ⅔ to the preferred dividends allows for the fact that preferred dividends are not income-tax deductible, whereas interest charges are so deductible.

C. OPTIONAL TEST FOR PUBLIC-UTILITY OPERATING COMPANY BONDS AND PREFERREDS

Earnings after Income Taxes for the past ten years should average 1¾ times charges (for bonds), or 2 times Fixed Charges plus Preferred Dividends (for preferred stocks). These coverage figures are computed by the financial services and investment manuals.

D. OTHER CATEGORIES OF BONDS AND PREFERREDS

The standards given above are not applicable to (a) public-utility holding companies, (b) financial companies, (c) real-estate companies. Requirements for these special groups are omitted here.

IX

—◆◇◆—

Stock Selection for the
Defensive Investor

IT IS TIME to turn to some practical applications of the techniques of security analysis. Since we have already described in general terms the investment policies recommended for our two categories of investors, it would be logical for us now to indicate how security analysis comes into play in order to implement these policies. The defensive investor who follows our suggestions will purchase only United States government bonds plus a diversified list of leading common stocks. He is to make sure that the price at which he bought the latter is not unduly high as judged by historical standards.

That program would call for only a minimum of aid from the security analyst. He would be asked only to supply a list of large, long-established and prosperous companies and to certify that the individual stock price of each, or perhaps the group or average price, is not high in the light of experience.

Yet even the latter assignment would confront the security analyst with something of a problem if he were facing it at the time these pages are written. Is the price of the Dow-Jones Industrial Average historically high at the level of, say, 175, about which it has fluctuated between September, 1946, and the present? Viewed in the simplest way, the answer is likely to be "yes." For the stock market has been above its 1948 level only twice before 1945—first in 1928–30, and then briefly in 1937. The long-term projection of past markets, as shown in the chart on page 32, would appear to place the 175 level safely in middle ground; but these lines show far from a convincing fit as applied to the market's behavior since 1925.

The analyst would seek to supplement his concept of past implications by looking guardedly into the future. In doing this he is bound to give weight to the rise in the price level brought on by the Second World War—apparently similar to that following the First World War—and to the general expectation of a physical volume of production far exceeding that of pre-1941. Thus he might well expect average earnings of about $14 for the unit, as against a figure of about $9 pre-war. If these are capitalized at a 6⅔ per cent basis—or with a multiplier of about 15—the resultant central value indicated would be above 200. (What we are doing here is to treat the thirty issues in the Dow-Jones list as if they were one gigantic company.)

Our initial excursion into practical security analysis is found to have yielded somewhat inconclusive results. The 175 level for the Dow-Jones Industrial Average seems indeed comparatively high if attention is focused exclusively on the past behavior of the price level. But if allowance is made for the known advent of new conditions—a necessary step in sound analysis—then the conclusion becomes quite otherwise. We believe the experienced analyst would feel justified in advising the defensive investor that he would not be overpaying for stocks of the Dow-Jones type at the 175 level, or moderately higher. The analyst would hasten to add that this statement contains no assurance against the possibility of a temporary decline to substantially lower figures. It is not the function of the security analyst to guarantee that such a decline either will or will not take place—nor can anyone be relied on to give such an undertaking. The analyst can express an opinion as to whether the investor will be getting adequate long-term *value* at present levels. That opinion, we believe, should be in the affirmative.

Our next assignment for the security analyst is the application of the four rules of common-stock selection which we recommended in Chapter IX. How would the thirty stocks in the Dow-Jones Industrial List fare under these tests? The first requirement—that of diversification—would be met, of course, unless too many of the issues were excluded by the other criteria. All the companies are large and prominent and would thus meet our second test.

In order to apply the other two rules, and mainly for the later purposes of this book, we are setting forth in the "Table of Basic Data re 30 Stocks in the Dow-Jones Industrial Average," on the two pages following, a statistical comparison under no less than nine headings:

1. Price on December 31, 1947
2. Percentage price change since the end of 1936
3. Year since which continuous dividends have been paid
4. Earnings per share—1929
5. Earnings per share—1931–33 (average)
6. Earnings per share—1936–40 (average)
7. Earnings per share—1947
8. Dividend paid in 1947
9. Net tangible assets per share at the end of 1947

In order to bring out the relative performance clearly, all the dollar figures are stated as a percentage of the December 1947 market price, that is, as the amount applicable to a $100 investment in each issue.

If we follow our third suggested rule—that an eligible common stock must have paid continuous dividends beginning at least in 1936—then three companies of the thirty would have to be excluded: Bethlehem Steel, Goodyear, and U. S. Steel. It is interesting to observe that the first two rank among the five best in terms of their gain in market price since 1936, and they also show up unusually well in their 1947 earnings. This indicates that a conservative approach may carry with it the rejection of really attractive investment opportunities. Such a possible disadvantage is inherent in the role of the defensive investor, and he must accept it philosophically.

Our fourth rule was designed to protect against possible paying too high a price for a "good stock." It suggested that an upper limit be set equal to 25 times the average earnings of 1936–40. (When a five-year post-war record becomes available—beginning with 1946–50—the maximum price should be 20 times such average earnings.) This last rule would exclude six of the Dow-Jones list if analyzed at their December 1947 prices: Du Pont, Eastman Kodak, Johns Manville, Sears, Roebuck, Standard Oil of California, and Union Carbide. As was to be expected, all these are popular issues, and their prices reflect the confident expectation of an unusually prosperous future. Nevertheless, we feel that the defensive investor would be wise to apply a

BASIC DATA RE 30 STOCKS IN THE DOW-JONES INDUSTRIAL AVERAGE

(ALL PER-SHARE FIGURES ARE GIVEN IN PERCENTAGE OF 1947
YEAR END PRICE)   N.A. — Figures not available

	Price 12/31/47	Price Change Since 12/31/36	Some Dividen Paid Sin
Allied Chemical	189-½	−16.4%	1921
American Can	70-⅛	−39.8	1923
American Smelting & Refining	56-¼	−27.5	1936
American Tel. & Tel.	151-⅜	−18.0	1881
American Tobacco B	68-½	−28.8	1905
Bethlehem Steel	34-⅜	36.9	1939
Chrysler	63-¾	10.0	1926
Corn Products	63-½	−6.6	1920
Du Pont	187	8.0	1915
Eastman Kodak	44-¾	27.9	1902
General Electric	35-¾	−34.7	1899
General Foods	35-¾	−9.8	1922
General Motors	58-¼	−8.2	1917
Goodyear	43-½	51.2	1937
International Harvester	89	-15.5	1918
International Nickel	26-¾	−58.0	1934
Johns Manville	40-¼	−19.8	1935
Loews, Inc.	18-⅜	−16.5	1923
National Distillers	20-⅞	131.5	1935
National Steel	91	27.2	1930
Procter & Gamble	69-½	24.0	1891
Sears, Roebuck	37-⅞	81.5	1935
Standard Oil of Calif.	62-⅞	42.1	1912
Standard Oil of N.J.	79-⅜	15.5	1882
Texas Co.	60-⅛	9.9	1902
Union Carbide & Carbon	103	−0.6	1918
United Aircraft	23-⅝	−17.1	1936
U.S. Steel	78-⅛	—	1940
Westinghouse Electric	30-¼	−17.8	1935
Woolworth	46	−27.0	1912

BASIC DATA RE 30 STOCKS IN THE DOW-JONES INDUSTRIAL AVERAGE

(ALL PER-SHARE FIGURES ARE GIVEN IN PERCENTAGE OF 1947 YEAR END PRICE)

1929 arnings	Average Earnings 1931–1933	Average Earnings 1936–1940	1947 Earnings	1947 Dividend	Net Tangible Assets 1947
6.65%	2.8%	5.0%	9.5%	4.75%	64.0%
4.3	6.4	8.1	10.9	4.3	90.5
4.8	Deficit	7.5	22.5	7.4	84.1
8.3	5.3	6.5	4.8	5.9	88.0
8.4	10.0	7.1	8.3	5.1	53.3
0.7	Deficit	5.65	14.5	5.8	171.5
3.8	0.2	7.4	12.1	4.5	58.6
8.6	5.3	5.0	9.6	4.7	56.4
3.7	1.6	3.6	5.3	4.3	48.3
4.3	1.9	3.8	7.7	3.5	49.0
6.3	2.0	4.5	9.2	4.5	47.0
0.3	7.0	7.0	8.9	5.6	58.5
9.4	2.0	7.0	10.8	5.15	47.7
1.5	Deficit	7.0	33.5	9.2	183.0
8.0	Deficit	4.7	11.3	4.1	114.0
5.5	0.7	9.5	8.9	7.5	63.3
6.7	Deficit	3.8	7.9	3.5	74.4
4.5	8.7	11.6	12.3	8.2	151.0
0.8	2.1	5.8	21.9	9.6	87.9
N.A.	1.5	6.5	13.2	4.4	99.7
1.4	3.0	5.0	11.0	5.8	46.8
4.4	1.0	3.7	12.1	4.6	53.0
5.8	0.9	3.3	13.1	5.1	89.8
6.0	0.6	5.1	12.4	5.0	87.0
8.15	Deficit	6.0	16.7	5.0	106.9
3.8	1.5	3.9	7.7	3.6	40.4
N.A.	N.A.	10.5	13.6	5.3	151.6
7.1	Deficit	4.7	15.0	6.4	192.5
8.4	Deficit	4.8	13.9	4.1	86.8
8.0	6.9	6.6	9.4	5.4	59.5

clear-cut rule of the kind we are discussing, let the chips fall where they may. Though some good security purchases may thus be forgone, the general result will be to assure him that the portfolio is acquired at reasonable cost.

It is only proper to point out that the prime investment favorite of all—American Telephone & Telegraph—might logically be excluded by our reasoning. In 1947 it earned only 4.8 per cent on the year-end price. Since 1947 is considered to have been an extraordinarily prosperous year, there would appear real danger that A.T. & T. will fail in the future to average earnings of 5 per cent on a price of 151. The market level of this issue has been supported by its unusually liberal dividend policy. One may hardly ignore the fact that the company paid out more than it earned in 1947, a year when most other companies moved toward the other extreme. We are willing to wager that no one is going to suffer a serious loss by buying A.T. & T. at 151. But objective analysis suggests that other leading issues now offer considerably more for the money—except for the current dividend, which cannot be relied upon when not buttressed by earning power.

Thus, carrying our method to its conclusion, we find that twenty out of the thirty Dow-Jones issues would meet our standards for the defensive investor at the close of 1947. If he divided his money about equally among these he would obtain the following percentages on his cost:

Dividend Yield 1947	5.54%
Earned 1947	12.32%
Earned 1936–40 (average)	6.92%
Tangible Asset Value	80.7%

(These are averages of the separate percentages shown by each stock.)

There is no reason to be dissatisfied with any of these figures. Nor, on the other hand, should any special claims of virtue be made for this list of twenty stocks, except that they represent large and successful concerns and they all meet certain reasonable investment standards.

Many other assortments of leading common stocks, which would meet the stipulated requirements and would reflect certain preferences and expectations of the compiler, could be assembled. It is natural for the investor to inquire whether we believe his list should be limited to so-called industrial companies, or whether it could or should include representative common stocks of railroads, public utilities, and financial enterprises. In our view there is no superior advantage in any fixed pattern of diversification. It is not essential to spread the risk around, in pre-established proportions, so that each of the major categories of American enterprise is included. What is essential is that a reasonable diversity of industries be achieved, so that the investor can feel he has his stake in a fairly good cross section of the economy. This being so, it follows that a railroad, utility, bank, or insurance-company stock may be accepted or rejected by the compiler of the list in the same way, and on the same principles, as he would act toward a steel or department-store stock.

There are some factors in the choice of railroad and utility issues which deserve special mention. On the one side, the factor of prominence or substantial size is not so important for the defensive investor in these two divisions as it is in the buying of industrial stocks. A medium-sized railroad or public utility has as much inherent stability as a very large one, provided its financial structure is sound and it has no special operating problems which show up in an unduly low profit margin.

Even strong railroad and utility companies are characterized by the presence of a considerable amount of debt and preferred stock. (By contrast, most of the best industrials are debt-free, though this is by no means a necessary requirement for a satisfactory common-stock investment.) Obviously, no common stock should be bought by the defensive investor unless the company's credit rating is very high, as shown by a relatively low interest yield on its bond issues. More logically, the good credit should be demonstrated by a fully adequate coverage of interest charges plus preferred dividends—and that over a considerable period of time. The investor should ask the framer of his list to make particularly sure on this point. There are probably not more than half a dozen railroad common stocks in 1948 which have past records that qualify them for inclusion in a conservative portfolio. The list of suitable public utility issues is much longer, and their price level (during 1948) appears eminently reasonable.

Selectivity for the Defensive Investor

Every investor would like his list to be better or more promising than the average. Hence the reader will ask whether, if he gets himself a competent adviser or security analyst, he should not be able to count on being presented with an investment package of really superior merits. "After all," he may say, "the rules just outlined are pretty simple and easy-going. A highly-trained analyst ought to be able to use all his skill and techniques to improve substantially on something as obvious as the Dow-Jones list. If not, what good are all his statistics, calculations, and pontifical judgments?"

Suppose, as a practical test, we had confined our inquiry to the choice of the "best" five stocks in the Dow-Jones Average, to be bought as at the end of 1947. We are quite sure that if a large number of practicing security analysts had been assigned this job very few would have come up with identical choices, and many of the lists would have differed completely from each other.

This is not so surprising as it may at first appear. The underlying reason is that the current price of each prominent stock pretty well reflects the salient factors in its financial record plus the general opinion as to its future prospects. Hence the view of any analyst that one stock is a better buy than the rest must arise to a great extent from his personal partialities and expectations, or from the placing of his emphasis on one set of factors rather than on another in his work of evaluation. If all analysts were agreed that one particular stock was better than all the rest, that issue would quickly advance to a price which offsets all of its previous advantages.

Our statement that the current price reflects both known facts and future expectations was intended to emphasize the double basis for market valuations. Corresponding with these two kinds of value elements there are two basically different approaches to security analysis. To be sure, every competent analyst looks forward to the future rather than backward to the past, and he realizes that his work will prove good or bad depending on what *will* happen and not on what *has* happened. Nevertheless, the future itself can be approached in two different ways, which may be called the way of prediction (or projection) and the way of protection.

Those who emphasize prediction will endeavor to anticipate fairly accurately just what the company will accomplish in future years—in particular whether earnings will show pronounced and persistent growth. These conclusions may be based on a very careful study of such factors as supply and demand in the industry—or volume, price, and costs—or else they may be derived from a rather naïve projection of the line of past growth into the future. If these authorities are convinced that the fairly long-term prospects are unusually favorable, they will almost always recommend the stock for purchase without paying too much regard to the level at which it is selling. Such, for example, has been the general attitude for many years with respect to the air-transport stocks—an attitude which persisted through 1948 despite the distressingly bad results shown for 1947 and 1948.

By contrast, those who emphasize protection are always especially concerned with the price of the issue at the time of study. Their main effort is to assure themselves of a substantial margin of indicated present value above the market price—which margin could absorb unfavorable developments in the future. Generally speaking, therefore, it is not so necessary for them to be enthusiastic over the company's long-run prospects as it is to be reasonably confident that the enterprise will get along.

The first, or predictive, approach could also be called the qualitative approach, since it emphasizes prospects, management, and other non-measurable, albeit highly important, factors that go under the heading of quality. The second, or protective, approach may be called the quantitative or statistical approach, since it emphasizes the measurable relationships between selling price and earnings, assets, dividends, and so forth. Incidentally, the quantitative method is really an extension—into the field of common stocks—of the viewpoint which security analysis has found to be sound in the selection of bonds and preferred stocks for investment.

In our own attitude and professional work we are committed to the quantitative approach. From the first we want to make sure that we are getting ample value for our money in concrete, demonstrable terms. We are not willing to accept the prospects and promises of the future as compensation for a lack of sufficient value in hand. This is by no means the standard viewpoint among investment authorities; in fact, the majority would probably subscribe to the view that prospects, quality of management, other intangibles, and "the human factor" far outweigh the indications supplied by any study of the past record, the balance sheet, and all the other cold figures.

Thus this matter of choosing the "best" stocks is at bottom a highly controversial one. Our advice to the defensive investor is that he let it alone. Let him emphasize diversification more than individual selection. Incidentally, the universally accepted idea of diversification is, in part at least, the negation of the ambitious pretensions of selectivity. If one *could* select the best stocks unerringly, one would only lose by diversifying. Yet within the limits of the four rules of common-stock selection suggested for the defensive investor there is room for a rather considerable freedom of preference. At the worst the indulgence of such preferences should do no harm; beyond that, it may add something worth while to the results.

Later we intend to develop further a combined quantitative-qualitative approach to the selection of common stocks. But this is a subject for study by the enterprising investor, to whose requirements we now turn.

X

◄◆►

Stock Selection for the Enterprising Investor: the Appraisal Method

We shall now develop an approach to common-stock investment which differs significantly from traditional ideas. It is difficult to describe exactly how most investors go about the business of choosing common stocks. By exactly what mental processes does A decide that he wants Bethlehem Steel at 35, while B prefers Woolworth at 46, and C selects Allied Chemical at 190? The operation seems to be something like choosing a wife. A number of concrete factors are weighed more or less carefully, to which is then added a strong and perhaps controlling component of unreasoning favoritism.

It is our suggestion that common-stock selection be done systematically through a process of appraisal. The aggressive investor should obtain the best available estimates of what a number of stocks are *worth*, apart from their market price. He will then make his choices from among those which are selling at the largest discounts from their indicated values. These values will be based chiefly upon the expected average future earning power, capitalized at a rate which reflects the quality of the issue in view.

This technique will not sound so strange to many of the initiated as it would have seemed a decade ago. In recent years there has been a steady expansion of the role of common-stock appraisal. It began in gift-tax and estate-tax cases, the purpose being to determine the "fair market value" of stocks for which there was an inadequate market or none at all. It was then adopted by the Interstate Commerce Commission (I.C.C.) as the basis for its approval of railroad reorganization plans. Since then it has become a central aspect of much of the important work of the S.E.C. in the field of corporate readjustment, including its far-reaching decisions in many cases under the Public Utility Holding Company Act of 1935.

Most important is the fact that all these valuations are intended, by legal theory, to be "realistic"; that is, they are supposed to reflect the most expert formulation available of what the company or the stock *should* sell for in a normal market ruled by intelligent buyers and sellers. In some now classic Supreme Court decisions, that tribunal has ruled that valuations of this sort are to be based ordinarily on what the business may be expected to earn in the future—which is the same idea that Wall Street has of the basis of security values.

The idea of a formal valuation of a company as the key to investment in its common stock has finally entered brokerage-house practice in its application to public utilities. The reasoning has run something like this: If the S.E.C. can do a good job of valuing utility stocks for the purpose of setting up recapitalization and dissolution plans, why should not security analysts follow the same procedure in order to decide whether a stock is cheap or dear in the market? The public-utility issues have been regarded as best suited to this valuation approach, because their operations have great underlying stability; here, therefore, estimates of future earnings can be made with a large measure of confidence in their reasonableness.

Security analysts have hesitated to extend the appraisal method to industrial and even to railroad stocks, because they dislike the idea of committing themselves in writing to a guess of future earning power which may well prove wide of the mark. The future operations of a typical industrial are indeed much less predictable than those of an electric and gas concern—for the latter enjoys a local monopoly, a steadily increasing demand, and a return on its invested capital which is more or less fixed by the process of rate regulation. Industrial results, on the other hand, are subject to uncontrolled variations in prices, costs, demand, and competitive supply.

Although fully recognizing these obstacles to the satisfactory prediction of industrial earnings, we believe nevertheless that a sufficiently dependable job can be done to warrant its use in security selection. This work is actually being carried on, as witness the 1945 estimates of future earnings of the Dow-Jones list given on page 129. Its defects or hazards can be largely offset by two sovereign devices—first, adequate diversification; and, second, a margin of safety in each individual choice. Finally, we believe that its basis is sounder and its results more satisfactory than those associated with the alternative methods now current, which are largely of the hit-or-miss variety.

After this longish introduction, let us now proceed to our illustrations. The subject matter is ready to hand, in that very Dow-Jones Industrial List to which we have already paid so much attention. (Incidentally, such attention is by no means undeserved, since the thirty issues in that group had at the end of 1947 a total market value of no less than $21 billion, which is fully half the total market value of the remaining 934 common stocks listed on the New York Stock Exchange.)

The valuation of the thirty stocks is by no means a complicated process, at least on the surface. It consists merely of placing a figure for the estimated average per-share earnings for the seven-year period 1947–53 and another figure by which to multiply this earning power.[1] The earnings figure we have used is a straight mean or compromise between the 1947 results—which are clearly the product of boom conditions—and the 1936–40 average, which must now be thought of as "subnormal." The multipliers range from a minimum of 10 to a maximum of 20. Thus we assume that Goodyear is fairly worth only 10 times our expected seven-year earnings of $8.80 per share, whereas Du Pont is worth as much as 20 times its earning power of $8.25.

Naturally these multipliers, or capitalization rates, are highly arbitrary. They are based on the "quality" of each issue, largely as it appears in the eyes of Wall Street and has been reflected in the market's own valuations over some years past. This "quality," in turn, is at bottom a rather vague formulation of the earning power over a longer term which goes beyond the 1947–53 period.[2] By our own decision we have set the highest multiplier at 20, because we believe that the investor who pays more than such a price for a highly promising issue is really turning himself into a speculator on the extent of its future prosperity.

[1] We expect these seven years to contain the elements of a full business cycle, including a boom, a depression, and a "normal" period.

[2] In the case of Goodyear the low multiplier also reflects the relatively large amount of bonds and preferred stock ahead of the common. This factor has an important bearing on "quality."

TABLE XIII. APPRAISAL OF STOCKS IN THE DOW-JONES INDUSTRIAL
AVERAGE AS OF DECEMBER 31, 1947

	Estimated Average Earnings 1947–53[1]	Multiplier	Appraisal Value Without Adjustment for Assets (Col. 2 times Col. 3)	Appraisal Value After Adjustment for Assets	Appraisal Value After Adjustment for Assets	Ratio of Adjusted Appraisal to Dec. 1947 Price
Allied Chemical	13.80	17	220		220	116%
American Can	6.70	15	101		101	144
American Smelting & Refining	8.40	13	109	—8	101	180
American Tel. & Tel.	8.60	16	137		137	91
American Tobacco B	5.30	16	85	—5	80	117
Bethlehem Steel	3.50	13	45		45	131
Chrysler	6.20	14	87	—3	84	132
Corn Products	4.60	16	74	—3	71	112
Du Pont	8.30	20	166		166	89
Eastman Kodak	2.60	20	52		52	116
General Electric	2.50	18	44	—3	41	115
General Foods	2.90	16	46	—1	45	126
General Motors	5.20	15	78	—5	73	125
Goodyear	8.80	10	88		88	202
International Harvester	7.10	15	107		107	120
International Nickel	2.50	15	37	—1	36	134
Johns Manville	2.40	14	33		33	82
Loews, Inc.	2.20	13	29		29	158
National Distillers	2.90	10	29		29	139

(Continued)

TABLE XIII. APPRAISAL OF STOCKS IN THE DOW-JONES INDUSTRIAL
AVERAGE AS OF DECEMBER 31, 1947 *(Continued)*

	Estimated Average Earnings 1947–53[1]	Multiplier	Appraisal Value Without Adjustment for Assets (Col. 2 times Col. 3)	Appraisal Value After Adjustment for Assets	Ratio of Adjusted Appraisal to Dec. 1947 Price
National Steel	9.00	13	117		117	129
Procter & Gamble	5.70	16	91	—7	84	121
Sears, Roebuck	3.00	17	51	—3	48	127
Standard Oil of Calif.	5.20	15	78		78	˙124
Standard Oil of N.J.	6.90	15	104		104	131
Texas Co.	. 6.80	14	95		95	158
Union Carbide & Carbon	6.00	18	108	—6	102	99
United Aircraft	3.00	12	36		36	152
U.S. Steel	7.70	11	85		85	109
Westinghouse Electric	2.80	15	42		42	139
Woolworth	3.70	16	59		59	128
	164.3		2433	—45	2388	
Average for 30 Stocks[2]	14.95		221		217	120%

[1]Based 50% on 1936–40 average and 50% on 1947 results.
[2]Because of past adjustments, the divisor is 11 instead of 30.

Table XIII gives the details of our valuations of the Dow-Jones Industrial
List as at the end of 1947. It will be observed that the list as a whole was selling
at some 20 per cent less than the sum of our valuations. This fact supports our
earlier statement that the rather stationary market level for this group between

September, 1946, and early 1949, was not a statistically high one and was therefore suitable for purchase by both the defensive and the enterprising investor.

Selection of the "Cheapest" and the "Dearest" Stocks

When we compare the individual appraisals with the corresponding market prices at the beginning of 1948 we find a wide range of variation. Three of the issues were selling at more than our appraisal values, five were selling at less than two-thirds of appraisal, and the remainder ranked in between. These relationships suggest that we have here at least one possible answer to the problem stated in the previous chapter—that of selecting the five "best" stocks in the Dow-Jones Industrial Average. The five issues appraised at 50 per cent or more above the market stand out quantitatively from the rest. Let us call them Group A and then add up the statistical data relating to them. Similarly, for purposes of contrast, let us supply such data for the three issues selling above appraisal— which we shall call Group B. The results are shown in Table XIV.

TABLE XIV

GROUP A: AMERICAN SMELTING, GOODYEAR, LOEW'S, TEXAS COMPANY, UNITED AIRCRAFT.

GROUP B: AMERICAN TELEPHONE & TELEGRAPH, DU PONT, JOHNS MANVILLE.

| | Totals of 1 share of each stock: | |
	Group A	Group B
December, 1947, Price	$200	$378
Our Appraised Value	358	337
Tangible Asset Value	257	253
1947 Dividend	13.92	18.40
1947 Earnings	42.75	20.29
1936–40 Earnings (average)	15.72	18.09
1929 Earnings	25.31[1]	22.21
Future Earnings (Collins's Estimate, p. 129)	31.16	25.92

[1]Excluding United Aircraft, formed in 1936.
Note: Appraisal values taken are without adjustment for assets.

Let us now turn to Table XV and see what the purchaser would have received had he placed $1,000 in Group A as against the same sum placed in Group B.

TABLE XV

	Per $1,000 Invested December 31, 1947		
	Group A	Group B	Ratio A/B
Appraised Value	$1760	$890	2 times
Asset Value	1290	670	1.9 "
1947 Dividend	69	49	1.4 "
1947 Earnings	214	54	4.0 "
1936–40 Earnings	79	48	1.6 "
1929 Earnings	146[1]	59	2.5 "
Future Earnings (Collins's Estimate, p. 129)	155	69	2.3 "

[1] On price of 4 issues.
Note: Appraisal values taken are without adjustment for assets.

The process of selection just illustrated is based primarily on quantitative factors. Although the multipliers—which greatly favor Group B—give expression to qualitative considerations, their effect in that respect has been limited through their conversion into figures. As it happens, the three "dear" stocks do not form a homogeneous group, since Johns Manville does not rank in so-called "investment quality" with A.T. & T. and Du Pont. The latter two have a definite superiority over our Group A list in their record during the 1931–33 depression and in their history of continuous dividends.[2] The multipliers chosen are intended to reflect these as well as other factors; hence, in logic, they should not be further determinative of the investor's decision.

It is worth pointing out that the long-term price behavior of the two groups is clearly irrelevant to the problem of selection. As appears in Table XIV, three of the issues in Group A show moderate declines between the end of 1936 and the end of 1947, whereas the two remaining issues have had a

[2] It is not practical, statistically, to give figures contrasting the 1931–33 performances on a group basis, because per-share deficits are not comparable as between companies.

large advance. In the case of Group B there are two declines and one advance. A price decline, in and of itself, is more of an inducement to buy in the thinking of the true investor than is a price advance. But neither one nor the other means much as compared with more appropriate indicators of value.

Let us observe also that one of the issues, Goodyear, which would appear attractive to the aggressive investor, was eliminated from our list for the defensive investor because it did not pay a dividend in 1936. Such contrary decisions would be natural for the two categories, since they are guided by different considerations. But *all three* of the issues in Group B, which appear too high in price in the present analysis, were rejected also for the defensive investor's list. This, too, is natural, since in our view both classes of investors should endeavor to avoid the purchase of "good stocks" at what may be an unsound price level.

Asset-Value Factor

In the table on page 141 we have added a column showing the value of the net assets (or net worth) behind each share of stock, which figure may be compared both with the market price and the appraised value based on expected earning power. What is the significance, if any, of the asset figure? A generation ago it was considered of first importance. The net tangible worth, as shown by the balance sheet, was supposed to be the starting point in investment valuations and decisions, just as even today it is the starting point in the valuation of an ordinary private or closely owned business. But in quoted securities the pendulum has swung completely the other way. The price is governed by current or expected earnings, by quality or "general prospects," and by the dividend rate. In the typical common stock it is difficult to find that any influence at all is exerted upon the market price by the book value of the available assets.

Thus we find that New York Central Railroad shares have $131 of assets behind them, but they sold in 1947 as low as 12; Coca-Cola common, on the other hand, has sold at 191 while backed by only $22 per share of tangible investment.

In our own thinking we have never been willing to turn our back completely on the asset figure. We do not like the idea of paying $5 for $1 of tangible assets, and we find it rather interesting to be offered $5 of assets for $1. The difficulty lies in formulating this general feeling in terms sufficiently concrete to assist the intelligent investor. After careful study of the point for many years, we hesitate to go any farther than to suggest that a substantial deficiency of asset value below price should be taken as a "minus factor" in rating the security.

If the reader insists on some arithmetical expression of this idea, he might consider reducing the appraisal value, based on earning power—that is the "earning power value" by one-quarter of the amount by which it exceeds *twice* the asset value. Example: Our earning-power value for American Smelting exceeds twice the asset value by $34 per share. The appraisal figure would then be reduced from 110 to 101. The adjustment for assets would affect only American Smelting in our list of "cheapest stocks." It would add Union Carbide to the list of stocks selling above appraisal value.

If the asset value *exceeds* the earning-power value, that is hardly a matter of interest to the investor, for fixed assets without corresponding profit-making power carry no recognizable weight. An exception to this statement, however, should be noted with respect to cases where the net current assets, or working capital, alone substantially exceed the earning-power value or the market price. This would not occur in any of the leading and prosperous companies, but it is a frequent phenomenon among secondary companies. In these we often see the common stock selling well below its current-asset value alone, with less than nothing being paid for plant and good will.

The difference between stock-market valuations and private-business valuations appears more clearly at this point than perhaps at any other. In a private business the lowest level for appraising its worth, even as applied to a small minority interest, would certainly be the cash on hand less all liabilities. Not so in Wall Street. People apparently think nothing of selling out their shares for as little as one-half their cash asset value, disregarding all other property of the corporation, if the business as a whole no longer appeals to them.[3] Nor does this apply only to clearly second-rate enterprises. The reader will recall that A. & P. common sold for less than the working capital alone in 1938. An even larger business—Swift & Company—sold continuously on such a basis before the war, and no one paid much attention to the fact. In 1947–1949 there were numerous issues in this category that had fairly impressive records of earnings, at least since 1940.

---

[3] A striking example of this kind is presented by Westmoreland Coal in the years before 1941. We discuss this situation in the 1940 edition of *Security Analysis*, pp. 608–609.

In the work of appraising and selecting common stocks, we recommend that an excess of current-asset value be considered as a definite "plus factor." If it can be found in conjunction with a satisfactory earning-power situation, it affords a strong added argument for purchase. For those who insist on putting this into a formula, we might suggest—as the counterpart of the deduction made for insufficient assets—that in an appraisal the earning-power value be *increased* by one-half of the excess of current-asset value over earning-power value.

Disclaimer

This is probably the place for a little expression of modesty. We have tried to be definite and unequivocal in our statement of principles and techniques. Not only that, we have been indiscreet enough to illustrate them with examples current as we write,[4] instead of resorting to past examples which have already worked out as we want them to. All this may give the impression of a self-confidence bordering on the cocksure. This is far from true. No one can be certain of the answers to questions of investment policy, when the right answer means a profit and the wrong one a loss. Our method of appraisal does not guarantee that the so-called "undervalued" Group A will prove a wiser purchase than Group B. We do claim for this technique that it is rational and practical, that it has yielded satisfactory results in the past, and that there is no reason to think that it is inferior to the current habit of picking stocks largely on the basis of partialities and prejudices.

Our estimate of future earnings and the related multipliers cannot be expected to prove entirely accurate. Other authorities, of course, would use different figures. But the use of this method in classroom work with practicing security analysts has satisfied us that the final valuation figure found for a given company by a number of practitioners is not likely to vary over a wide range. The key to the successful use of the method undoubtedly lies in the margin-of-safety feature. If the investor will buy only at prices at least one-third under the indicated value, he will acquire a cushion that should be ade-

---

[4]Incidentally, to eschew hindsight, we have not withdrawn or adjusted any of our examples because of price developments since their choice in early 1948.

quate to absorb the shock of the unexpected or the miscalculated event. In our view the margin-of-safety idea is an indispensable part of an operation in secondary stocks.

But in any single instance even a substantial margin of safety is not sufficient to guarantee a successful outcome. That is why diversification is fully as essential as the use of sound methods in making individual choices. For no one investment operation is ever a matter of certainty, but all of them can and should be matters of intelligent calculation. In this respect investment is much like the fascinating game of bridge. When an individual case is to be judged, it is not the result of the play but its conformity with sound principles that marks the competent player. The results do count, of course, both in bridge and in investment—but they must be measured in the aggregate and over the years.

Primary and Secondary Common Stocks

The chief practical difference between the defensive and the enterprising investor is that the former limits himself to large and leading companies whereas the latter will buy any stock if his judgment and his technique tell him it is sufficiently attractive. We do not consider it essential that the defensive investor be guided by our appraisal method, or something equivalent to it, in making his selections among the leading issues. This may involve more bother than he is willing to assume. It may be quite enough if he buys a well-diversified cross section at any time except when the general market level has advanced into an area that cannot be justified by established standards of value.

The enterprising investor, on the other hand, if he buys into leading or primary enterprises, will assuredly want to demonstrate his independent judgment by picking out the "best" from among them. He may wish to apply our appraisal method for this purpose, or he may prefer to follow some other technique of selection which appeals more strongly to him and his advisers. Whatever the process followed, we urge upon him that in each case he satisfy himself that the market valuation for the company as a whole, as represented by the price he is paying for the shares, is not an unduly high one in the light of the actual record.

The field of secondary stocks cannot be delimited precisely. It includes perhaps two thousand listed issues and many thousands more of unlisted ones which are not generally recognized as belonging in the aristocratic category of "large and prosperous market leaders." Obviously there must be at all times a number of marginal cases about the placing of which opinions will differ. But ordinarily the investor will have no doubt whether the issue presented for his consideration falls in the primary or in the secondary class.

The intelligent investor can operate successfully in secondary common stocks provided he buys them only on a bargain basis. This means that he should rarely buy them when their short-term prospects look bright—which is about the only time that the ordinary purchaser is likely to be interested in them at all. On those occasions the market price is likely to climb close to, and even to exceed, the indicated long-term value. Obviously that is an opportunity to sell on advantageous terms, rather than to buy.

It is during the colorless and even the somewhat unpromising periods in the careers of these secondary companies that price levels are created which should appeal to the enterprising investor. It is not hard at such times to find a large choice of issues that appear to be worth intrinsically even twice as much as they sell for. The appraisal method can be used to good advantage to establish the indicated fair value. If the investor makes sure that he is not paying more than 67 cents for each dollar of such value, and preferably less, he has good reason to expect a satisfactory outcome in the ensuing years.

The technique of selecting secondary common stocks was illustrated by our brief analysis of National Department Stores as of January 31, 1948, given in Chapter VI (page 98). Here are two further examples:

A. Stewart Warner Corporation, considered at the end of 1947, the price being 14.

This is a long-established company, prominent in the manufacture of auto parts, radios, and various other products. Its sole capitalization consists of about 1,300,000 shares of common. At 14, the entire company was valued at $18.2 million.

The working capital, plus a cash fund for plant rehabilitation, totaled $18.7 million. The total tangible assets for the stock were $27 million, or $21 per share. Sales in 1947 were $77 million; the net after taxes and the inventory reserve was $2,437,000, or $1.88 per share. The reported earnings for the eleven years 1936–47 averaged $1.20 per share. A comparison of the surplus and reserve accounts will increase this figure to $1.45.

In this case a comparison between 1936 and 1947 is significant. The average price in 1936 was 20½, the sales $27 million, and the net after taxes $1.70 per share. The working capital then was only $7.1 million, and the net assets for the stock were $15.1 million, or $12 per share.

Stewart Warner has greatly increased its sales, its net before taxes and reserves, and its asset value; but the 1947 price was much lower than the 1936 average. The net after taxes in 1947 was not so impressive as that of many other companies. In this case projections of the future sales volume and profit margins might warrant expectation of somewhat higher average earnings for 1947–53—say $2 per share. A multiplier of 12 would yield an appraised value of 24. This is sufficiently above the price of 14 to indicate that the stock was undervalued at its December, 1947, price.

B. White Dental Manufacturing Company, considered in July, 1948, at 25.

This concern is the largest in the field of dental appliances and supplies. The business was established in 1844 and incorporated in 1881. It has paid dividends in every year since its incorporation.

The sole capitalization consists of 300,000 shares of stock, par $20. At a price of 25 the company was valued at $7,500,000. On June 30, 1948, the balance sheet showed $8,878,000 ($28.9 per share) of working capital alone, and $12,564,000 ($41.88 per share) of net tangible assets ("book value").

In the twelve months to June, 1948, sales were $19 million, and the net after taxes was $1,227,000, or $4.09 per share. The dividend was $1.60. The average earnings for 10½ years were $2.30 per share.

In the 1936 calendar year the sales were about $8.5 million, and the net after taxes was $406,000—or $1.35 per share. At that time, the working capital was $19 per share and the net tangible assets were $28.6. The average market price was $17.50.

In contrast with Stewart Warner, the current earnings are high, but the pre-war figure is comparatively low. Assuming an average future volume of $16 millions, the net for the stock might be estimated at $900,000, or $3 per share. This figure would justify an appraisal of 35–40, which is less than the book value and about 50 per cent above the July, 1948, price.

A company of this caliber, with its long dividend record, should clearly be worth at least the amount of its net current assets alone. At 25, therefore, the stock would qualify as an undervalued secondary issue.

It is possible, of course, that any individual analysis of such companies as National Department Stores, Stewart Warner, or White Dental may be proved unsound by adverse future developments. But when group investments are made in accordance with this technique—with a diversification of ten or more issues—we have confidence that the over-all result will be satisfactory.

Rules for the Appraisal of Common Stocks

The eleven statements with which we conclude this chapter provide a set of rules to guide the investor or security analyst in his appraisal work. Since the procedure is still a comparatively new one, we may expect that improvements will be made in a number of directions. In any case, these suggestions are intended to be helpful rather than definitive.

1. The appraised value is determined by (a) estimating the earning power, (b) applying thereto a suitable multiplier, and (c) adjusting, if necessary, for asset value.

2. The earning power should ordinarily represent an estimate of average earnings for the next five years.

3. The above estimate should be developed preferably from a projection of the dollar volume and the profit margin. The starting point is the actual exhibit over some period in the past. Under conditions existing in early 1949 there is no "normal period" of past years which can be accepted as a direct measure of future earning power. However, an averaging of the results of an unusually good period and a subnormal period might be acceptable—for example, giving 50 per cent weight to the 1936–40 average after taxes and 50 per cent weight to 1947–48 or 1946–48.

4. When figures of earlier years enter into the calculation, proper adjustment should be made for subsequent changes in capitalization.

5. The multiplier should reflect prospective longer-term changes in earnings. A multiplier of 12 is suitable for stocks with neutral prospects. Increases or decreases from this figure must depend on the judgment and preferences of the appraiser. In all but the most exceptional cases, however, the maximum multiplier should be 20 and the minimum should be 8.

6. If the tangible-asset value is less than the earning-power value (earning power times multiplier), the latter may be reduced by some arbitrary factor to reflect this deficiency. Our suggested factor is as follows: Deduct one-quarter of the amount by which the earning-power value exceeds twice the asset value. (This permits a 100 per cent premium over tangible assets without penalty.)

7. If the net-current-asset value exceeds the earning-power value, the latter may be increased by 50 per cent of the excess to give the final appraised value.

8. Where extraordinary conditions prevail—such as war profits or war restrictions, or a temporary royalty or rental situation—the amount of the total probable gain or loss per share due to such conditions should be estimated and added to, or subtracted from, the appraised value as determined without considering the abnormal conditions.

9. Where the capitalization structure is highly speculative—that is, where the total of senior securities is disproportionately large—then the value of the entire enterprise should first be determined as if it had common stock only. This value should be apportioned between the senior securities and the common stock on a basis which recognizes the going-concern value of the senior claims. (Note difference between this treatment and a valuation based on dissolution rights of the senior securities.) If an adjustment is needed for extraordinary conditions, as referred to in (8), this should be made in the total enterprise value, not on a per-share-of-common basis.

10. The more speculative the position of the common stock—for whatever reason—the less practical dependence can be accorded to the appraised value found.

11. Appraised values should be taken as a definite guide to current purchase or sale only if they exceed or fall below the market price by at least one-third. In other cases they may be useful as a supplemental fact in analysis and investment decisions.

XI

—◆◇◆—

Detection of Undervalued
Issues by Security
Analysis: Three Examples

ATTRACTIVE BUYING OPPORTUNITIES for the enterprising investor arise through a variety of causes. The standard or recurrent reasons are (a) a low level of the general market and (b) the carrying to an extreme of popular disfavor toward individual issues. Sometimes, but much more rarely, we have the failure of the market to respond to an important improvement in the company's affairs and in the value of its stock. Frequently we find a discrepancy between price and value which arises from the public's failure to realize the true situation of a company—this in turn being due to some complicated aspects of accounting or corporate relationships.

It is the function of competent security analysis to unravel such complexities and to bring the true facts and values to light. In the present chapter we shall present three examples of this kind of analytical activity, drawn respectively from the railroad, the utility, and the industrial field. Again we shall be rash enough to choose illustrations that are current and may therefore work out differently marketwise than our conclusions would indicate. But we happen to think that no analysis has illustrative value, or is even a quite honest one, unless it reflects fully the uncertainties of the time to which it applies—in other words, unless it runs its inescapable risk of proving wrong.

EXAMPLE I. Northern Pacific Railway Common Stock
Price on December 31, 1947—20
Price on December 31, 1948—16¾

General Statement

For many years prior to the First World War the Northern Pacific was regarded as one of the stronger railroads. Between 1901 and 1930 it paid dividends of not less than $5 annually. The company was hard hit by the depression of the 1930's. It avoided receivership, but in the pre-war period 1936–40 it earned very little for the stock and paid nothing. The large earnings generated since 1940, however, have brought a tremendous improvement in the Northern Pacific's position. These benefits were not reflected to any extent in the price at the end of 1947—which was below the average of the year 1937. For this backwardness there appear to be two main reasons: first, the failure to pay more than a $1 dividend since 1942—a rate which in turn seems to control the average price of the shares—and, second, the understatement of the true earnings for Northern Pacific stock in the company's reports, because a number of important profit items are excluded from the income account.

There are four elements of additional earning power for Northern Pacific beyond the stated earnings per share. Their nature and effect are shown in Table XVI and the explanatory comment.

On the basis of the Table XVI, Northern Pacific was selling at only three times the company's true average annual earnings for the past ten years—and at less than one-third of the $68 per share added to the common-stock equity by earnings retained during the period. The most important adjustment made in our computation is the addition of the equity in the Burlington (C., B. & Q.). Both the Northern Pacific and the Great Northern own slightly under 50 per cent of that very prosperous carrier. By technical accounting rules, the Northern Pacific's share of the undistributed earnings of the C., B. & Q. need not be reported to N.P. stockholders; but in the last analysis they are just as real as the earnings of the N.P. itself. In actuality the gross and net earnings of the Burlington mean as much in dollars to Northern Pacific's stockholders as do its direct operations.

In a situation of this kind it is the job of the security analyst to present a more informing picture of a company than that which emerges from its own report. The condensed income account presented in Table XVII shows the results for Northern Pacific stockholders on two bases: (a) the conventional statement of the company to the I.C.C. and its security holders; and (b) a consolidated return, including its pro-rata share of the gross and net of the Burlington and the S.P. & S. and crediting land department profits to income.

TABLE XVI. TEN-YEAR EARNINGS FOR NORTHERN PACIFIC RAILWAY STOCK 1938–47 (AS REPORTED, AND AS ADJUSTED TO REFLECT ADDITIONAL EQUITIES)

	Total 10-Year Figures	Annual Average Per Share
Net Income as Reported	$94,000,000	$3.80
Additional Equities:		
(1) N.P.'s share (48.6%) of undistributed earnings of C., B. & Q.	59,300,000	2.40
(2) N.P.'s share (50%) of undistributed earnings of Spokane S. & N. R.R., less estimated tax	9,600,000	.39
(3) Undistributed Earnings of Northwest Improvement Co. (100% owned)	1,100,000	.05
(4) Profits of Land Department (the company credits these to surplus instead of to income)	12,800,000	.51
Total Earnings, as Adjusted	$178,200,000	$7.15
Dividends Paid	14,900,000	.60
Added to Common Stock Equity	$163,300,000	$6.55
		(10 yrs.: $65.50)

The consolidated figures show not only a large increase above the reported earnings per share but also the fact that both the operating ratio and the credit position of the Northern Pacific have become fundamentally strong ones. The 30 per cent reduction in combined fixed charges since 1937 is of the highest importance.

Another factor in the Northern Pacific situation should be brought out by the analyst. This is its large ownership of equipment, from which it regularly derives a large income through rental payments by other carriers. (In 1947 the road received $5,216,000 net for rentals of various sorts.) During the war period the road spent no less than $40 million on additional equipment; this it wrote down to zero by means of the special depreciation or amortization charges permitted by war-time accounting. In the ten years the total depreciation charged to income by Northern Pacific itself were $98 million—a total of $40 per share of stock. This means that the company has a large amount of new physical assets which are carried in the balance sheet at a very small net figure.

TABLE XVII. NORTHERN PACIFIC RY. RESULTS (IN THOUSANDS)

| | 1947 | | 1937 | |
	As Reported	As Adjusted	As Reported	As Adjusted
Operating Revenue ("gross")	$142,600	$253,000	$64,900	$118,000
Available for Charges (before income tax)	27,100	50,300	14,500	20,900
Fixed Charges	10,500	13,300	14,400	19,100
Income Tax	3,200	12,400	. . . . .	200
Balance for Common	13,400	24,600	100	1,600
Per Share	$5.40	$9.90	$.06	$.65
Charges Earned (before income tax)	2.58 times	3.75 times	1.01 times	1.09 times

Conclusion

Our Northern Pacific example illustrates two main points of interest to the alert investor. The first is that security prices are influenced to a considerable extent by conventional accounting methods, which in some cases may fail to portray the true performance and position of a common stock. The second is that a low dividend rate in relation to earnings, when long continued, tends to create more and more of a bargain situation; for the low dividend holds down the price while at the same time it permits the piling up of ever increasing equities in the form of undistributed earnings.

The price of Northern Pacific common at the end of 1947 was undoubtedly affected by both of these factors. They combined to create what seems to be a clear case of undervaluation. Unless the future works much more unfavorably for the railroads than the general market was expecting, the buyer of Northern Pacific at 20 could look forward to an eventual correction of the disparity between its price and its performance. The subsequent price decline to 14, despite the dividend increase to $1½, makes this seem a rash prediction. We are willing to stand on it.

EXAMPLE II. Standard Power and Light $7 Preferred Stock
    (Accumulated Dividends to end of 1947—$90 per share)
    Price on December 31, 1947—106

General Statement

This is a more complicated example of security analysis than any of our others. We are including it in order to give our readers an idea of the intricacies of corporate affairs. It may well be skipped by those who do not care to bother too much about the technical side of investment. We shall greatly foreshorten our analysis for brevity's sake.

Standard Power and Light is a "top holding company" of a public-utility holding-company system which is being broken up under the Holding Company Act of 1935. Its chief assets are prior preferred and common shares of Standard Gas & Electric. The latter, in turn, owns shares in a number of companies, the most important of which is the Philadelphia Company. This, too, is a holding company controlling utilities in the Pittsburgh area, notably Duquesne Light.

There have been long delays in working out simplification or dissolution plans for the various tiers in the Standard Power set-up. Much of the difficulty has been due to conflicting interests of Standard Gas preferred and common holders. At the beginning of 1948 the S.E.C. was exerting some pressure for greater speed.

The salient elements in the Standard Power situation is summarized in Table XVIII.

TABLE XVIII. STANDARD POWER SET-UP

	Market Value Dec. 31, 1947	Estimated "Work-Out" Value
Assets of Standard Power:		
40,751 sh. Standard		
Gas $7 Prior Pfd.	@ 100 $4,075,000	@ 160 $6,520,000
1,160,000 sh.		
Standard Gas Common	@ 1⅜ 1,595,000	@ 2½ 3,990,000
Misc. Bonds and Stocks	est. 1,300,000	... 1,300,000
Total	$6,970,000	$11,810,000
Less: Estimated reduction		
for settlement of claims	270,000	270,000
Balance of Assets	$6,700,000	$11,540,000
Capitalization:		
34,054 sh. Standard		
Power Pfd. (at $100 per sh.)	3,405,000	
Accumulated Dividends		
($90 per sh.)	3,065,000	
Total Claim of Preferred	6,470,000	6,470,000
Balance for 1,760,000 sh.		
of common	$ 230,000	$ 5,070,000

The key figures in the above table are the estimated "work-out" values. These are taken from a study prepared by an expert public-utility analyst and published by a New York Stock Exchange house[1] in February, 1948. They are derived from the estimated earning power of the companies in the Standard Gas system, capitalized at conservative rates. The total value found for all the Standard Gas stock issues has been divided 70 per cent to the prior preferred, 25 per cent to the junior preferred, and 5 per cent to the common. This allocation, in turn, reflects the analyst's view of how the legal preferences of the senior issues will be reduced in the process of carrying through a practicable plan.

Indicated Value of Standard Power Preferred

On the basis of the above valuation of Standard Power's assets there are ample values to pay the preferred stock its full claim of $190 per share for principal and back dividends. If it works out this way the purchase of the preferred at 106 per share will prove extremely profitable. But the experienced investor would allow for the probability that the preferred will not be paid off in full. It is more likely to receive securities which are theoretically worth that amount for purposes of the plan but will have a smaller market or realizable value. The loss here involved may run as high as 25 per cent— but that would still leave a pay-out of $143 per share for Standard Power Preferred (plus a $7 dividend rate since December, 1947), as against the price of 106.

If the past history of these proceedings is studied, we find another indication of the value of Standard Power preferred. In a reorganization plan approved by the S.E.C. in 1945 each share of this issue was awarded 14½ shares of common stock of the recapitalized company, whereas Standard Gas $7 preferred received 10½ shares. This established a value ratio of 14½ to 10½ for the two issues. Although the new plan will be entirely different from the old, it is fair to assume that the relative values of these senior securities may not be changed appreciably. On that basis the December 31, 1947, market price of Standard Gas $7 Preferred would warrant a corresponding price of 133 for the Standard Power issue. This fact indicates that the latter stock

[1]Josephthal & Co.

was being comparatively neglected in the market—mainly, perhaps, because it was not nearly so well known as the Standard Gas issues.

Conclusion

Past experience would indicate that Standard Gas $7 preferred will itself eventually work out at a considerably higher value than its selling price while the proceedings are dragging on. Thus we feel justified in concluding that all indications point to a still better ultimate result for Standard Power preferred.

What are the hazards or drawbacks that may weaken this conclusion? First, there is the time element. No one can tell how long it will take for this situation to work out, and it may well be two years or more. Though this would be enough to repel the speculator, it is by no means a serious matter for the true investor; for if the value is established at anywhere near the figure indicated he would have an exceedingly satisfactory annual return, even if the operation took as long as three years from December, 1947.

The real hazard is the possibility that while the proceedings are pending economic conditions may worsen and the values of the underlying operating-company stocks may be sharply reduced. This danger is present, but in a degree not very different from that in the case of an ordinary investment in a utility common stock. Since the purchase of Standard Power preferred carries a large margin of safety in the form of a present underlying value greatly in excess of the price, the chance of final loss through untoward developments in the utility picture is correspondingly reduced.

Thus this type of bargain purchase, based on a rather elaborate analysis of a complicated situation, is likely to result profitably in the great majority of instances.

EXAMPLE III. American Hawaiian Steamship Company

In this situation the analysis turns not on the underlying earning power—which is the key element in the two preceding discussions—but on the development of an extraordinary balance-sheet position.

A. The Picture as It Appeared in the Financial Services

At the end of 1947 American Hawaiian Steamship stock was selling at 39½. During that year it reported earnings of $3.85 per share and paid dividends of $3. For the years 1940–47 the reported earnings averaged $4.25 per share, and the dividends averaged $3.30. In the nine years before the war there were hardly any profits. The net asset value, or equity, per share, as computed by a large investment service at the end of 1947, was about $62.

On the basis of these figures the stock of American Hawaiian showed no great attraction. Most secondary corporations, other than public utilities, were earning a much larger percentage on the market price. The future of the American merchant marine was represented in the company's annual report as uncertain and even unpromising.

B. The Figures as Adjusted by the Security Analyst

1. *The Balance-Sheet Position.* The company has additional assets, equivalent to cash holdings, not shown in the balance sheet but for the most part disclosed in footnotes thereto. These represent: (a) Compensation previously tendered to the company by the government but rejected as insufficient. The company was suing for larger amounts and presumably would recover at least the sums previously offered it. (b) Claims for boats taken over and not yet paid for, even in part. (c) Increased market value of stocks owned over cost. (d) Tax overpayment allowed by the tax court but not finally settled.

These items indicate additional cash values of about $8,000,000 before taxes, and of about $5,500,000 after taxes. On 396,000 common shares—the only securities outstanding—this would add $14 per share.

More significant than the total amount of the applicable assets is their composition. Of a total of some $30 million in net assets, including items not listed in the balance sheet, about $28 million are current, and by far the greater part of these assets are in the form of cash equivalents. This means that for each dollar of market price there are close to $2 of highly liquid assets. It means further that by far the greater part of the 1947 earnings were derived from the use of a small amount of capital in the shipping business, whereas the huge holdings of United States bonds and similar cash assets probably produced only about $1 per share after taxes.

The balance-sheet position at the close of 1947, as corrected, is summarized in Table XIX.

2. *The Historical Record, as Revised.* At the end of 1939 the company had about $10 per share in working capital and $12½ more in fixed assets—a total of $22½ per share. The stock closed that year at $28½. Eight years later the fixed and miscellaneous assets were down to about $5 per share, but the net current assets, as adjusted above, had risen to no less than $72 per share. Thus in that period the company paid $26½ in dividends and added $62 to liquid assets.

It is clear that the stockholder's position had improved since 1939 to an extent in no wise reflected in the "financial-service figures" quoted at the outset. The main reason for this extraordinary creation of cash values was the conversion of ship tonnage into money at very high rates. The company had been carrying its boats on its books at a depreciated cost of a dollar or two a ton; under war conditions it was able to realize—through insurance and requisition payments—a value of some $50 per ton *after* tax provision. These gains were not shown in the earnings figures, and the latter were further understated because the company reported as earned only 75 per cent of the compensation tendered it by the government for charter hire. (Because of the company's protest it received only the 75 per cent in cash, the balance being now subject to legal determination.)

3. *The Analyst's Conclusion.* It is difficult, if not impossible, to avoid the conclusion that American Hawaiian Steamship shares were fairly worth considerably more than $40 per share at the end of 1947. Not only had a much larger total of cash assets been amassed, as a result of war conditions, but the management had also shown a determination not to commit this cash into boat acquisitions unless the purchase price and the indicated operating conditions were such as to make these purchases attractive from the stockholders' standpoint. Both the operating results and the dividend in 1947 were satisfactory, considering that nearly all the capital was kept liquid and thus earning a minimum return.

There was the possibility, of course, that these cash assets might be invested unprofitably and thus effectively dissipated. Every investment has its adverse possibilities, but investment for profit has to be made on the basis of the weighing of *probabilities.* Judged by this standard there was a considerable basis for confidence—though not for certainty—in the ability of the management to conserve what the stockholders now possessed. American

Hawaiian's history went back to 1899; it had paid dividends continuously since 1902, except—oddly enough—in the prosperity period of 1926–28. Its dividend payments during the First World War were enormous.

TABLE XIX. BALANCE SHEET POSITION OF AMERICAN-HAWAIIAN
STEAMSHIP COMPANY

December 31, 1947

Ordinary Cash		$4,506,000
Special Cash Funds		17,503,000
Marketable Securities		4,510,000
Receivables and Inventory		6,739,000
		33,258,000
Less: Current Liabilities	$6,474,000	
Reserve for Capital		
Gains Tax	3,820,000	
		10,294,000
Net Liquid Assets, as Reported		22,964,000
Add: Claims and Current		
Values not stated	est. 8,000,000	
Less taxes there against	est. 2,500,000	5,500,000
Total Liquid Assets for Capital Stock		28,464,000
Fixed Assets		813,000
Prepaid Accounts		1,287,000
Total Assets for Capital Stock		$30,564,000
	Per Share	$77.

At the end of 1947 the shares were clearly a bargain at a total valuation for the company of only $15,700,000, when the company held cash and an equivalent net of about $29 million and total net assets of nearly $31 million.

XII

—◈—

The Pattern of Change in
Stock Earnings and
Stock Prices

THE VALUE APPROACH to common-stock investment starts from the principle that a given issue is fairly "worth" some suitable multiplier of its indicated earning power. The latter is properly defined as the expectable average future earnings. The notion of earning power carries with it an allowance for variations in the figures of separate years, due to the alternation of good times and bad. Hence, in theory at least, the "worth," or intrinsic value, of a common stock will neither decline when earnings fall in depression periods nor advance when they improve in times of prosperity. The value will change only with the advent of new long-term developments or influences which were not reflected in the original appraisal.

The behavior of stock prices departs radically from this concept of intrinsic worth. On the whole, prices respond vigorously to any significant change in either current earnings or short-term earning prospects. It appears to be an axiom of the market that stocks should and do sell much higher when the "situation is favorable" than when it is unfavorable. The fact that both favorable and unfavorable situations are part of any normal long-term picture—and as a consequence both should be accepted without undue excitement—is evidently not part of the stock market's philosophy. The latter seems to be grounded on the feeling that, since nothing is really permanent, it is logical enough to treat the temporary as if it were going to be permanent—even though we know it is not.

The action of the stock market must necessarily be puzzling at times, since otherwise everyone who studies it only a little would be able to make money in it consistently. The puzzlement arises, we believe, from a simple circumstance—the fact that sometimes the market reflects what is *now* happening in business and sometimes it reflects what is expected to happen *later*. Thus it operates somewhat in the manner of the once universally familiar "shell game." The pea—namely, the next movement of prices—is deftly manipulated by fortune so as to fall either under the shell marked "This Year's Business" or under that marked "Next Year's Business"; the follower of the market, of course, often puts his money on the wrong shell.

As the reader knows by now, we are firmly convinced that investors cannot, by taking thought, learn to beat this shell game of the stock market. It is not that they are deficient in intelligence or the capacity to learn the ropes. The trouble is just the opposite. Too many clever and experienced people are engaged simultaneously in trying to outwit one another in the market. The result, we believe, is that all their skill and efforts tend to be self-neutralizing, or to "cancel out," so that each expert and highly-informed conclusion ends up by being no more dependable than the toss of a coin.

We once likened the activities of the host of stock-market analysts to a tournament of bridge experts. Everyone is very brilliant indeed, but scarcely anyone is so superior to the rest as to be certain of winning a prize. An added quirk in Wall Street is that the prominent market analysts freely communicate and exchange their views almost from day to day. The result is somewhat as if all the participants in a bridge tournament, while each hand was being played out, gathered around and argued about the proper strategy.

Modern stock-market movements, in fine, are the result of a concentration of tremendous skill in a limited area, where profits can be made by smart people only at the expense of other people who are almost equally smart. The pattern of price changes has therefore a peculiarly tricky quality. The farther away you get from it the more regular it appears—and the casier to profit by. But, when you try to make these easy profits and in the try-ing come to close grips with the actualities of the market, you find the pat-tern to be full of irregularities, deceptions, and hazards.

Thus we reach our conclusion, with its overtones of a scriptural paradox, that the investor can profit from market fluctuations only by paying them lit-tle heed. He must fix his eye not on what the market has been doing—or what it apparently is going to do—but only on the *result* of its action as ex-pressed in the relationship between the price level and the level of underly-ing or central values.

Let us study some of the characteristic results of the tendency of the mar-ket to fluctuate over wide limits and in a basically emotional rather than a ra-tional manner. If the investor is going to acquire and hold an assortment of common stocks he should at least be sophisticated enough to know what has been their pattern of price changes over a number of years in the past. With this knowledge before him he can decide to what extent, if any, his own plans of purchase and sale should be related to the price variations of, say, the last quarter century.

No one can foretell the approximate limits of the price fluctuations of the future by studying the record of 1924–48. But it is a persuasive assumption that the general character of future markets is much more likely to resemble this pattern than to depart completely from it. Thus, even if the investor is unable or unwilling to use this knowledge of typical price fluctuations for his financial advantage, it is nonetheless essential to have it as part of his psy-chological preparedness for what the future may bring.

PATTERN I. Price Changes of Common Stocks with Highly Stable Earnings

Chart III gives the record of earnings and dividends of S. H. Kress—the well-known chain-store enterprise—for 1924–45, and indicates also the more extreme price variations during that period.

The stability of the annual earnings per share of common stock is ex-traordinary. In sixteen out of the twenty-two years they varied only between $1.93 and $2.32. In the other six, including the boom and deepest depression years, the range widened only to $1.38–$2.88. It may properly be concluded that this record at no point showed any definite indications of permanent change for either the better or the worse in the company's affairs or prospects. Hence the variations in market price must have been entirely psychological

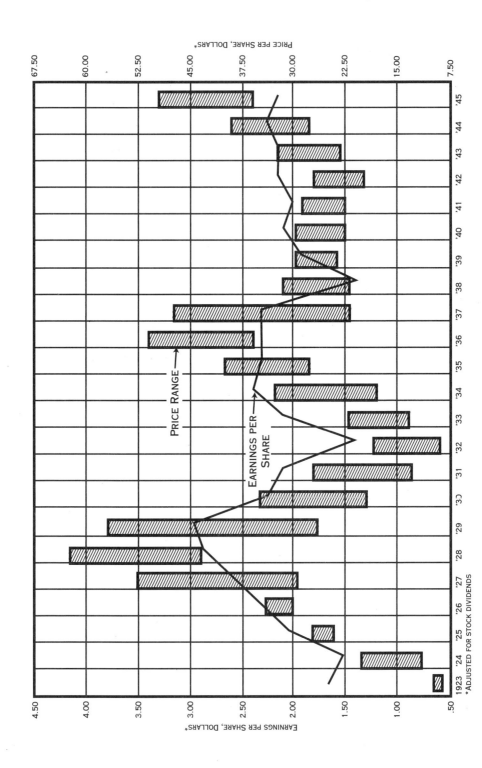

in their origin. They offer a fairly accurate measurement of the breadth of price change ascribable to the mere vagaries of the stock market—while the "article valued" changed its character not at all.

Under the circumstances, the range of price changes must be considered extraordinary. We have a rise from 12 to 62, a fall to 9, a rise to 48, a fall to 20, and a rise to 49. For the five years 1933–37 the earnings varied only between $2.11 and $2.31 per share, whereas the price ranged from 13½ to 47½. In the six years 1939–45 the earnings varied between $1.93 and $2.25, but the price ranged from 19½ to 49¼.

A similar picture is shown by Columbian Carbon. In fifteen of the twenty-four years between 1922 and 1945 its earnings held within a range of $5 to $7 per share; yet in these fifteen years the price rose from 36 to 135, fell to 65, rose to 136½, and fell again to 54. (In 1929 the earnings were $8.40 and the price rose to 344. In 1932 the earnings were $1.77 and the price fell to 13½.) In the public-utility field the earnings per share of Pacific Gas & Electric common show like stability, and its price a wide range of fluctuation.

Even if we set aside the extreme price variations engendered by the irrational stock market of 1928–33, our picture indicates that a common stock, *without visible change in its underlying value,* will be appraised in bull markets at from two to three times its price in bear markets. No investor who buys common stocks should be unaware of this inherent characteristic of the securities market.

PATTERN II. Price Fluctuations of Common Stocks with Typical Variations in Earnings Per Share

A. Leading Company: General Motors

This enterprise is the largest in the country, and no doubt in the world, in terms of annual sales. Its record illustrates the sharp vicissitudes of even our major companies. In spite of an underlying stability of *average* earning power and *average* value—growing out of its commanding industrial position and the flexibility of its managerial policies—General Motors has been subject to wide changes in its *annual* earnings and much wider changes in current market price.

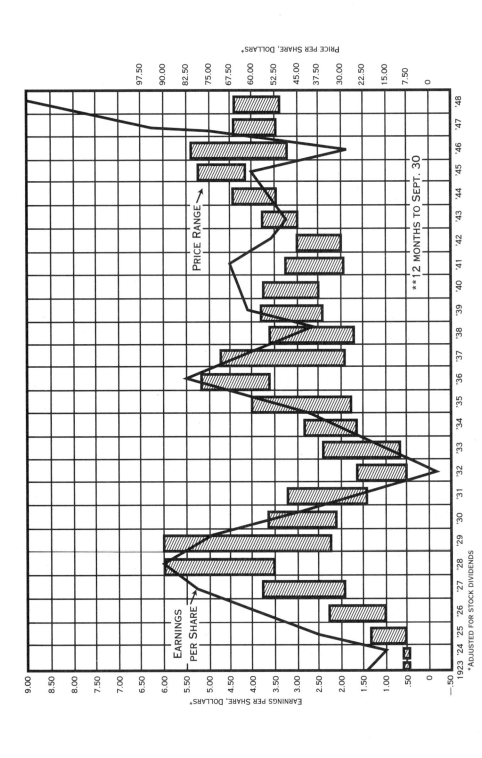

PRICE PER SHARE, DOLLARS*

EARNINGS PER SHARE, DOLLARS*

PRICE RANGE

EARNINGS PER SHARE

**12 MONTHS TO SEPT. 30

*ADJUSTED FOR STOCK DIVIDENDS

The twenty-five-year record of earnings, dividends, and market variations is given in Chart IV.

It is interesting to observe that General Motors' price at the end of 1947 was about the same as it was twenty years before, although in the meantime its sales had exactly tripled and it had doubled the asset value behind each share. But the impact of a lower profit margin and much higher income taxes had cut the gain in net earnings per share to only 20 per cent. In this simple arithmetic we have a condensed picture of the profit-reducing forces against which American corporations have had to contend since the end of the boom of the 1920's. They have had to run very fast to keep in the same place.

The market fluctuations of General Motors common are almost unbelievable for an issue of its prime importance and quality. It rose from 13 in 1925 to 92 in 1929; collapsed to 7½ in 1932; climbed back to 77 in 1936; relapsed to 25½ in 1938; then mounted to 80½ in 1946 and fell back to 48 in the very same year. There is some reason to argue from this price history that the stock has had a central value of from 50 to 60 throughout the last quarter century. Certainly in the past it has proved unwise to pay much above those figures, and purchases made well below them have turned out to be sound and profitable.

Can the investor be sure that this pattern will be followed in the future, even very roughly? If we could answer "yes," the basic problems of common-stock investment would all be solved on the spot. The investor could then wait with joyous confidence for his assured opportunity, first to buy General Motors at 40 and then to sell it out at 80. Unfortunately, a past record carries no guarantees for the future, but only suggestions. In this, as in most other cases, however, it issues an emphatic warning that investors should beware of paying prices that cannot be justified by either the record of the longer past or by a *conservative* projection into the future.

Beyond that, the record appears to carry considerable encouragement for the strong-minded person who refuses to buy any security—either primary or secondary—except when the market insists upon offering it to him at considerably less than its indicated true value. We must repeat our doubts whether the average common-stock buyer has sufficiently conclusive evidence on this point to warrant his adopting and adhering to a program of waiting to buy General Motors at 40 and then being prepared to sell it at

80.[1] It may prove less shrewd, but more comfortable and sensible, to buy stocks of the type of General Motors when the investor has money available for such securities and when they are obtainable at a reasonable price. The choice between the two policies must be made by the investor himself.

B. Price Fluctuations of Atchison Common Stock

As an addendum to the price figures given for General Motors, let us summarize those of a leading railroad—the Atchison, Topeka & Santa Fe. Here the common rose from 18 in 1900 to 125 in 1909, receded to 75 in 1917 (and 1921), soared to 299 in 1929, collapsed to 18 in 1932, recovered to 95 in 1937, made a new low of 13 in 1940, climbed to 121 in 1946, fell back to 66 the next year, and moved up again to 120 in 1948. Note the startling resemblance between the sevenfold advance of 1900–09 and the ninefold rise of 1940–46—history repeating itself after forty years.

C. A Typical Small-Sized Listed Company: Intertype Corporation

Intertype is a specialty manufacturer of line-casting machines and related products. It sells to the printing and publishing trade. The company was formed in 1916, and the shares were listed in 1923. In 1947 its sales were $7,745,000, its net after taxes was $703,000 and the invested capital was about $6,500,000. Chart V shows a usual type of fluctuation in earning power over the past twenty-five years, except for the fact that the best earnings were reported as far back as 1923. This point would apparently mark it as in a "declining industry," and according to the "growth stock" school of thought it should have had no investment appeal at any time since it was listed.

Actually the company has operated as a well-established and soundly

---

[1] Note that our appraisal of General Motors, given in the table on p. 150, indicates a future central value of as high as 73, which is considerably above the central value of about 50 indicated by the long-term past record. This difference reflects our own expectation, based on general economic considerations, that average earnings and values after the Second World War will be appreciably higher than before 1941.

managed business. It has been able to build up the equity for its common stock over the years, retiring its initial preferred stock issue and greatly expanding its working capital.

TABLE XX. AVERAGE OF YEARLY HIGH AND LOW

	Kress	General Motors	Intertype
1923	9	12	24
1940	26	47	7
1947	52	59	24

From the standpoint of security analysis, the stock has been an undervalued security on many occasions in its history, and it has amply rewarded the investor who purchased it at those times. During the entire five-year period 1938–42 its quotation fluctuated around $9, although there were about $20 in current assets alone behind each share and the average earnings were over 10 per cent on the price.

The moral to be drawn from the record of Intertype, as shown on the chart, is both obvious and little heeded. It is *not* wise to buy companies of this kind when their earnings have improved, their short-term prospects look good, and their price is several times the low of a few years previously. It *is* intelligent to buy such shares in neutral markets when they are relatively neglected and their price is much lower than the underlying facts will warrant.

Some comparative price data for the three companies just discussed may suggest interesting conclusions. Table XX gives the average prices for three widely separated years.

The best long-term result, pricewise, is shown by Kress. (The high price in 1947 is related to a large increase in post-war earnings, which does not appear on our chart.) For many years Kress had been a stable stock rather than a growth stock in the accepted sense; yet after two decades of horizontal earning power it was able to move into the growth-stock class. But the best profit opportunities indicated by the above comparison were presented by the purchase of Intertype at its 1940 level. The relatively unattractive record of Intertype at that time resulted in a price low enough to create an exceptional investment value.

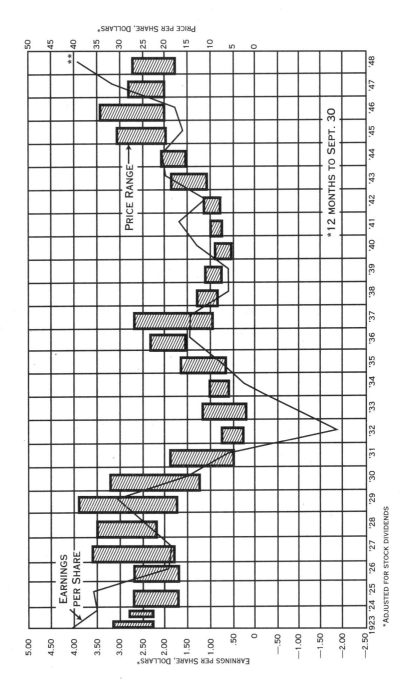

CHART V. INTERTYPE CORPORATION

These conclusions hardly fit into conventional ideas of investment policy. They suggest that open-mindedness and independent thinking will pay big dividends in Wall Street.

PATTERN III. Extreme Vicissitudes

The examples which follow may not be called typical in the sense that they represent a permanent and easily found segment of the securities market. Extreme cases are by definition unusual, but they should be useful to the investor in revealing to him how extraordinarily wide is the range of fluctuations in corporate affairs. Most people think of such phenomenal changes in terms of the definitive success or failure of the enterprise. Thus we read of the enormous increase in the value of each dollar originally invested in the Ford Motor Company. Conversely, there is the familiar story of all the millions lost by those who regarded New Haven Railroad stock as a high-grade investment and then were wiped out by its eventual bankruptcy.

We get a deeper insight into the forces affecting American business and the investments made in it from a study of the extreme ups and downs experienced in one and the same enterprise. The illustrations below show forth different types of such vicissitudes in corporate affairs and the related security values. To each we shall append some observations which may have a general application.

A. St. Louis Southwestern Railway (the Cotton Belt)

The story of Lazarus has been re-enacted in the case of St. Louis Southwestern shares. By June, 1947, the preferred and common had twice been pronounced dead and valueless by the highest authority of the land—the United States Supreme Court. Yet a month after the latter of these coroner's verdicts the corpse not only opened its eyes and stirred; it rose up completely cured of every vestige of financial ill. The bankruptcy was ended; all matured debts and interest were paid; the stockholders took over again as if nothing had happened. In the following year the common stock received its first dividend in the company's fifty-seven-year history. During the bankruptcy the stock had been suspended from New York Stock Exchange dealings as presumably worthless, and it had actually sold for next to nothing in the "over-the-counter" market. Now it was restored to exchange trading, and in addition its price rose to *138—which made it one of the highest-priced railroad issues in the market.*

How did these reversals come about? Before 1929 the Cotton Belt had been one of the weaker roads, with an irregular record. In the eleven years from 1930 to 1940 it reported continuous deficits. After allowing for preferred dividends (which were non-cumulative) the computed losses aggregated $130 per share of common stock. In 1935 trustees in bankruptcy were appointed. By 1941 the I.C.C. had approved a reorganization plan which scaled down the debt drastically and completely wiped out both the preferred and the common stocks. This plan was approved by the United States District Court, and it was upheld by the next higher court on appeal. The stockholders then went to the United States Supreme Court, which declined to review the case. The stockholders tried their last resort—a request to the Supreme Court for a rehearing. This too was denied, in June, 1947. By every legal precedent the case was now finished and the stock issues were extinct.

But, while all this legal maneuvering was taking its tedious course, the financial position of the Cotton Belt was being revolutionized by the impact of war and post-war traffic. In the 7-year period 1941–47 the road made phenomenal earnings, which were equivalent to over $200 a share on the common—an annual average of $34 per share. It had now become one of the most economically operated carriers in the country, as measured by the ratio of net to gross.

Thus the Cotton Belt stockholders lost every legal battle but won their war. There was now enough cash to restore the company to a completely solvent condition. Instead of carrying out the reorganization plan, which the Supreme Court had just upheld and which wiped out both stock issues, the lower court was readily persuaded to dismiss the bankruptcy proceedings altogether. Just as in an old-fashioned melodrama, the hero rode up with the mortgage money in the nick of time and the homestead was saved.

We should hardly recommend the general purchase of stocks of bankrupt concerns on the strength of the Cotton Belt resurrection. Many more of such issues perish than survive. But there is an *a fortiori* moral here. If a company hopelessly insolvent in appearance can come back so strongly, there must be many excellent opportunities for large recoveries of value in the field of depressed but *not* financially embarrassed enterprises.

B. Bankers Securities Corporation Common Stock

This company is interesting as an illustration not only of the vicissitudes of the past twenty years but also of the long-term change in investors' attitudes. The Bankers Securities Corporation was floated as an "investment trust" in 1928, in the heyday of financial legerdemain. Investors and speculators, who in those days were even more indistinguishable than they are now, were convinced that financiers could create values miraculously by merely forming a new investment fund or by shuffling old ones around. The miracles proved to be mirages. The disillusionment of the investors was a bitter thing, and it still shows itself in what we should style a wholesome mistrust of the ability of financiers to perform tricks with other people's money.

The changes in the asset value and market price of Bankers Securities Corporation common stock between 1928 and 1947 are summarized in Table XXI.

Thus in twenty years the asset value of the common has fluctuated twice between positive and negative values, but it has now reached a figure far higher than anything in its days of popularity. The variations in market price have also been tremendous. At the end of 1928 the indicated liquidating value was only 30 per cent of the market price. Nineteen years later—the closing price being about 110—there was almost the same ratio in the opposite direction.

TABLE XXI

	Year-End Asset Value of Common Stock	High or Low Price in Year
1928	$65	High 218
1932	def. 55	Low ¾
1936	31	High 44 (1937)
1941	def. 9	Low 3½
1947	259	High 135 (1946)

The Bankers Securities Corporation has some features which distinguish it from the more usual investment company operation. The preferred stock has a participating feature, by which it appropriates 60 per cent of the increase in asset values. Without that arrangement, the book value of the common would have risen to $510 per share at the end of 1947. The company has concentrated its investments in the department-store and real-estate fields, in addition to holding a fair-sized general portfolio. In the earlier years it borrowed considerable money and thus intensified the leverage of the common. When that issue sold at 75 cents per share in 1932, it was apparently worth $55 less than nothing; no self-respecting security buyer would have given it a second look. The situation was similar in 1941. As we see by the sequel, in both cases there were opportunities for enormous profits as compared with the risk of loss.

C. Textile Finishing Machinery Preferred

Here is an extreme example of a paradoxical but not unusual development—one in which a decision to throw up the sponge and withdraw from business creates a large increase in the price and value of the stock. This is not so surprising as it seems at first glance. If a company is unsuccessful, reporting no earnings and paying no dividends, the price of its shares tends to approach the vanishing point. The market pays virtually no attention to the possible realizable value of the company's assets. But once the concern decides to sell out, or liquidate, the asset values become the controlling factor. Sometimes these bring in little; if the company has relatively large debts it may be basically insolvent and the stockholders may receive nothing. In a large number of cases, however, there are substantial salable assets when operations cease. The creditors are easily paid off, and a considerable balance remains for the stock.

The Textile Finishing Machinery Company was a small concern of this kind which in the course of time lost its profit-making ability. In 1940 the preferred stock was quoted at about $3 and the common at about $1. In 1943 the stockholders voted to liquidate. In 1944 and 1945 the preferred stock received payments in liquidation totaling $110 per share. In May, 1948, it was announced that about $80 more would be received.

Thus the $3 in 1940 has grown to $190 by the process of corporate suicide. Interestingly enough, the common stock is not participating in this bonanza. The accumulated unpaid dividends of $91 per share on the preferred, plus its claim for $100 of principal, are just about enough to absorb all the funds realized.

Because of a similarity in the name of another concern, some curious readers might wish to compare with the above the contemporaneous developments in United States Finishing preferred, which was selling around $1 a share in October, 1940. After continuous operating losses throughout 1930–40, the war turned the business picture around and large profits were realized. The market value of the preferred advanced to 202 in 1947. Thus almost equally spectacular gains were recorded in the two cases, in the first by the company's quitting business and in the second by its refusing to quit.

D. Two Briefer Examples

Here is a brief summary of the vicissitudes Reo Motors, Inc., has experienced since 1920. Between 1920 and 1929 it enjoyed continuous profits, totaling $38 million. Between 1930 and 1940 it had continuous losses, totaling $22 million, and it was temporarily in receivership. Between 1941 and 1947 it again had continuous profits, totaling $15 million.

The capital and surplus rose from $14 million in 1919 to $32 million in 1928, fell to $2 million in 1940, then recovered to $16 million in 1947. The market price of the stock issue rose from $11 million in 1920 to $70 million in 1928, fell to $1 million in 1941, then recovered to $17 million in 1946.

Finally, consider the record of Clinchfield Coal Corporation common, listed on the New York Curb Exchange. Between 1928 and 1939 the company reported losses in each year, except for a small gain in 1934. In 1940 it earned 1 cent per share, and the average price of the stock was under 2. The profits then rose to the equivalent of $23 per share in 1947, and in 1948 the (split-up) stock sold at the equivalent of 234.

Undoubtedly, the largest theoretical gains in the stock market are to be made not out of the continuously prosperous companies but out of those which experience wide vicissitudes—by buying their stocks at their depths and selling them at their heights. Profits of such amplitude are realized only in the paper calculations of hindsight. Yet these examples have practical significance for the intelligent investor. They should confirm his conviction that the outstanding characteristic of the stock market is its tendency to react *excessively* to favorable and unfavorable influences. The word "excessive" applied to the stock market's reactions indicates that they create many sound counter-opportunities for the investor with sense and courage.

PATTERN IV. Behavior of Growth Stocks

 This final section differs from the preceding ones in that it stresses differences rather than similarities in the performance of the issues now to be described. A growth stock is identified as such because it has an especially satisfactory past record coupled with the expectation that this will continue. As Mead & Grodinsky have pointed out, it is the inherent nature of corporate growth eventually to taper off or to cease entirely. Thus, if the stock market possessed the penetrating qualities popularly accorded to it, many growth stocks would begin to lose their high price level some time *before* any decline in their earning power had become apparent.

We have been unable to discover any traces of such a prescient market pattern in the field of growth stocks. What seems to happen, rather, is that the price remains high until the earnings actually show a definite falling off—which invariably seems to take the followers of the issue by surprise. Then we have the market decline usually associated with a disappointing development—a decline perhaps intensified by the fact that the price level of the growth stock had been dangerously high.

Sometimes, either because of a certain stubbornness or a real insight into the long-term future on the part of investors, the price of such a deteriorated growth stock remains higher than its current performance would justify. The airline issues in 1947–48 provide examples of this phenomenon.

A. Continued Growth: Minnesota Mining & Manufacturing Company ("Scotch Tape," etc.)

TABLE XXII

	Net Earnings for Common	Per Share of Present Stock	High Price (Adj. to Present Stock)
1929	$1,317,000	.71	7¼
1939	4,365,000	2.27	30
1947	10,715,000	5.49	70¾

This concern shows an impressive and completely satisfactory record. The market price indicates confidence that the company will continue to prosper in future years. Today the stock is relatively more popular than it was in 1929. It is worth noting that in 1929 the entire company was valued at a maximum of $14 million; at the end of 1947 the company was selling for close to $160 million. The high enterprise valuations that come with continued success carry their own hazards.

B. Spectacular Growth Followed by Decline in Profits: Philip Morris & Co.

TABLE XXIII

(SALES AND NET IN THOUSANDS)

Year[1]	Sales	Net before Taxes	Net after Taxes	Price Record
1929	. . . . . .	$479	$426	1929 High 23
1939	$73,344	9,140	7,436	1938 " 144
1942	112,565	14,254	7,792	1942 Low 55½
1946	170,906	8,251	4,958	1946 High 142 (adj.)
				1948 Low 50 (adj.)

[1]Earnings data are for fiscal year ending the following March 31st.

The twentyfold increase in net before taxes between 1929 and 1939 was an extraordinary achievement, which was duly recognized in a spectacular price advance that ran counter to the general market. Seven years later the net earnings had clearly turned downward, but the market's enthusiasm continued. The 1946 high was actually 27 times the earnings of the previous year and 35 times the earnings of the current year. From that level, however, the price receded nearly two-thirds in early 1948—a much greater loss than that of other leading stocks—apparently reflecting a belated realization that the company had entered a new and more difficult stage of its business history.

C. *Enthusiasm Belied by Results: Transcontinental & Western Airlines (TWA)*

TWA illustrates, in a heightened degree, the history of our airlines as a whole. After a number of developmental years ending in 1937, the business entered on a period of ultra-rapid expansion. Operating revenues advanced from $5 million in 1937 to $25 million in 1944, and then to $79 million in 1947. With respect to traffic volume the companies in the air-transport industry have fulfilled the high hope held for them. But the history of TWA's net earnings has been a far different story. From a loss of $960,000 in 1937 the profits advanced unspectacularly to a high of $2,753,000 in 1944. Then, along with the enormous rise of gross revenues in 1946 and 1947, came operating losses of staggering proportions. In the two years the deficits aggregated over $23 million. The result of this was to wipe out completely the stockholders' book equity, which had been about $18 million at the end of 1945, and to plunge this leading "growth company" into virtual insolvency.

As might have been expected, the price gyrations of the stock have been extraordinary. In 1937 it declined from 27⅝ to 4. It then advanced to 79 in 1945. That figure was 27 times the record high earnings, and it reflected speculative confidence in still better results to come. The price then fell to a low of 13½ in 1947.

Contrary to the usual behavior of stocks, the price collapse of TWA was less severe than the change in the earnings results and in the company's financial picture. In 1948 the quotation recovered to 22, indicating a valuation of $22 million for the stock issue—which was a far from negligible figure for a company that had more debts than assets. Thus even the deflated price reflected the persistence of a considerable degree of market optimism on the future of the industry and of this important factor in it.

It is instructive to contrast the financial records and the price behavior of Transcontinental & Western and with that of Northern Pacific over the past ten years. In one case enormous profits resulted in no net increase in market value; in the other case enormous *deficits* produced no net decline in price. To the security analyst these contradictions illustrate how strong and irrational are the prejudices and partialities of the security-buying public. It is possible, of course, that they represent the superior ability of the mass mind to look ahead ten or fifteen years. Past experience offers little to support such a view.

Summary

The last three examples have been given to demonstrate that the growth-stock principle of investment carries with it a real danger of miscalculations. We believe the average investor is likely to be most enthusiastic about such companies at the wrong time. In the next chapter we shall develop this theme from another angle, by presenting evidence that past trends are generally an unsound basis for investment decisions.

XIII

—◀◇▶—

Group Studies of
Earnings and Price
Developments

THERE ARE many intelligent questions which the investor may ask about securities and for which the answers are not forthcoming because the proper research has not been conducted. It should be possible to tell the investor how
different kinds of security operations have worked out in practice over the
years. This information should be gathered in two complementary ways: (a) by
studying the actual results of numerous investments made in a particular type
of security purchase, and (b) by tracing through the behavior of large market
samples, from which hypothetical investment results can be calculated.

We know of practically no published investment studies which show the actual results of following a given theory, or technique, or plan of selection over a
fairly long period of time.[1] We do have a mass of raw material, in the form of the
operating and portfolio data of some two hundred investment funds, from
which some such studies might be made. But that work remains to be done. In

---

[1]One of the few such examples available is the result of the operation of a common-stock fund by
Vassar College from 1938 to date in accordance with a definite formula timing plan.

the meantime there is nothing in the archives of investment analysis which corresponds to the huge accumulation of clinical observation and experimental data which has contributed so much to the progress of medical science. Hypothetical studies—as distinct from the systematic recording of actual experience—are more plentiful in the securities field. There are good comparisons of the over-all behavior of bonds with that of common stocks—for example, those compiled by E. L. Smith and by the Cowles Commission. An elaborate investigation into the comparative performance of different grades of corporate bonds is now under way. There are a number of studies—not too well integrated, as yet—relating to the investor's experience with preferred stocks. No doubt, more and better data of this kind will gradually emerge out of the research activities of the graduate schools of business and finance. On the whole, however, the inquiring investor has far fewer inductive studies at his disposal than he has a right to expect in view of the importance of the general subject.

In our own work in securities we have had occasion to make or direct a number of group studies with a bearing on problems of investment policy. In this chapter we shall present the results of some of them, with comments on their significance to the security buyer.

1. Long-Range Variations within a Corporate Group

It is instructive to compare the list of railroad stocks on the New York Stock Exchange at the turn of the century with the same list in 1948. A number of the companies have disappeared through merger or some other form of acquisition, but nearly all the more important issues can readily be traced through to their present status. The facts that stand out are that practically every stock which sold above par in 1900 has since lost the major part of its value and, conversely, that all the roads which have been selling above par in 1948 were valued at comparatively low figures in 1900. Table XXIV gives the comparative prices for the common stock values issues which were listed on the New York Stock Exchange on both dates and which sold above par on either date.

The complete reversal of the position of strong and weak roads indicated by these price records is an extreme example of the inherent tendency of corporate issues to change their investment quality over the years. It is probably too much to say of them, with Scriptural force, that the last shall be first and the first shall be last. But we may invoke the lines which Horace applied long ago to the poems of his day (and which we have used as the epigraph of our book *Security Analysis*):

"Many shall be revived that now are fallen, and many fall that are now in honor."

TABLE XXIV. SOME PRICE COMPARISONS OF RAILROAD COMMON STOCKS

1900 VS. 1948

	Price—	Price—
A. Issues that sold above par in	*Jan. 1900*	*June 30, 1948*
January, 1900:	*(% of Par)*	*(% of Par)*
Central R.R. of N.J.	119	27
Chic., Milw. & St. Paul	118	..[1]
Chic., N.W.	172	..[1]
Chic., R.I. & Pac.	107	..[1]
Del. & Hudson	108	48
Gt. Northern Pfd.[2]	173	47
Del., Lack. & Western	178	48[3]
Ill. Central	113	41
N.Y. Central	135	16½
N.Y., New Haven & Hart.	215	..[1]
Pennsylvania	132	41[3]

	Price—	Price—
B. Issues that sold above par in	*Jan. 1900*	*June 30, 1948*
June, 1948:	*(% of Par)*	*(% of Par)*
Atchison, T. & Sante Fe	19	114
Chesapeake & Ohio	31	151[4]
Norfolk & Western	24	242[4]
St. Louis, S.W.	10	127
Union Pacific	46	191

[1] The shares quoted in 1900 were wiped out in bankruptcy.
[2] Actually a common stock.
[3] Par is $50.
[4] Par is $25.

These drastic changes in position set a premium value on investor alertness and on freedom from ingrained prejudices or preferences. There is more to the problem, of course, than merely identifying those companies which have been forging ahead and those which have been retrogressing. One must be reasonably sure, besides, that these changes in relative performance and in prospects have not already reflected themselves fully in a corresponding change in market price. Some light may be thrown on this question by the section that follows.

2. Results of Portfolio Changes to Improve Quality

The history of the Dow-Jones Industrial Average supplies material for interesting studies on the subject of portfolio switches. In the fifty-odd years for which this average has been computed, its composition has changed frequently and drastically.[2] The announced purpose of these changes has been to keep the list diversified as to industries and representative of the active and important issues on the exchange. A study of the individual substitutions, however, indicates a further purpose to build up quality by dropping components that have become unpopular because they have been relatively unsuccessful and replacing them by issues with a better current reputation. (The changes are handled in such a way as not to affect the dollar value of the average on the day of the switch.)

In this respect the formulators of the Dow-Jones Industrial Average have been acting very much like the typical conservative stock investor who is anxious to maintain and improve the quality of his portfolio and therefore periodically makes changes with that object in view. How profitable do such substitutions prove? A simple test may be applied by comparing the value of the average, including the effect of the substitutions, with the value it would have had if no changes had been made. We could also compare the progress of the Dow-Jones values with those of another index which was held substantially constant through the years. Such an index is that of 354 Industrial Stocks compiled by Standard and Poor's Corporation, for which we have figures since 1918. The comparison works out as shown in Table XXV.

[2]Of the twelve issues in the original list of May, 1896, only two—American Tobacco and General Electric—remain. Of the twenty issues in the enlargement of September, 1916, seven remain. Of the thirty issues in the enlargement of October, 1928, eighteen remain.

TABLE XXV

	Standard-Poor's 354 Industrials (1935–9 = 100)	Dow-Jones Industrials (1935–9 = 100)	Dow-Jones Industrials (actual figures)
Year 1918	31.2	55.9	(91.0)
Year 1928	139.4	156.1	(226.2)
Av. 1935–39	100.0	100.0	(144.9)
Dec. 1947	129.2	123.4	(179.2)

The Dow-Jones list did slightly better than the larger index from 1918 to 1928, but in every other period in the comparison the Standard-Poor's list shows up better. None of the differences is impressively large, and what they prove is largely negative. They suggest that nothing is to be gained from the obvious kind of selectivity which consists in buying only the popular issues and in substituting new leaders for the less active issues regardless of relative price. Apparently one can fare at least as well by buying a little of everything, without analysis or judgment. (The reader is reminded here of the material given in Chapter VI, p. 92, regarding the laggard price behavior of the five most popular stocks selected by investment experts in 1939.)

We have made some additional tests on issues confined to the Dow-Jones list. If the investor had held on to the original list of twenty issues from the time it was set up in September, 1916, it would have been worth only 121 at the end of 1947, whereas by making the numerous changes precisely as was done in the Dow-Jones Industrial Average he would have increased the value to 181. But a similar comparison starting with the first list of thirty stocks— which was set up in October, 1928—would have yielded a different conclusion. The unchanged list would have been worth 193 at the end of 1947, as against 181 for the list as modified by the thirty-eight individual substitutions made between 1928 and 1939. What this seems to prove is that the 1916 list was of subnormal quality and that even conventional substitutions proved beneficial.

Let us summarize our practical suggestions in the matter of security switches as follows:

The investor who begins with a list of standard, first-grade common stocks must expect some of them to lose quality through the years. His aim should be to replace these, with a minimum sacrifice of dividend return and with a fair chance of recouping any loss of principal value resulting from their sale. The best means of accomplishing this is by seeking out attractive issues in the secondary group. A competent security analyst is usually in a position to recommend a number of such issues which by objective tests appear to be worth substantially above their selling price. The fundamental principle of every security replacement should be the following: Each dollar paid for the issue bought should appear to obtain more intrinsic value than was represented by a dollar's worth of the issue sold.

We believe, in sum, that quality may be approached soundly by way of value. If the value is abundant, the quality may be deemed sufficient.

3. How Permanent Are Trends?

Wall Street's judgment has been influenced by past trends more than by any other single factor related to security values. The avowed object of people in the market is to anticipate *future* developments, and the past is held to have no significance except as it aids in such anticipation. Yet in practice it is almost the universal habit to base forecasts of future happenings on a projection of past trends. This is notoriously true of both the professional's and the public's view of market prospects. Nearly everyone is optimistic (or "bullish") because the market has been enjoying a spirited advance and pessimistic (or "bearish") after a decline. In the same way an industry or a company which has grown in the past is almost always expected to keep on progressing; those which have been on the downgrade are expected to get worse and worse.

The last attitude is expressed in categorical fashion on page 458 of Mead & Grodinsky's book *The Ebb and Flow of Investment Value*, as follows: "Declining industries, therefore, usually continue to decline until they reach the point where they pay nothing to the investor."

Our own thinking during the past thirty years has been out of sympathy with this viewpoint. It is true that every established trend has a certain momentum, so that it is more likely to continue for *at least a while longer* than it is to reverse itself at the moment of observation. But this is far from saying that any trend may be relied upon to continue long enough to create a profit for those who "get aboard." Rather extensive studies which we have made of the subject lead us to conclude that reversals of trend in every part of the financial picture occur so frequently as to make reliance on a trend a particularly dangerous matter. There must be strong *independent* reasons for investing money on the expectation of a continuance of past tendencies, and the investor must beware lest his weighing of future probabilities be unduly influenced by the trend line of the past.

We shall not discuss here whether money can be made on balance by following the trend of the general market. The subject is too complicated and controversial to admit of our treating it here with our own selection of statistical evidence. But it is appropriate to point out (a) that playing the trend is the standard formula of stockmarket trading by the general public and (b) that the general public loses money in the stock market.

The public has a similar tendency to speculate in those industrial groups which have established the best market records in the recent past. It is easy to show that this naïve effort to exploit a historical trend is dangerous. The following figures are probably typical. They trace the subsequent market action of the five industrial groups that acted best from January, 1939, to September, 1946.

Price Index (January, 1939 = 100)

Industry	9/14/46	12/31/47
Aviation Transport	373.8	205.0
Amusement	347.4	210.5
Paper	207.8	244.5
Tire and Rubber	185.3	141.7
Investment Companies	170.6	177.7
Average of Five Best	257.0	195.9 Decline 24%
General Market	128.6	124.5 " 3%

Although two of the favored groups continued to act in satisfactory fashion, the performance of the other three created a loss for the five groups far larger than that of the market generally. (These figures are from the monthly bulletins of the S.E.C.) Some additional material on the price behavior of various industrial groups during this period may be of interest. The four industries in the list which were most generally recognized as being in the growth class in 1939 were air transport, chemicals, electrical machinery and equipment, and tobacco products (mainly cigarettes). In addition, aircraft manufacture would be expected to benefit most from a long war. The index of performance to the end of 1948 is shown in Table XXVI.

TABLE XXVI

	Price—Dec. 31, 1948 (Jan. 1939 = 100)
Air Transport[1]	181.3
Chemicals	122.1
Electrical Machinery, etc.	96.7
Tobacco Products	79.2
Aircraft Manufacture	73.6
General Market	120.9

[1]An anomaly in these figures is the showing made by the air-transport stocks. Their price index is one of the highest of all the groups, but their earnings performance is probably the poorest.

Standard and Poor's Corporation made a selection of 35 war stocks, for which it kept a separate price index. If the investor had bought these issues at the outbreak of the war and held them to its end, he would have had a price advance of just 3 per cent. Had he bought practically everything—that is, the large index of 402 stocks—he would have had an advance of 31 per cent.

The trend of industry profits is no more reliable than that of industry prices. Take, for example, the behavior of the aggregate profits of different industries in 1926, 1930, and 1936. The data have been compiled by Standard Statistics-Poor's. They show that the total profits of all industries were about equal in each of the three years. Hence those which had larger earnings in 1930 than in 1926 had a good trend at that time, and those which had smaller earnings showed a bad trend. To what extent were these trends continued or reversed when 1930 is compared with 1936? Figures we have compiled show that the reversals outnumbered the continuances by about two to one.

TABLE XXVII. 1929 RETURN ON NET WORTH COMPARED WITH 1947

	1929 Return	1947 Return
A. Five Best Industries in 1929:		
Automobiles	23.5%	20.8%
Printing and Publishing	21.5	21.3
Merchandise Chains	19.9	18.8
Metal Mines	19.6	11.5
Chemicals	18.0	17.2
Average	20.5%	17.9%
B. Five Poorest Industries in 1929:		
Coal Mining	2.3%	12.3%
Rubber Goods	3.9	16.1
Cotton Goods	4.0	36.1
Department Stores	10.2	14.7
Petroleum Products	11.1	19.9
Average	6.3%	19.8%

Again, let us take figures of earnings as a percentage of invested capital. These figures have been compiled for many years by the National City Bank of New York. The comparisons, as shown in Table XXVII, are startling.

If a similar comparison is made between 1939 and 1947 we find that the average of the five best industries declined from 24.6 per cent to 17.7 per cent, whereas that of the five poorest advanced from 4.2 per cent to 18.5 per cent.

War conditions and their aftermath, of course, have played an important part in bringing about this extraordinary change in the relative position of prosperous and non-prosperous industries. There are many unexpected reasons for the changed performance; the important thing is that performance trends do change and investment values with them.

4. Investment in Giant Enterprises

In 1947 Business Week ran a little article on the "Billion Dollar Club," in which it referred to American businesses with either assets or sales exceeding $1 billion. In addition to thirty-one banks and insurance companies there were six railroads, three utilities, and nine industrials in this category, as follows:

Railroads: Atchison, B. & O., N.Y. Central, Pennsylvania, Southern Pacific, and Union Pacific.

Utilities: American Tel. & Tel., Commonwealth & Southern, and Consolidated Edison of N.Y.

Industrials: Armour, Great Atlantic & Pacific, Du Pont, General Motors, Sears, Roebuck, Standard Oil of N.J., Swift, U.S. Steel.

All of these enterprises have achieved enormous size, and by that token they have presumably made a great success. But how successful are they from the standpoint of the investor? We must first supply our definition of success in this context:

"A successful listed company is one which earns sufficient to justify an average valuation of its shares in excess of the invested capital behind them."

This means that to be really successful (or prosperous) the company must have an earning-power value which exceeds the amount invested by and for the stockholder. In the aggregate the industrial issues listed on the New York Stock Exchange sold for more than book value in 1947, and this was true for about three-quarters of the companies in the Dow-Jones Industrial List. The companies in the "billion-dollar club," however, do not show up so well. Only four of the industrials, one of the utilities, and *none* of the rails sold on the average in 1947 as high as book value. Similarly, most of these issues sold at lower prices in 1947 than they did in 1927. Far from showing the dynamic qualities of growth issues, the group as a whole was unable to maintain its market position vis-à-vis common stocks generally.

If similar data were compiled for the nineteen banking institutions in the billion-dollar class, we are sure they would fail to meet our tests of prosperous operation from the stockholder's standpoint.

It is evident from this analysis that the biggest companies are not the best companies to invest in. (Federal Trade Commission data on the percentage earned on invested capital support this conclusion.) It is equally true that small-sized companies are not suited to the needs of the average investor, although there may be remarkable opportunities in individual concerns in this field. There is some basis here for suggesting that defensive investors show preference to companies in the asset range between $50 million and $250 million, although we have no idea of propounding this as a hard-and-fast rule.

PART III

The Investor as Business Owner

XIV

—◄◇►—

Stockholders and
Managements

THE SITUATION in respect to stockholder-management relationships should be described on three levels, each of which gives a different picture.

The first level is that of legal rights and legal machinery. Here the stockholders as a class are king. Acting as a majority they can hire and fire managements and bend them completely to their will. Though ownership may be widely scattered there is no legal obstacle to many stockholders' joining forces so as to create an effective majority voice on any issue that may arise. Indeed, the S.E.C. has adopted proxy rules designed to facilitate the expression of any stockholder's viewpoint and the solicitation of support from his fellows. (These rules apply to nearly all corporations in which there is a widespread public interest.)

The second level is that of the assertion of stockholders' rights in practice. Here the stockholders are a complete washout. As a class they show neither intelligence nor alertness. They vote in sheeplike fashion for whatever the management recommends and no matter how poor the management's record of accomplishment may be.

In an increasing number of cases efforts are being made by individual stockholders, or groups, to pass resolutions or to supplant incumbent administrations. Some of these appear to have little significance, others to be self-seeking, still others to be worthy of support. If the insurgent stockholders have a large proportion of the shares to begin with, they may win their battle. Otherwise, regardless of the merits of their case, they always lose. We do not know of a single instance where a proposition opposed by the management has been carried primarily by the votes of the *rank and file* of the stockholders.

The third level is that of the stockholders' actual treatment by managements. Here the picture is by no means a bad one. The typical management is honest, competent, and fair-minded. It does the right thing, even though it could easily get away with the wrong thing. It might be seriously remarked here that our generally good managements have produced stupid stockholders. If inefficient or dishonest managements were the rule, it would not take long for the country's stockholders to wake up.

If conditions are so good, why all the fuss? Conditions are indeed good on the whole—but there are far too many exceptions. If in one company out of ten either the management is incompetent or the stockholders are not getting proper treatment, we have a situation that requires intelligent action by the owners of the nation's large businesses. This figure of 10 per cent is probably not too wide of the mark. It can grow much larger if stockholders continue supine; it can be sensibly diminished if stockholders begin to act like proprietors.

Our approach to this problem may be concentrated and simplified by pointing out that there are just two basic questions to which stockholders should turn their attention:

1. Is the management reasonably efficient?
2. Are the interests of the average *outside* stockholder receiving proper recognition?

Strangely enough, neither of these questions has received proper presentation, even in stockholder-management disputes. Such disputes have turned mainly on matters of managerial compensation and of alleged improper dealings by those in control. Excessive compensation to officers is by no means a negligible matter. There are real abuses here, especially through the use of stock options at inadequate prices and sometimes through unduly liberal pension plans. But in relation to the question of managerial efficiency that of managerial compensation becomes unimportant. Good managements are rarely overcompensated to an extent that makes any significant difference with respect to the stockholders' position. Poor managements are always overcompensated, because they are worth less than nothing to the owners.

A. *Efficiency of Management*

The attitude of the financial world toward good and bad management seems to this writer to be utterly childish. First, we have the solemn assurance that quality of management is the most important consideration in selecting an investment. Second, we have the complete absence of any serious effort to determine the quality of management by any rational tests. It is all a matter of hearsay and obvious deductions from the degree of success of the company. Third, we find no interest of any kind in the common-sense objective of improving or replacing weak managements—even though their existence is freely admitted. The first and last word of wisdom to the owners of American business is: "If you don't like the management, sell your stock."[1]

We cannot resist pointing out the paradoxical fact that Jesus seems to have been a more practical businessman than are American stockholders. In at least four parables in the Gospels there is reference to a highly critical relationship between a man of wealth and those he puts in charge of his property. Most to the point are the words that "a certain rich man" speaks to his steward or manager, who is accused of wasting his goods: "Give an account of thy stewardship, for thou mayest be no longer steward" (Luke, 16:2).

The first requisite for a healthy relationship between stockholders and managements is some interest on the part of the owners in whether their servants are "good and faithful." The second is that there be some simple tests by which good management may be distinguished from bad. As it happens, we do have some excellent prima facie indications which can readily

---

[1]This viewpoint finds expression in the generally excellent pamphlet of Merrill Lynch et al., *How to Invest*, as follows: "It is the investor's continuing job to keep an eye on the industry and the company so that he can *withdraw* if economic conditions or *inept management* threaten the company's future" (italics ours), p. 6.

identify those cases where an investigation of managerial competence is in order. There are three clear-cut signs that a management has been unsuccessful and is presumably inefficient unless it can convince the proprietors otherwise. These are:

1. Its failure to earn a satisfactory return on the stockholders' investment during a period of several years in which *the industry as a whole* is prosperous.
2. Its failure to maintain its approximate share of the total sales volume of the industry.
3. Its failure to show a profit margin on sales reasonably close to that of the industry as a whole.

When all three of these unfavorable signals are present the stockholders are clearly entitled to an accounting of the management's stewardship. Actually the presence of any one of these factors justifies the asking of searching questions at stockholder meetings or by correspondence. If managements were properly educated by their shareholders, they would freely acknowledge that these matters require an explanation—and they would hasten to supply it before they are asked.

How does a stockholder, or his adviser, go about determining whether any of the three unsatisfactory conditions exist? This is much easier than one might expect. We now have available industry studies, going back to 1936, which show how the performance of each listed company compares with that of its industry as a unit. These have been compiled by the Securities and Exchange Commission and are not hard to obtain or to inspect. They include a comparative presentation of salaries paid to the executive force. Nearly every industry shows one or two companies that fall far below the average level of performance; but so far as we know the comparative material provided in these compilations has been all but completely neglected.

The first public use of these comparative statistics of performance to test the competence of management appears to have been made in 1948. Oddly enough it was made by the management of a company, and it appears in the annual report of Philip Morris & Co. for 1947 (that is, for its fiscal year ended March, 1948). This contains a ten-year analysis of operating results, covering 1938–47, not only for Philip Morris but also for its four large competitors combined. Certain of the figures for the first and last years are summarized in Table XXVIII.

TABLE XXVIII. EFFICIENCY INDICATORS

PHILIP MORRIS[1] VS. FOUR COMPETING COMPANIES

	1938		1947	
	P.M.	4 Other Companies	P.M.	4 Other Companies
Net Income as % of Net Worth	24.6%	13.4%	8.6%	13.3%
Net Income as % of Net Sales (excl. revenue stamps)	20.6	17.0	7.1	8.8
Increase in Net Sales: 1947 vs. 1938 (incl. revenue stamps)			170%	156%

[1]Philip Morris figures are for years ended the following March.

The Philip Morris figures show a good comparative gain in sales in the nine years. The other and more basic figures, however, are unfavorable. Ten years ago Philip Morris showed excellent earnings both on sales and on capital, substantially surpassing the record of its competitors. By 1947 these advantages had been completely lost, in spite of the company's success in expanding the volume. Though earnings of 8.6 per cent on net worth, after taxes, constitute a respectable figure, it is far from glamorous—in fact, it is less than that of manufacturing companies generally in 1947. Furthermore, in that year Philip Morris stock had the benefit of a large amount of borrowed capital, at a net cost of less than 2 per cent after taxes.

This ten-year exhibit may possibly provide us with a classic portrayal of the manner in which a spectacular growth enterprise is transformed into the ordinary kind of company that has to pay toll to competitive forces.

It is entirely characteristic of management-stockholder relations that these revealing figures were provided in the Philip Morris report with no comment of any kind which indicates an awareness of their significance to the owners of the business. The decline in earning power is not even mentioned, nor is the fact that the company has now fallen behind its competitors in the key indicators of operating efficiency. Apparently the splendid increase in sales is regarded as a sufficient achievement to evoke the plaudits of the stockholders. This is the only explanation we can think of for the publication of these highly informing, but rather accusatory, comparative figures.

The clear moral of the Philip Morris story is that it is up to the stockholders to keep track of management efficiency and management results. This will not be done for them by the managers themselves in any critical fashion unless the results are good. Naturally it is desirable that a good performance be called to the owners' attention, in order that it may be clearly recognized and liberally rewarded. But stockholders and their advisers should appreciate the significance of similar figures when they indicate declining success or definite inadequacy. They should then be made the basis of a concerted demand for either a suitable explanation or a change in conditions.

It is time now to say a word about the role of boards of directors in the determination of managerial ability. One reason why stockholders have largely ignored this question is their belief that the directors they elect are the ones who have both the duty and the opportunity to pass critical judgment on the executive staff. Since the stockholders are much farther removed from the scene than are the directors, their traditional inertia is reinforced by a certain logic, which limits their expression of ownership to voting for the directors whose names appear on the official proxy statement. The rest is then up to the directors.

The trouble with this idea is that directors are rarely independent of management. They should be, of course, but it does not work out that way. Our observation is that the officers choose the directors more often than the directors choose the officers. In many cases the executives actually constitute a majority of the board. Where this occurs the notion that the directors serve as a check on the management is patently incorrect. But in most of the other cases the situation is not really different, for even the non-officer directors are generally bound closely to the executives by ties of friendship and often of business dealings. When a president has outlived his usefulness or fails to measure up to the growing requirements of his job, he is not going to be removed by his personal friends.

What, then, are the concrete and practical steps by which stockholders can obtain efficient managers in place of poor ones? First, we think, a few of the more substantial stockholders should become convinced that a change is needed and should be willing to work toward that end. Second, the rank and file of the stockholders should be open-minded enough to read the proxy material and to weigh the arguments on both sides. They must at least be able to know when their company has been unsuccessful and be ready to demand more than artful platitudes as a vindication of the incumbent management. Third, it would be most helpful, when the figures clearly show that the results are well below average, if it became the custom to call in outside business engineers to pass upon the policies and competence of the management. Once this approach was established as the normal and sensible thing to do under such circumstances, the detection and strengthening of weak managements would become a comparatively simple thing to accomplish—instead of appearing next to impossible, as it does at present.

The engineering firm preferably should not be engaged by the existing board of directors, nor should the report be made to the board. The firm should be selected by an independent committee of stockholders soliciting proxies for this purpose, and the report should be submitted directly to the stockholders. The cost of the study should be borne by the company.

There are many existing financial agencies which could contribute mightily to the improvement of corporate managements. They have experience in these matters, as well as great influence with stockholders. They include the leading investment funds, the Association of Stock Exchange Firms, the New York Society of Security Analysts, the financial services, and the important investment-counsel firms. All of these have shied away from that field of activity as troublesome and unrewarding. We think they are missing a great opportunity for rendering service to the investing public and for obtaining its good will.

It is by no means necessary that such agencies take the initiative in demanding an investigation of management efficiency even where this seems to be justified—although it would be entirely appropriate for an investing fund owning shares in such a concern to do so. What is needed from these agencies is a willingness to support a demand of this kind when it is put forward with persuasive evidence by substantial stockholders. Their recommendation behind a stockholders' resolution will probably mean its adoption if the stock control lies in the general public. Without such support, public stockholders are likely to remain apathetic and swayed by the management's propaganda.[2]

---

[2]The Massachusetts Investors Trust, the largest of the investment funds, indicated in its report for 1941 a determination to use its influence in the direction of improving managements and otherwise protecting the interests of itself and its fellow stockholders.

As an alternative to the outside engineering survey, there are advantages to be gained through the selection of one or more professional and independent directors. These should be men of wide business experience who can turn a fresh and expert eye on the problems of the enterprise. They should receive adequate compensation for their time and skill. They should submit a separate annual report, addressed directly to the stockholders and containing their views on the major question which concerns the owners of the enterprise: "Is the business showing the results for the outside stockholder which could be expected of it under proper management? If not, why—and what should be done about it?"

Our suggestion for either the engineering report or the specialized directorship is obviously not intended to be applied to corporations generally. Both are merely devices for dealing with what on its face seems to be an unsatisfactory situation, as indicated by comparative operating results. Let us return here to the point we made in Chapter II—that a disappointing *average* market price is itself strong and easily recognized evidence that the stockholders have something to look into.

The average market price may fairly be called deficient (a) if it is well below the stockholders' equity—that is, the "book value" and (b) if the average ratio of price to book value in the *industry* is much better than in the one company under scrutiny. The first criterion alone is not conclusive, for in certain industries—for example, railroads and steel—even well-managed units may not earn enough to support the book value. In most cases the average market price reflects fairly well the composite view of the financial community as to the quality of the management. Hence, if the price record is unsatisfactory, as judged by both of the stated tests, it is reasonable to conclude that the management is not considered up to par. It would seem only common sense to go on from there into a critical study of the management, but thus far stockholders have shown no interest in anything so logical as that.

B. *Fair Treatment of the Average Stockholder*

The management may be efficient but still fail to act in the best interests of the outside stockholders. There are a number of ways in which this may occur. The most important of these are the following:

(a) Failure to pay dividends commensurate both with earnings and with the value of the stockholders' equity
(b) Use of stockholders' money in a relatively unprofitable manner
(c) Use of stockholders' money to buy back their stock at an inadequate price
(d) Maintenance of a holding-company set-up, in face of the fact that outside stockholders would be much better off if they owned the underlying assets directly.

Before discussing these points, we should say something about our use of the term "outside stockholders." These are the owners who should not and do not consider themselves as participating directly in the control of corporate policies. Obviously, more than 99 per cent of the stockholders of every large publicly held enterprise are outsiders. The inside owners must be very few in number, yet in most cases—but not all—they hold a substantial stock interest.

Although in some important respects the inside and outside stockholders have identical interests, in others their viewpoints may be different and even basically opposed. Both groups, of course, would like to see large earnings and a large underlying value for the shares. But the insiders will not ordinarily be willing to change the management to improve the earnings picture, for that would mean discharging themselves. Furthermore, the insiders often have a special view of their own on the two questions which touch the outside stockholder most directly—the dividend payments and the average market price of the stock.

There is no truth more fundamental in investment than the simple statement that dividends and market value are the *only* concrete returns which a public stockholder ever gets for the money he puts into a company. Earnings, financial strength, increased asset values—all these may be of vital importance to him, but only because they will immediately or ultimately affect his dividend and his market price. This means that what is or is not in the outside stockholders' interest must be judged in the light of an additional factor of prime importance—the *time element*. If an advantage is going to be deferred for many years, it may be of little value to the public owners.

In the first place, there is the arithmetical discount that must be applied in order to ascertain the present value of a future benefit. If the period of postponement is indefinite and may possibly be a very long one—which is frequently true of the "benefit" to be derived, for example, from paying an inadequate dividend—then that very uncertainty makes for so large a discount factor in practice as virtually to eliminate the future value as a present influence.

Again, in accordance with the nature of publicly held companies, there is a substantial turnover of shares and transfer of ownership during the course of years. When policies are followed which are certain to depress the current market value—ostensibly for the sake of values to be created sometime in the future—those who sell their shares in the long interval are going to take an unnecessary loss, perhaps one of large magnitude. Managements sometimes assert (in private conversation) that they owe no duty to anyone so faithless or so speculative-minded as to sell his stock. This view is inexcusable. An important inducement to the public for investing in shares is that they will have a ready market in case they want to sell. To sell out is just as legitimate as to buy. Every stockholder is entitled not only to the promised marketplace when he wants to sell but also to a fair chance of getting a fair price—to the extent that reasonable corporate policies can give him that chance.

Why is it that insiders may have no interest of their own in following policies designed to provide an adequate dividend return and an adequate average market price? It is strange how little this point is understood. Insiders do not depend on dividends and market quotations to establish the practical value of their holdings. The value to them is measured by what they can do with the business when and if they want to do it. If they need a higher dividend to establish this value, they can raise the dividend. If the value is to be established by selling the business to some other company, or by recapitalizing it, or by withdrawing unneeded cash assets, or by dissolving it as a holding concern, they can do any of these things at a time appropriate to themselves.

Insiders never suffer loss from an unduly low market price which it is in their power to correct. If by any chance they should want to sell, they can and will always correct the situation first. In the meantime they may benefit from the opportunity to acquire more shares at a bargain level, or to pay gift (and prospective estate) taxes on a small valuation, or to save heavy surtaxes on larger dividend payments, which *for them* would mean only transferring money from one place where they control it into another.

Holding Companies

The broadest illustration of the wide gap which frequently exists between the basic position of insiders and that of outsiders is found in the corporate group commonly known as holding companies. We do not mean the type of holding companies which represent simply a convenient method of carrying on business operations in a number of different states or in different fields of activity. Thus U. S. Steel, General Motors, and American Telephone & Telegraph technically are holding companies, but not in the sense that Wall Street commonly uses and understands the term. That sense applies to the formation of a new enterprise for the primary purpose of acquiring a controlling interest in one or more previously existing concerns.

Holding companies of this familiar type developed in large numbers during the period of rampant speculation and large-scale corporate manipulation of the 1920's. Their shares were very popular in Wall Street, because there was always something spectacular going on in their affairs. Thus the shares sold in the market for at least as much as the underlying stocks, and people were quite ready to turn in their holdings in operating companies in exchange for holding-company securities. (Often the turned-in stocks themselves represented holding companies which were being taken over by super-holding companies. This happened most frequently in the public-utility field. The notorious Insull pyramid superimposed no less than six successive tiers of holding companies above the actual operating enterprises.)

After the debacle of 1929–33, holding companies lost all their popularity. This can well be understood, since the losses taken by "investors" in these concoctions were colossal. It became an established axiom of the marketplace that holding-company securities owned by a non-controlling stockholder were worth *less* than the value of the assets behind them.[3] In other words, they sold persistently at substantial discounts from their liquidating values.

What this situation means is that holding-company shares now have one value for outside stockholders and another value—about 40 to 50 per cent higher—for those in control; for the latter can eliminate the discount whenever it suits them, by the simple expedient of moving to dissolve the holding

---

[3]This fact received explicit judicial recognition in a gift-tax case involving shares of Christiana Securities Company, the holding company for Du Pont shares.

company. There are many instances in which they have done this; in such cases the outside stockholders *at that particular moment* also enjoy a substantial increase in the market price of their shares. But, since this is an arbitrary and unpredictable matter, countless outside stockholders are destined to sell out at the wrong time. So far as anyone can tell there is no reason why a given holding company, with its attendant price discount, may not go on indefinitely.

The major dissolutions of holding companies have been effected in the field of public utilities under the compulsions of law, as embodied in the Public Utility Holding Company Act of 1935. The history of these proceedings is not without its sardonic side. The utility managements have fought the "death sentence" bitterly; they have tried to enlist the support of their stockholders to prevent the passage of the act itself, and in their annual reports they have recounted their (unsuccessful) efforts to defeat it in the courts as though they were thereby protecting the interests of the owners of the securities. Yet for years the course of market prices has proclaimed eloquently that the holding-company stockholders would gain and not lose from these dreaded dissolutions. For, once they receive the shares of the operating companies in place of the parent-company securities, the persistent discount on the latter disappears and the aggregate value of what they own is materially improved.

All the holding-company stockholders who know anything about market prices have been aware of this situation. Nevertheless, there is no indication that they have made any effort to compel their managements to accept dissolution instead of fighting it. They just keep on signing the proxies that come to them each year.

Mission Corporation

As an example of how outside stockholders fare in holding-company setups we have selected Mission Corporation, the shares of which are listed on the New York Stock Exchange. In addition to the standard attributes of the genre, this concern offers some special points of interest. It was organized at the beginning of 1935 to hold two large blocks of oil-company shares—Tidewater Associated and Skelly Oil. The usual market discount developed promptly; by the end of 1937 it had reached 35 per cent, which was about the average figure for the next ten years. The inherent unattractiveness of holding-company shares to the general public is demonstrated here by the surprising fact that this large discount between asset value and market price was established during the very time that another oil company, Pacific Western, was acquiring working control (45 per cent) of Mission by buying up hundreds of thousands of shares.

In 1947 steps were initiated to terminate the existence of Mission by way of merging it with still another concern—Sunray Oil. The merger terms were unusual. The controlling stockholders of Pacific Western—which in turn controlled Mission—were to get about $79 million in cash for their stock. The outside Mission stockholders were to get Sunray Oil common stock, which had large amounts of bonds and preferred ahead of it. Should they accept such terms? The terms did not seem equitable; yet they offered more in market value than Mission shares were selling for, because of the huge discount on the latter.

At this point a new factor entered. The recently resigned president of Mission, who was also president of Skelly, denounced the merger as grossly unfair and took legal steps to enjoin it. The merger fell through. By the end of 1947 the price of Mission again showed its customary discount of 35 per cent from break-up value.

Most significant of the many statements made in the contest over the merger was the promise made by the former president that, if the deal was prevented, he would take prompt steps to bring about the *liquidation* of Mission, in order that each stockholder might have direct ownership of his interest in Skelly and Tidewater. This was a virtual admission by one who had been part of the inside group that the existence of the holding-company arrangement was contrary to the interest of the outside public. (However, no steps calling for the liquidation of Mission have been taken, up to the end of 1948.)

We should point out that the Mission stockholders have fared reasonably well in recent years, despite the holding-company discount. This situation has resulted from a great increase in the earnings and market price of Skelly Oil and—to a lesser degree—of Tidewater Associated. We find no evidence that the controlling interests in Mission had anything to do with these favorable developments, but the facts recounted above indicate how great have been the advantages that their inside position has given them over the outside stockholders.[4]

In the next chapter we shall discuss a clear-cut example of the creation of an unsatisfactory situation for outside stockholders through inadequate dividends. Let us now refer briefly to the matter of surplus holdings of cash. Many relatively unsuccessful or unpopular businesses accumulate a considerable amount of extra cash assets as the years go by. Sometimes this comes from stock financing in former years of activity and is now held as unneeded capital. Sometimes it comes from the accrual of substantial depreciation and depletion reserves, which are actually the transfer into cash of the original capital assets. Sometimes it comes from large temporary earnings not disbursed as dividends and not really needed for the smaller amount of business now done. Such cash assets produce very small income—their usual form of investment is in United States Treasury issues—and, since the company itself is not doing very well, the market price tends to reflect the small earning power rather than the large holdings of liquid assets.

So long as this surplus cash remains with the company the outside stockholder gets little benefit from it, either in his dividends or in his market price. A favorite use for a portion of the surplus cash is the purchase of outside shareholdings at prices considerably less than their fair value.[5] Here again the insiders can count the cash assets as worth their full value *to them*. For the funds are under their control, and if they wish to obtain their pro-rata share of them they can easily arrange a distribution.

Since 1929, a corporation's repurchase of its own shares has become a standard and widespread practice. Financial authorities have given little attention to the questions about fair treatment which arise in such repur-

---

[4]At the time this chapter was written, another example of the same genre was being created. Stockholders of Patino Mines received a free distribution of shares of Patican Co., Ltd., an investment company dominated by Patino and holding interests in other mining enterprises. *The Patican shares immediately sold at a discount of 46 per cent from the market value of the portfolio*—that is, the price of Patican was 3½, as against a net asset value in United States funds of about $6.50.

[5]Some readers may wish to look up the examples of White Motors in 1931 and Westmoreland Coal in 1935–38, described on pp. 605–609 of *Security Analysis*, by Graham & Dodd. In these instances the price paid for the shares bought in was far below their interest in the applicable *cash holdings alone*.

chases; the stockholders themselves have not thought about it at all. It is time that a basic principle was adopted here—the principle that a corporation should deal fairly with *all* its owners and that it should pay a fair price to those who are selling their interest back to it.

If a fair price is well above the market quotation—as usually happens in cases of this kind—then the repurchase should be made by inviting competitive tenders at a maximum announced figure equal to such fair price or value.

Some inequitable repurchase policies have been prohibited by S.E.C. regulation in the field of investment funds and public-utility holding-company systems. These are the only areas in which the Commission has been given jurisdiction over the buying in of shares. If we could raise the level of stockholder intelligence in these matters, the demand for just and sound treatment would come from them—instead of by paternalistic law—and it would apply to every publicly held corporation.

It might be pointed out that the American-Hawaiian Steamship Company, described on page 171 as a definitely undervalued situation, is an example of both of the conditions we have just discussed. Its cash assets do not reflect themselves in the market price, because they produce small income and because the current or prospective operating results are not viewed with favor. A moderate part of these cash assets has been employed continuously to repurchase shares at less than their fair value; about 20 per cent of the capital has been bought back in this way.

Concept of Financial Efficiency

The two main subdivisions treated in this chapter may be brought together with the aid of the notion of "financial efficiency." A company's management may run the business well and yet not give the outside stockholders the right results for them, because its efficiency is confined to operations and does not extend to the best use of the capital. The objective of efficient *operation* is to produce at low cost and to find the most profitable articles to sell. Efficient *finance* requires that the stockholders' money be working in forms most suitable to their interest. This is a question in which management, as such, has little interest. Actually, it almost always wants as much capital from the owners as it can possibly get, in order to minimize its own financial problems. Thus the typical management will operate with more capital than is necessary, if the stockholders permit it—which they often do.

It is not to be expected that public owners of a large business will strive as hard to get the maximum use and profit from their capital as will a young and energetic entrepreneur. We are not offering any counsels of perfection or suggesting that stockholders should make exacting demands upon their superintendents. We do suggest, however, that failure of the existing capital to earn enough to support its full value in the marketplace is sufficient justification for a critical spirit on the part of the stockholders. Their inquiry should then extend to the question of whether the amount of capital used is suited to the results and to the reasonable needs of the business.

For the controlling stockholders the retention of excessive capital is not a detriment, especially since they have the power to draw it out when they wish. As pointed out above, this is one of the major factors that give insiders important and unwarranted benefits over outsiders. If the ordinary public stockholders hold a majority of the stock, they have the power—by use of their votes—to enforce appropriate standards of capital efficiency in their own interest. To bring this about they will need more knowledge and gumption than they now exhibit. Where the insiders have sufficient stock to constitute effective voting control, the outside stockholders have no power even if they do have the urge to protect themselves. To meet this fairly frequent situation there is need, we believe, for a further development of the existing body of law defining the trusteeship responsibilities of those in control of a business toward those owners who are without an effective voice in its affairs.

S.E.C. and Investor Protection

It is well known that the Securities and Exchange Commission was constituted, by 1933 and later legislation, to correct financial abuses and to protect the investing public. The S.E.C. is a powerful and active body, with many different functions and with many accomplishments to its credit. Yet it would be a mistake to regard the Commission as a *general* protector of investor rights and interests. Its work proceeds in accordance with the provisions of eight different statutes, each of which gives it specific but limited duties.[6]

The Commission's powers in relation to new security issues are extensive, but they all relate to matters of information. It has no duty to examine into the merits of a security offering or into the fairness of the selling price. Similarly, it has wide powers to investigate and punish manipulative actions on the security exchanges, but it has no responsibility for the level of security prices. (It has somewhat similar powers and duties in connection with unlisted trading.) Under Chapter X it takes an active part in working out corporate reorganizations and endeavors to bring about plans that are both fair and financially sound to the various security holders. Yet in this field it has no direct jurisdiction but acts in an advisory capacity to the court. Its duties in the matter of investment companies, investment advisers, and indenture trustees are mainly to make sure that the various provisions of the relevant statutes are being obeyed.

The Public Utility Holding Company Act gave the Commission functions far wider in scope than it exercises in any other field relating to securities. On the one hand it was given the duty of reforming a generally unsatisfactory corporate picture. This has involved the breaking up of pyramided holding companies and of systems too widely spread out in space, as well as the recapitalization of companies with insufficient common stock equities and the equitable re-allocation of voting power as between preferred and common interests. Besides this, the Commission was given the widest powers over the financial transactions of all the constituent units in the holding-company systems. This applies to the terms of issuance of new securities and the retirement of old ones and to various accounting entries and so forth (except to the extent that state public-utility commissions have local jurisdiction).

The Commission has the power to require periodic reports, in forms prescribed by it, from companies which have sold new securities or have issues

---

[6]These statutes are: (1) The Securities Act of 1933, relating to new issues of securities. (2) The Securities Exchanges Act of 1934, relating to trading on organized exchanges. This was enlarged by (3) the "Maloney Act" of 1938, conferring jurisdiction over unlisted trading. (4) The Public Utility Holding Company Act of 1935, to reform abuses in that field. (5) The Chandler Act of 1938, which added Chapter X to the Bankruptcy Act, setting up new procedures for corporate reorganizations. (6) The Trust Indenture Act of 1939, which defines the responsibilities of corporate bond trustees. (7) The Investment Company Act of 1940, which regulates publicly held investment funds. (8) The companion Investment Advisers Act of 1940.

listed on exchanges. It regulates the solicitation of proxies to be voted at annual or special meetings. It also collects and publishes reports of purchases
or sales by so-called "insiders"—officers, directors, and large stockholders—
in the securities of their own companies.

This list of powers and responsibilities is a formidable one, and we do not
wish to minimize the importance of the S.E.C. as a regulator of the financial
behavior of those in control of corporations. Nevertheless, the protection it
affords investors is not only incomplete—which was to be expected—but ir-
regularly distributed as well. Take the matter of recapitalization plans, as an
example. If they come under the Public Utility Holding Company Act, then
every detail is subject to S.E.C. supervision and approval; even though security holders may be anxious to accept a plan the Commission will not permit
them to do so if it thinks the terms are not completely fair. But in the case of
solvent industrial companies it has no obligation or power to pass upon such
plans and its function is limited to making sure that the disclosures in the
proxy statements are adequate.

There is a similar inconsistency in the general legal attitude toward the
ability of security owners to make sound decisions. In the case of insolvent
corporations it is now the settled view of the law that the bondholders and
stockholders cannot be trusted to take care of themselves and that it is necessary for the courts, the Commission, and the disinterested trustee to determine what is fair and proper. Here elaborate machinery is set up to protect
investors against unfair proposals that may emanate from the former managements and controlling interests. But in the ordinary solvent corporation
the law assumes that the outside stockholder will pass independent and intelligent judgment on the management's proposals, including the question of
its continuance in office. Experience indicates that security holders are no
more capable of looking out for themselves intelligently in the one case than
in the other.

The functions of the S.E.C. do not include any effective protection of investors with respect to the two main issues which may arise between them
and their managements—the efficiency of management and the proper treatment of outside stockholders by the insiders. (We are speaking now of the
ordinary, solvent corporation.) The Commission's powers and labors in this
field have been confined to setting forth proxy rules which will make it easier for an outside stockholder to bring his viewpoint to the attention of his
fellows. In this area progress has been made. But it is still almost impossible

for an outsider to have any action adopted by stockholders against the opposition of management, unless he and his group control a large proportion of the stock. This is true, in part, because managements may spend a virtually unlimited amount of the corporation's money to campaign against the outsider's proposals. An equally important reason is that stockholders are lazy, indifferent, accustomed to obey the management, and suspicious of outside suggestions.

If the Commission were directed to render advisory opinions on matters in controversy, upon the request of a designated percentage of the stockholders, an important element that is now lacking would be supplied, namely, an authoritative and impartial viewpoint to which security holders would pay respectful attention.[7]

OPINIONS OF SECURITY ANALYSTS ON STOCKHOLDER-MANAGEMENT RELATIONSHIPS

In June, 1947, the author circulated among the members of the New York Society of Security Analysts a questionnaire on stockholder-management relationships. The replies received totaled 573. The detailed results of the questionnaire are presented and commented upon in the *Analysts' Journal* for the fourth quarter of 1947.

The following summary of the seven questions asked and the replies received should be of interest:

Question 1: Do you believe that the competence of management is a practical consideration in the selection of securities?

Nearly all the analysts answered "yes."

Question 2: Of 100 listed companies taken at random, about what percentage do you think would have a fully satisfactory management?

The replies varied widely, but the mid-point of the estimates was under 50 per cent.

Question 3: Do you favor cumulative voting for directors?

The answers favored the affirmative by two to one.

---

[7]There is provision now in the Investment Company Act of 1940 for an advisory opinion by the S.E.C. on a recapitalization plan of any such company, when the opinion is requested by the management or by holders of 25 per cent of any class of its securities. A simple change in existing legislation could extend this function to cover the whole field of stockholder-management controversies.

Question 4: Do you believe that a majority (or a substantial minority) of the directors of the typical corporation should be independent of the operating management—in particular, that they should not be recipients of salaries or other substantial income from the corporation?

The replies were as follows:

A majority	291
A substantial minority	120
Neither	80
No answer	82

Question 5: If a company's average earnings fail to show a reasonable return on the stockholders' equity, and if they are substantially lower than in the industry as a whole, do you believe that this fact calls for inquiry by shareholders?

Nearly all the answers were "yes."

Question 6: Do you believe that it is the duty of the directors to pay such dividends, within the average earnings of the business, as will be reasonably commensurate with the intrinsic value of the shares, as they determine such value?

The replies favored the affirmative by two to one.

Question 7: Do you believe that it is the duty of the management to transmit to stockholders any offer to purchase a substantial number of shares at more than the current market price?

The replies favored the affirmative by seven to one.

XV

—◄◇►—

A Study of Stockholder-
Management Relations in
Two Industries

To GIVE more concrete expression to the ideas set forth in the preceding chapter we propose now to examine two industries from the standpoint of the stockholders' position and treatment. The two financial groups are: (a) the closed-end investment funds, and (b) the fire and casualty insurance companies.

Both industries present a challenge to their owners and their managements by reason of the fact that their shares sell persistently in the market for less than the amounts that could be realized on sale or liquidation of the business involved. In the continued—and presumably considered—judgment of the marketplace, nearly all of these companies would be worth more dead than alive. What are the implications of this curious fact? Is it to be presumed that the market's verdict is a mere irrationality and has no practical or theoretical significance to the stockholder-owners of these enterprises? Or does it, rather, carry an emphatic and meaningful message to these owners, admonishing them to look with critical eyes on the way their businesses are set up and managed?

Any intelligent person must admit that the latter is true and not the former. For what the market says over a long period of time has at least a strong presumption of being correct. Furthermore, the average market price is of primary importance to outside stockholders, because in large measure it determines the success or failure of their individual investments. Investors, as buyers and sellers of securities, are completely and sometimes excessively aware of this truth. But the same investors, as stockholders and owners of their companies, act in precisely the contrary fashion. From what they do and fail to do it would appear that they believed implicitly that the verdict of the market is either wrong or irrelevant and that any inquiry into the competence or policies of management—regardless of how badly the stockholders may be faring—is unnecessary and impertinent.

This chapter is being written with a dash of acerbity which may seem out of harmony with the sweet reasonableness of our earlier discussion. The change of tone is intentional. Years of experience has taught us that the only way to inspire the average American stockholder to take any *independently* intelligent action would be by exploding a firecracker under him. Hence the mild pyrotechnical display that follows. (As a matter of courtesy, we shall identify individual companies by letter instead of by name.)

A. Closed-End Investment Funds

The price discount on the shares of these companies may be viewed as an expensive monument erected to the inertia and stupidity of stockholders. It has cost the owners of these businesses countless millions of dollars, yet it has been totally unnecessary. It could have been terminated at any time by the mere passing of a resolution at a stockholders' meeting. Yet the matter never seems even to have been brought up for discussion.

We have here a clear-cut illustration of management's domination of stockholder thinking. The resolution to abolish the discount would merely instruct the management to repurchase shares when tendered or available at a price equal to their net asset value—in other words, to place the closed-end company on an open-end basis. If such a resolution were presented by a *management* it would be passed with enthusiasm. But managements are opposed to such a policy, because it would mean using up part of the corporation's resources, contracting its size, and impairing their own position. Since the managements do not recommend any such action, the stockholders do not vote it or even discuss it. It never occurs to the owners of these funds that an open-end, no-discount arrangement might be good for *them*, even though the management did not like it. In fact, the very idea of taking any independent action in their own interest is so alien to stockholders' thinking that if someone proposed such a resolution it would no doubt be voted down automatically at the request of the management.

Let us expand the previous argument a little under the three headings of (1) facts, (2) reasons, and (3) remedies.

1. Extent of the Market Discounts. The leading source of information on the statistics of investment funds is the comprehensive *Manual of Investment Companies*, published annually by Arthur Wiesenberger and Co. Page 94 of the 1948 edition sets forth the average discount of market price from net asset value for twenty-four leading companies, as shown in Table XXIX.

TABLE XXIX

Date	Average Discount
December 31, 1936	26 %
1941	41%
1942	37%
1943	33%
1944	28%
1945	23%
1946	29%
1947	29%

Over the last fifteen years these discounts have doubtlessly averaged at least 30 per cent. This means that typical shares with $100 of realizable value behind them could be sold by their owners for only $70. The picture has varied, of course, as between different funds, but for most of them the 30 per cent figure would be about right. Only in one or two cases in recent years, where the performance and reputation have been outstanding—the Lehman Corporation, for example—have the shares *ever* sold as high as their net asset value. (We exclude here certain low-priced, highly leveraged shares, which have a special *speculative* status.)

2. Cause of the Discount. Is the discount explained by the poor performance of these companies? The figures argue otherwise. Table XXX presents some composite results, for two representative periods, as calculated in the Wiesenberger Manual.

TABLE XXX

MANAGEMENT RESULTS

	11 Years 1937–1947	4 Years 1944–1947
Closed-End Funds	66%	62½%
Open-End Funds	54	54
Dow-Jones Composite Stocks	68	65
Standard-Poor's 90 Stocks	57	55

Note: These results include the annual reinvestment, and consequent compounding, of dividends received. Thus they give higher results than the basis of calculation used in this book on page 25.

The figures shown are not very impressive in either direction. They suggest that, on the whole, the managerial ability of investment funds has been just about able to absorb the expense burden and the drag of uninvested cash. Whether this is satisfactory or mildly disappointing depends on the viewpoint of those who own the shares.

In our opinion the cause of the price depreciation in closed-end companies is found not in their performance but in their corporate set-up. They are not well suited to the desires and needs of any important group of buyers. The small and unsophisticated investor will buy only what is actively sold to him, and that means the shares of the open-end funds which have an energetic sales effort behind them. The larger and more experienced investor is not attracted by a performance about on a par with the market averages. He believes—rightly or wrongly—that he can do at least as well with his own choices. Speculators have little interest in the ordinary closed-end company, because it has no individual prospect or appeal to arouse their enthusiasm.[1]

---

[1] Note as a rule-proving exception the case of Chicago Corporation, which struck out into original paths of industrial development. Its shares sell at a high *premium* over the stated book value.

Perhaps another way of saying the same thing is to point out that the closed-end investment fund is a special form of the holding company and suffers from the general unpopularity that now attaches to *indirect ownership* of securities. Thus buyers for their shares can be found only on bargain terms. (Pursuant to this view, in Chapter IV we recommended closed-end funds for consideration by the intelligent investor, *provided* they could be bought at a substantial discount.)

But whether our diagnosis of causes is correct or not is largely irrelevant. The discount exists and persists, and it places the stockholders of these funds under a serious disability in relation to the values that belong to them and should be realizable by them.

3. The Remedy. If the stockholders want the discount removed they have only to demand that it be done. Many of the funds are constantly buying in their own shares at low prices. For example, during 1947 the N Corporation, which has one of the poorest of performance records, bought in 37,000 shares (about 3 per cent of the total) at a discount of 47 per cent from net asset value. (Since the end of 1936 about 20 per cent of the common has been repurchased at a similar discount.) By resolution of the stockholders, the management can be directed to buy back their shares at a fair price—either at full value or at a discount of not more than 5 to 10 per cent.

The officers will object, of course, that such a policy would absorb most of their funds and possibly put the company out of business. To this the stockholders might well answer "So what?" That should be the management's problem, not the owners'. Perhaps the real solution is to convert these funds into a full open-end basis, with agency arrangements for the sale of new shares. It is significant that for many years the open-end, stock-selling funds have been expanding phenomenally in size, whereas the capitalization of all closed-end companies has steadily contracted.

It is the virtue of the free-enterprise system that the consumer dictates production by purchasing what he likes and rejecting what he does not care for. For years the verdict of the "consumer" has been against closed-end companies.[2]

---

[2]Figures published by the National Association of Investment Companies show the following: Between December, 1940, and December, 1948, the member open-end companies raised $953 million of new capital, net, from the public. In the same period the member closed-end companies had a net *decrease* of $207 million in capital funds, due to re-purchases from the public.

B. Fire and Casualty Insurance Companies

Like the closed-end investment funds, the insurance shares have proved relatively unpopular and unremunerative investments for at least the last ten years. This fact should be a surprising one, because the well-established insurance companies have enjoyed great inherent advantages. The industry has been basic and expanding. Although such enterprises entail the taking of risks, theirs is not a risky business. They achieve this paradox by the wide spreading of their individual commitments and by charging premiums that are nearly twice as large as the losses actually incurred. Unlike every other business, they can carry on all their operations with their customers' money—received in the form of premiums paid in advance. Their own capital, in fact, functions only as a kind of contingency fund. In addition to their underwriting business, which presumably should be reasonably profitable, they have the use of large funds for investment. These include not only their capital and surplus but in addition considerable sums belonging to their policyholders.

Despite these major elements of strength, the industry as a whole has not turned in a good performance for its stockholders in the past decade. As a better-than-average example, among the fire companies, let us look at the results of the N Insurance Company. This concern has paid dividends uninterruptedly ever since 1828, and its shares ought to be an attractive and rewarding medium for stock investment. Yet between December, 1936, and December, 1947, its over-all earnings have averaged scarcely 4 per cent on the stockholders' funds. Although its dividend policy has been unusually generous in relation to earnings and capital value, the market has viewed the shares without favor; their price has averaged less than liquidating value in every year since 1941. Most fire insurance companies have not done even this well in earnings, in dividends, and in average market price.

If one views the fire-insurance industry as a whole, he may well raise the question of whether the poor results are not a reflection on the caliber of the management. Has it shown sufficient resourcefulness in dealing with the problem of non-remunerative rates? Has it done an effective job in holding down expenses, which have been running at some 40 per cent of premium income? This is typically a situation in which the owners of the businesses would be justified in asking searching questions of those in charge.

Needless to say, such questions have not been asked by the insurance stockholders. In fact, their role has been even more feckless and fatuous than that of stockholders generally. Many of the fire concerns do not bother to send their stockholders any financial data other than an unintelligible balance sheet. Most of the others take advantage of the so-called "convention basis" of accounting to supply a ridiculously inadequate statement of income. Some managements go on losing money year after year in their insurance operations without feeling any need of even referring to this unpleasant circumstance in their reports. Too many companies have been operated for the apparent sole benefit of the insurance agencies, and others for the chief advantage of majority or controlling stockholders. The relatively few concerns which have succeeded in earning an average of 6 per cent or better on the stockholders' equity in 1943–47 have vitiated this achievement by failing to pay dividends as high as 4 per cent on book value. Even in these cases, therefore, the low dividend has produced a low average market value.

The insurance industry has so handled its accounts that the mere fact of its doing a great deal more business than before causes it to show operating losses.[3]

At the same time the expansion of volume causes it to need more capital, which it has raised by selling more common stock at prices far below the liquidating value of the old capital. Thus a dynamic expansion, which in other industries would be a welcome sign of health and promise to the stockholders, has been manhandled in a fashion to confuse and depress the supposed beneficiaries of the upsurge of business. A little frankness and ingenuity on the part of management could have avoided all these discouraging developments.

Let us now use two individual companies to illustrate the consequences of stockholder apathy in the face of (1) inadequate earnings and (2) inadequate dividends.

1. *An Example of Unprofitable Management.* The A Fire Insurance Company has 300,000 shares outstanding. On December 31, 1947, the stockholders' equity was computed as $38.55 per share, but the market price was only 15—a discount of 60 per cent. Eleven years earlier the equity was $51 per

---

[3]This is ascribed to insurance-department regulations which require them to charge off the full cost of acquiring business as a *current expense* in making up their reports to the authorities. But their reports to *stockholders* could have carried a proper portion of the unearned premiums as a *prepaid expense.* This has been done, in fact, in all analyses made by the financial services.

share. The dividends paid during that time were only $11.25, so that over the entire period the company actually lost money in the aggregate.[+] Since the company has had the benefit of an investment income averaging $1.90 per share, it is evident that its fire-insurance business has been very unprofitable.

This concern is managed by another corporation, which is in the insurance-agency and brokerage business and effectively controls the A Company by ownership of a large minority stock interest. The public's investment, which aggregates more than half the shares, is spread among some 3,500 stockholders.

All the surface indications point to the conclusion that the A Insurance Company is being operated for the advantage of the agency—which gets commissions on its business and other perquisites—and to the disadvantage of the public owners. Whether this is really so or not could be determined only through a competent and impartial investigation initiated and controlled by the outside stockholders. Thus we have here a perfect example of a prima facie case calling for independent inquiry and possible action by the stockholders whose money is being administered.

2. *An Example of an Inadequate Dividend.* In this illustration the stockholders were actually summoned to pass judgment on an issue of vital importance to them. They supported the management. Let us summarize the facts, and then add our own interpretation of the results.

The B Casualty Company has 500,000 shares outstanding. On December 31, 1947, the stockholders' equity was computed at $47.95 per share, but the market price was only 27½. At the end of 1936 the equity was $18.67 per share. Dividends paid in the eleven-year period were $9.55, so that the overall earnings work out as $38.83 per share, or an annual average of $3.53. Thus the company has been able to realize a reasonably good return on the stockholders' equity since 1936.

The dividend rate, however, did not keep pace with the rise in the stockholders' equity. In 1941 it paid 87½ cents per share on an average equity of $25.80. In 1948 it was paying only $1.00, which was but slightly more than 2 per cent on the then value of the owners' investment. This niggardly divi-

---

[+]In these figures we have followed long-established custom and given the company credit for prepaid expense equal to 40 per cent of the increase in unearned premiums. If the newer and more appropriate credit of 25 per cent were allowed, the earnings picture would be appreciably worse.

dend policy injured the stockholders in two primary respects. In the first place, their income return was inadequate, especially in the light of the huge increase in living costs which has prevailed since 1941. Since the typical outside investor places his money primarily to obtain a suitable income return, the low dividend of the B Company meant that the investment was not working out satisfactorily. Many of the stockholders were thus moved to sell their shares. At this point they were faced with the second discomfiture re sulting from the 2.1 per cent dividend yield on the equity value. The market price was itself largely governed by the dividend return. Instead of being quoted close to the asset value of $48 per share, as was perhaps justified by both earnings and prospects, their holdings were evaluated in the market at not much more than half that amount.[5] In the past few years several hundred of the shareholders were thus moved by the low dividend to sell, and because of the same low dividend they found themselves realizing an inordinately low price for their shares.

At the annual stockholders' meeting in the spring of 1948 a stockholder introduced a resolution disapproving the management's dividend policy as inadequate. Both sides sent out letters in which the issue was fully discussed. The management insisted that a conservative dividend policy was beneficial to both the company and its stockholders. It pointed to the losses taken in the 1929–32 debacle as demonstrating the need for building up the capital resources against possible future adversity, and it asserted that the great current expansion in premium volume made it desirable to hold on to earnings. The objecting stockholder stressed the disadvantages suffered by the owners because of the inadequate dividend. It was suggested that periodic stock dividends, in addition to the $1 payment in cash, would solve the problem of giving the owners a satisfactory return and still retaining the profits for business expansion. It was pointed out, also, that by merely paying the same *proportionate* dividend now as in 1941, the management would go far toward meeting the legitimate expectations of the stockholders.

---

[5]The relationship between dividend return and market price is summarized in the following excerpt from a study of insurance stocks issued in June, 1948, by Geyer & Co., one of the leading authorities in the field: ". . . Insurance stockholders received a return of only 2.89 per cent on invested capital last year. As this obviously is too meager a 'reward' for venture capital, the market continuously has evaluated the worth of capital invested in the insurance business at only 70 cents on the dollar." Since the B Company's dividend was only 2.1 per cent on the invested capital, the discount on its shares was greater than the average, even though its earnings were better than the average.

As stated above, the management won the contest. It was supported by about 70 per cent of the shares voted and by about 55 per cent of the stockholders voting. What is the significance of the result? It may mean that the analysis of the stockholders' interest in these matters, as presented in this and the preceding chapter, has been a fallacious one; the stockholders in a test case, having the issue fairly presented to them, exercised their considered judgment in favor of conservatism, even though it meant low income and a low average market price. On the other hand, it may mean that stockholders are not yet ready to reach an independent view on any matter of corporate policy; most of them will mechanically follow the management's recommendation no matter how cogent may be the arguments for a contrary action.

Before expressing our opinion on this matter, we must reveal that the "disgruntled stockholder" who introduced the resolution of disapproval was none other than our own investment fund. This fact should scarcely make any real difference in the present discussion, since our own thinking on stockholder-management relations—with whatever prejudices it involves—has already been amply set forth in the preceding pages. Naturally we think that those outside stockholders of the B Company who supported the management's view of dividend policy acted unwisely and contrary to their real interest. We believe they were moved in part by habit, in part by the prevalent myth of managerial infallibility, and in part by the superior campaign effort which the management was able to bring to bear on the matter.

To us the moral of the B Casualty Company case and many others is this: It will take a true stockholders' revolution to establish the owners of American corporations in an intelligent and effective position vis-à-vis their managements. This would be the counterpart and the antidote to what was described some years ago by James Burnham in his book, *The Managerial Revolution*,[6] and also in the classical work of Berle & Means, *The Modern Corporation and Private Property*. Both of these studies take for granted the abdication of the stockholder as an independent factor on the corporate scene. It is assumed that he will be dominated, and thus at least partially exploited, by the management. No doubt there is a great deal of truth in this viewpoint, with all its unfavorable connotations respecting the intelligence of investors when they assume the role of owners. The cause of sound stockholdership is thus seen to be desperate, but it is not yet lost.

[6]New York: G. P. Putnam's Sons, 1942.

To win this cause two things are needful: first, a persistent campaign to educate stockholders to act as true proprietors of the businesses they own; and second, organized counsel and leadership in the field of stockholder-management relationships. Stockholders will act to protect their interests if they are advised of the proper course by authoritative agencies they can trust.

PART IV

Conclusion

XVI

---◆◇◆---

"Margin of Safety" as the Central Concept of Investment

IN THE OLD LEGEND the wise men finally boiled down the history of mortal affairs into the single phrase, "This too will pass." Confronted with a like challenge to distill the secret of sound investment into three words, we venture the motto, MARGIN OF SAFETY. This is the thread that runs through all the preceding discussion of investment policy—often explicitly, sometimes in a less direct fashion. Let us try now, briefly, to trace that idea in a connected argument.

All experienced investors recognize that the margin-of-safety concept is essential to the choice of sound bonds and preferred stocks. For example, a railroad must have earned its total interest charges better than twice, taking a period of years, for its bonds to qualify as investment-grade issues. This *past* ability to earn in excess of interest requirements constitutes the margin of safety which is counted on to protect the investor against loss or discomfiture in the event of some *future* decline in net income. (The margin above charges may be stated in other ways—for example, in the percentage by which gross revenues may decline before the balance after interest disappears—but the underlying idea remains the same.)

The bond investor does not expect future average earnings to work out the same as in the past; if he were sure of that, the margin demanded might be small. Nor does he rely to any controlling extent on his judgment as to whether future earnings will be materially better or poorer than in the past; if he did that, he would have to measure his margin in terms of a carefully *projected* income account, instead of emphasizing the margin shown in the past record. Here the function of the margin of safety is, in essence, that of rendering unnecessary an accurate estimate of the future. If the margin is a large one, then it is enough to justify the assumption that future earnings will *roughly* approximate those of the past in order for an investor to feel sufficiently protected against the vicissitudes of time.

The margin of safety for bonds may be calculated, alternatively, by comparing the total value of the enterprise with the amount of debt. (A similar calculation may be made for a preferred-stock issue.) If the business owes $10 million and is fairly worth $30 million, there is room for a shrinkage of two-thirds in value—at least theoretically—before the bondholders will suffer loss. The amount of this extra value, or "cushion," above the debt may be approximated by using the average market price of the junior stock issues over a period of years. Since average stock prices are generally related to average earning power, the margin of "enterprise value" over debt and the margin of earnings over charges will in most cases yield similar results.

So much for the margin-of-safety concept as applied to "fixed-value investments." Can it be carried over into the field of common stocks? Yes, but with some necessary modifications.

There are instances where a common stock may be considered sound because it enjoys a margin of safety as large as that of a good bond. This will occur, for example, when a company has outstanding only common stock which under depression conditions is selling for less than the amount of bonds that could safely be issued against its property and earning power. That was the position of a host of strongly financed industrial companies at the low price levels of 1932–33. In such instances the investor can obtain the margin of safety associated with a bond, *plus* all the chances of larger income and principal appreciation inherent in a common stock. (The only thing he lacks is the legal power to insist on dividend payments "or else"—but this is a small drawback as compared with his advantages.) Common stocks bought under such circumstances will supply an ideal, though infrequent, combination of safety and profit opportunity.[1]

In the ordinary common stock, bought for investment under normal conditions, the margin of safety lies in an expected earning power considerably above the going rate for bonds. Assume in a typical case that the earning power is 8 per cent on the price and that the bond rate is 3 per cent; then the stock buyer will have an average annual margin of 5 per cent accruing in his favor. Some of the excess is paid to him in the dividend rate; even though spent, it enters into his over-all investment result. The undistributed balance is reinvested in the business for his account. In many cases such reinvested earnings fail to add commensurately to the earning power and value of his stock. (That is why the market has a stubborn habit of valuing earnings disbursed in dividends more generously than the portion retained in the business.) But, if the picture is viewed as a whole, there is a reasonably close connection between the growth of corporate surpluses through reinvested earnings and the growth of corporate values.

Over a ten-year period the typical excess of stock earning power over bond interest may aggregate 50 per cent of the price paid. This figure is sufficient to provide a very real margin of safety—which, under favorable conditions, will prevent or minimize a loss. If such a margin is present in each of a diversified list of twenty or more stocks, the probability of a favorable result under "fairly normal conditions" becomes very large. That is why the policy of investing in representative common stocks does not require high qualities of insight and foresight to work out successfully. If the purchases are made at the average level of the market over a span of years, the prices paid should carry with them assurance of an adequate margin of safety. The danger to investors lies in concentrating their purchases in the upper levels of the market or in buying non-representative common stocks which carry more than average risk of diminished earning power.

Observation over many years has taught us that the chief losses to investors come from the purchase of low-quality securities at times of favorable business conditions. The purchasers view the current good earnings as equivalent to "earning power" and assume that prosperity is synonymous

---

[1]Some readers may be interested in our analysis, along these lines, of American Laundry Machinery stock at its price of 7 in January, 1933, in *Security Analysis*, 1940 edition, pp. 593–594.

with safety. It is in those years that bonds and preferred stocks of inferior grade can be sold to the public at a price around par, because they carry a little higher income return or a deceptively attractive conversion privilege. It is then, also, that common stocks of obscure companies can be floated at prices far above the tangible investment, on the strength of two or three years of abnormally large profits.

These securities do not offer an adequate margin of safety in any admissible sense of the term. Coverage of interest charges and preferred dividends must be tested over a number of years, including a period of subnormal business. The same is ordinarily true of common-stock earnings if they are to qualify as indicators of earning power. Thus it follows that most of the fair-weather investments, acquired at fair-weather prices, are destined to suffer disturbing price declines when the horizon clouds over—and often sooner than that. Nor can the investor count with confidence on an eventual recovery—although this does come about in some proportion of the cases—for he has never had a real safety margin to tide him through adversity.

The philosophy of investment in growth stocks parallels in part and in part contravenes the margin-of-safety principle. The growth-stock buyer relies on an expected earning power which is greater than the average shown in the past. Thus he may be said to substitute these expected earnings for the past record in calculating his margin of safety. In investment theory there is no reason why carefully estimated future earnings should be a less reliable guide than the bare record of the past; in fact, security analysis is coming more and more to prefer a competently executed evaluation of the future. Thus the growth-stock approach may supply as dependable a margin of safety as is found in the ordinary investment—provided the calculation of the future actually shows a satisfactory margin in relation to the price paid.

The danger in a growth-stock program lies precisely here. For such favored issues the market has a tendency to set prices which will not be adequately protected by a *conservative* projection of future earnings. (It is a basic rule of prudent investment that all estimates, when they differ from actual performance, must err at least slightly on the side of understatement.) The margin of safety is always dependent on the price paid. It will be large at one price, small at some higher price, non-existent at some still higher price. If, as we suggest, the average market level of most growth stocks is too high to provide an adequate margin of safety for the buyer, then a simple technique of diversified buying in this field may not work out satisfactorily. A special degree of foresight and judgment will be needed, in order that wise individual selections may overcome the hazards inherent in the customary market level of such issues as a whole.

The margin-of-safety idea becomes much more evident when we apply it to the field of undervalued or bargain securities. We have here, by definition, a favorable difference between price on the one hand and indicated or appraised value on the other. That difference is the safety margin. It is available for absorbing the effect of miscalculations or worse-than-average luck. The buyer of bargain issues places particular emphasis on the ability of the investment to withstand adverse developments. For in most such cases he has no enthusiasm about the company's prospects. True, if the prospects are definitely bad the investor will prefer to avoid the security no matter how low the price. But the field of undervalued issues is made up of the many concerns—perhaps a majority of the total—for which the future appears neither distinctly promising nor distinctly unpromising. If these are bought on a bargain basis, even a moderate decline in the earning power need not prevent the investment from showing satisfactory results. The margin of safety will then have served its proper purpose.

Theory of Diversification

There is a close logical connection between the concept of a safety margin and the principle of diversification. One is correlative with the other. Even with a margin in the investor's favor, an individual security may work out badly. For the margin guarantees only that he has a better chance for profit than for loss—not that loss is impossible. But the more the number of such commitments is multiplied the more certain does it become that the aggregate of the profits will exceed the aggregate of the losses. That is the simple basis of the insurance-underwriting business.

Diversification is an established tenet of conservative investment. By accepting it so universally, investors are really demonstrating their acceptance of the margin-of-safety principle, to which diversification is the companion. This point may be made more colorful by a reference to the arithmetic of roulette. If a man bets $1 on a single number he is paid $31 profit when he wins—but the chances are 33 to 1 that he will lose. He has a "negative margin of safety." In his case diversification is foolish. The more numbers he bets

on, the smaller his chance of ending with a profit. If he regularly bets $1 on
every number (including "0" and "00") he is certain to lose $2 on each turn of
the wheel. But suppose the winner received $35 profit instead of $31. Then
he would have a small but important margin of safety. Therefore, the more
numbers he wagers on, the better his chance of gain. And he could be certain
of winning $2 on every spin by simply betting $1 each on all the numbers.
(Incidentally, the two examples given actually portray the respective posi-
tions of the patron and the proprietor of a wheel with "0" and "00.")

A Criterion of Investment vs. Speculation

Since there is no single definition of investment in general acceptance,
authorities have the right to define it pretty much as they please. Many of
them deny that there is any useful or dependable difference between the concepts of investment and of speculation. We think this scepticism is unnecessary and harmful. It is injurious because it lends encouragement to the
innate leaning of many people toward the excitement and hazards of stock-
market speculation. We suggest that the margin-of-safety concept may be
used to advantage as the touchstone to distinguish an investment operation
from a speculative one.

Probably most speculators believe they have the odds in their favor when
they take their chances, and therefore they may lay claim to a safety margin
in their proceedings. Each one has the feeling that the time is propitious for
his purchase, or that his skill is superior to the crowd's, or that his adviser or
system is trustworthy. But such claims are unconvincing. They rest on subjective judgment, unsupported by any body of favorable evidence or any conclusive line of reasoning. We greatly doubt whether the man who stakes
money on his view that the market is heading up or down can ever be said to
be protected by a margin of safety in any useful sense of the phrase.

By contrast, the investor's concept of the margin of safety—as developed
earlier in this chapter—rests upon simple and definite arithmetical reasoning from statistical data. We believe, also, that it is well supported by practical investment experience. There is no guaranty that this fundamental
quantitative approach will continue to show favorable results under the unknown conditions of the future. But, equally, there is no reason for pessimism
on this score.

Thus, in sum, we say that to have a true investment there must be present a true margin of safety. And a true margin of safety is one that can be demonstrated by figures, by persuasive reasoning, and by reference to a body of actual experience.

Extension of the Concept of Investment

To complete our discussion of the margin-of-safety principle we must now make a further distinction between conventional and unconventional investments. Conventional investments are appropriate for the typical portfolio. Under this heading come United States government issues and high-grade, dividend-paying common stocks. We have sometimes added state and municipal bonds for those who will benefit sufficiently by their tax-exempt features. Also included will be first-quality corporate bonds and preferred stocks when and if they can be bought to yield sufficiently more than United States Savings Bonds.

Unconventional investments are those which are suitable only for the enterprising investor. They cover a wide range. The broadest category is that of undervalued common stocks of secondary companies, which we recommend for purchase when they can be bought at two-thirds or less of their indicated value. Besides these, there is often a wide choice of medium-grade corporate bonds and preferred stocks when they are selling at such depressed prices as to be obtainable also at a considerable discount from their apparent value. In these cases the average investor would be inclined to call the securities speculative, because in his mind their lack of a first-quality rating is synonymous with a lack of investment merit.

It is our argument that a sufficiently low price can turn a security of mediocre quality into a sound investment opportunity—provided (a) that the buyer is informed and experienced and (b) that he practices adequate diversification. For, if the price is low enough to create a substantial margin of safety, the security thereby meets our criterion of investment. Our favorite supporting illustration is taken from the field of real-estate bonds. In the 1920's, billions of dollars' worth of these issues were sold at par and widely recommended as sound investments. A large proportion had so little margin of value over debt as to be in fact highly speculative in character. In the depression of the 1930's an enormous quantity of these bonds defaulted their interest, and their price collapsed—in some cases below 10 cents on the dollar. At that stage the same advisers who had recommended them at par as safe investments were rejecting them as paper of the most speculative and unattractive type. But as a matter of fact the price depreciation of about 90 per cent made many of these securities exceedingly attractive and reasonably safe—for the true values behind them were four or five times the market quotation.

The fact that the purchase of these bonds actually resulted in what is generally called "a large speculative profit" did not prevent them from having true investment qualities at their low prices. The "speculative" profit was the purchaser's reward for having made an unusually shrewd investment. They could properly be called *investment* opportunities, since a careful analysis would have shown that the excess of value over price proved a large margin of safety. Thus the very class of "fair-weather investments" which we stated above is a chief source of serious loss to naïve security buyers is likely to afford many sound profit opportunities to the sophisticated operator who may buy them later at pretty much his own price.

The whole field of "special situations" would come under our definition of investment operations, because the purchase is always predicated on a thoroughgoing analysis which promises a larger realization than the price paid. Again there are risk factors in each individual case, but these are allowed for in the calculations and absorbed in the over-all results of a diversified operation.

To carry this discussion to a logical extreme, we might suggest that a defensible investment operation could be set up by buying such intangible values as are represented by a group of "common-stock option warrants" selling at historically low prices. (This example is intended as somewhat of a shocker.) The entire value of these warrants rests on the possibility that the related stocks may some day advance above the option price. At the moment they have no exercisable value. Yet, since all investment rests on reasonable future expectations, it is proper to view these warrants in terms of the mathematical chances that some future bull market will create a large increase in their indicated value and in their price. Such a study might well yield the conclusion that there is much more to be gained in such an operation than to be lost and that the chances of an ultimate profit are much better than those of an ultimate loss. If that is so, there is a safety margin present even in this unprepossessing security form. A sufficiently enterprising investor could then include an option-warrant operation in his miscellany of unconventional investments.[2]

A Final Word

Investment is most intelligent when it is most *businesslike*. It is amazing to see how many capable businessmen try to operate in Wall Street with complete disregard of all the sound principles through which they have gained success in their own undertakings. Yet every corporate security may best be viewed, in the first instance, as an ownership interest in, or a claim against, a specific business enterprise. And, if a person sets out to make profits from security purchases and sales, he is embarking on a business venture of his own, which must be run in accordance with accepted business principles if it is to have a chance of success.

The first and most obvious of these principles is, "Know what you are doing—know your business." For the investor this means: Do not try to make "business profits" out of securities—that is, returns in excess of normal interest and dividend income—unless you know as much about security values as you would need to know about the value of merchandise that you proposed to deal in or manufacture.

A second business principle: "Do not let anyone else run your business, unless (a) you can supervise his performance with adequate care and comprehension or (b) you have unusually strong reasons for placing implicit confidence in his integrity and ability." For the investor this rule should determine the conditions under which he will permit someone else to decide what is done with his money.

A third business principle: "Do not enter upon an operation—that is, manufacturing or trading in an item—unless a reliable calculation shows that it has a fair chance to yield a reasonable profit. In particular, keep away from ventures in which you have little to gain and much to lose." For the enterprising investor this means that his operations for profit should be based

---

[2]This argument is supported by an article entitled "Speculative Opportunities in Stock-Purchase Warrants," by Paul Hallingsby, Jr., in the *Analysts' Journal* for the third quarter, 1947. Note also the similar implications in our table of prices and asset values of Bankers Securities Corporation common stock on p. 187.

not on optimism but on arithmetic. For every investor it means that when he limits his return to a small figure—as in a conventional bond or preferred stock—he must demand convincing evidence that he is not risking a substantial part of his principal.

A fourth business rule is more positive: "Have the courage of your knowledge and experience. If you have formed a conclusion from the facts and if you know your judgment is sound, act on it—even though others may hesitate or differ." (You are neither right nor wrong because the crowd disagrees with you. You are right because your data and reasoning are right.) Similarly, in the world of securities, courage becomes the supreme virtue *after* adequate knowledge and a tested judgment are at hand.

Fortunately for the typical investor it is by no means necessary for his success that he bring these qualities to bear upon his program—*provided* he limits his ambition to his capacity and confines his activities within the safe and narrow path of standard, defensive investment. To achieve *satisfactory* investment results is easier than most people realize; to achieve *superior* results is harder than it looks.

APPENDIX

A METHOD OF DETERMINING BUYING AND SELLING POINTS IN THE
GENERAL MARKET BY THE DETERMINATION OF A CENTRAL VALUE FOR
THE DOW-JONES INDUSTRIAL AVERAGE.

This method is predicated on the following basic assumptions:

(1) A reasonably sound central value, or intrinsic value, of the Dow-Jones list
can be ascertained by capitalizing the average earnings of the past ten years on a
basis equivalent to twice the current yield of high-grade bonds.

(2) It would be sound practice to purchase the Dow-Jones unit when obtainable at 80% of its central value and to sell out the unit when the price rises to
120% of such value.

The application of the above method has been worked out for the twenty-five
years, 1924–1948, as shown on the appended chart and table C, shown on pages
253–54. We are indebted to Mr. Robert L. Hatcher of Douglaston, N. Y. for the
detailed calculations. If the method had been consistently followed beginning in
1924, the operations shown in Table A below would have taken place.

TABLE A.

INDICATED BUYING AND SELLING OPERATIONS
BY "CENTRAL-VALUE METHOD"

1924–1948

Purchases		Sales	
Date	*Price of D-J Ind. Av.*	*Date*	*Price of D-J Ind. Av.*
March 1924	94.2	October 1925	155.5
September 1931	108.9	July 1936	165.8
March 1938	106.4	October 1938	154.7
March 1942	100.5		

The method indicates buying and selling points in other years than those shown in Table A as follows:

TABLE B.

ADDITIONAL BUYING AND SELLING OPERATIONS INDICATED
AT INTERMEDIATE PERIODS

Purchases		Sales	
Year	*Price of D-J Ind. Av.*	*Year*	*Price of D-J Ind. Av.*
		1926	162.8
		1927	160.6
		1928 (low)	193.0
		1929 (low)	199.0
		1930 (low)	160.0
1931	109.9		
1932 (high)	88.2		
1933	95.5		
1934	104.1		
		1937	150.9
		1939	148.3
		1940	135.3

An investor operating in accordance with Table A would not have followed the indications in Table B, since he would already have made his purchases or sales.

The results shown above must be regarded as quite satisfactory on the whole, even though the investor may have purchased well above the bottom and sold at well below the top. The pattern appears deficient in that it did not indicate a sale at or below the high point in 1946. This suggests various observations, as follows:

(1) Failure of the pattern to work in 1946 probably means that this idea, like all others of the kind, is not fully dependable. On the other hand it may be sufficiently dependable to be worth using for its overall results.

(2) It happens that the Dow-Jones average failed to rise as much in 1942–46 as the stock market generally. Had the investor been guided by the Standard Statistics Index covering 354 industrial stocks, he might actually have sold out in 1946. This observation indicates that techniques can always be improved by the application of hindsight. It probably has little practical value.

(3) There is a possibility that failure of the Dow-Jones list to reach a selling range in 1946 may mean that it did not complete its full bull market rise in that year. If so, the bull market may have been interrupted rather than completed in 1946. Only time will tell whether this optimistic interpretation is warranted.

TABLE C.
CALCULATION OF CENTRAL VALUE OF DOW-JONES INDUSTRIAL AVERAGE

1924–1948

Year	Average Earnings of 10 Previous Years	Yield of Moody's All Corporation AAA Bonds April of Same Year	Central Value: Average Earnings Divided by Twice Interest Rates	80% of Central Value	120% of Central Value	Range of D-J I.A Same Year High	Low
1924	11.99	5.08	118.0	94.4	141.6	120.5	88.3
1925	12.62	4.87	129.6	103.7	155.5	159.4	115.0
1926	12.86	4.74	135.7	108.5	162.8	167.0	136.0
1927	12.36	4.58	133.8	107.1	160.6	201.5	152.0
1928	11.28	4.46	126.5	101.2	151.8	300.0	193.0
1929	11.21	4.69	119.5	95.6	143.4	381.2	199.0

(Continued)

TABLE C.

CALCULATION OF CENTRAL VALUE OF DOW-JONES INDUSTRIAL AVERAGE

(Continued)

1924–1948

Year	Average Earnings of 10 Previous Years	Yield of Moody's All Corporation AAA Bonds April of Same Year	Central Value: Average Earnings Divided by Twice Interest Rates	80% of Central Value	120% of Central Value	Range of D-J I.A Same Year High	Low
1930	11.75	4.60	127.7	102.2	153.3	294.1	160.0
1931	11.98	4.40	136.1	108.9	163.4	193.0	74.6
1932	12.28	5.17	118.8	95.0	142.5	88.2	41.2
1933	11.41	4.78	119.4	95.5	143.2	108.5	50.2
1934	10.59	4.07	130.1	104.1	156.1	111.0	85.6
1935	9.86	3.66	134.7	107.8	161.6	149.9	96.7
1936	9.09	3.29	138.2	110.5	165.8	185.0	143.0
1937	8.60	3.42	125.7	100.6	150.9	194.4	113.0
1938	8.51	3.30	128.9	103.2	154.7	158.4	99.0
1939	7.45	3.02	123.3	98.7	148.0	155.9	121.5
1940	6.36	2.82	112.8	90.2	135.2	152.8	111.8
1941	6.35	2.82	112.6	90.1	135.1	133.6	106.3
1942	7.11	2.83	125.6	100.5	150.7	119.7	92.9
1943	8.08	2.76	146.4	117.1	175.7	145.8	119.3
1944	8.85	2.74	161.5	129.2	193.8	152.5	134.2
1945	9.46	2.61	181.2	145.0	217.5	195.8	151.4
1946	9.88	2.46	200.8	160.7	241.0	212.5	163.1
1947	10.24	2.53	202.4	161.9	242.8	186.9	163.2
1948	10.97	2.78	197.3	157.8	236.8	193.2	165.4

Everything considered, the results of the method outlined would appear sufficiently interesting to warrant giving more attention to this approach than it has received to date. Certainly it has the basic soundness of seeking to place the buying at low market values and the selling at high market values.

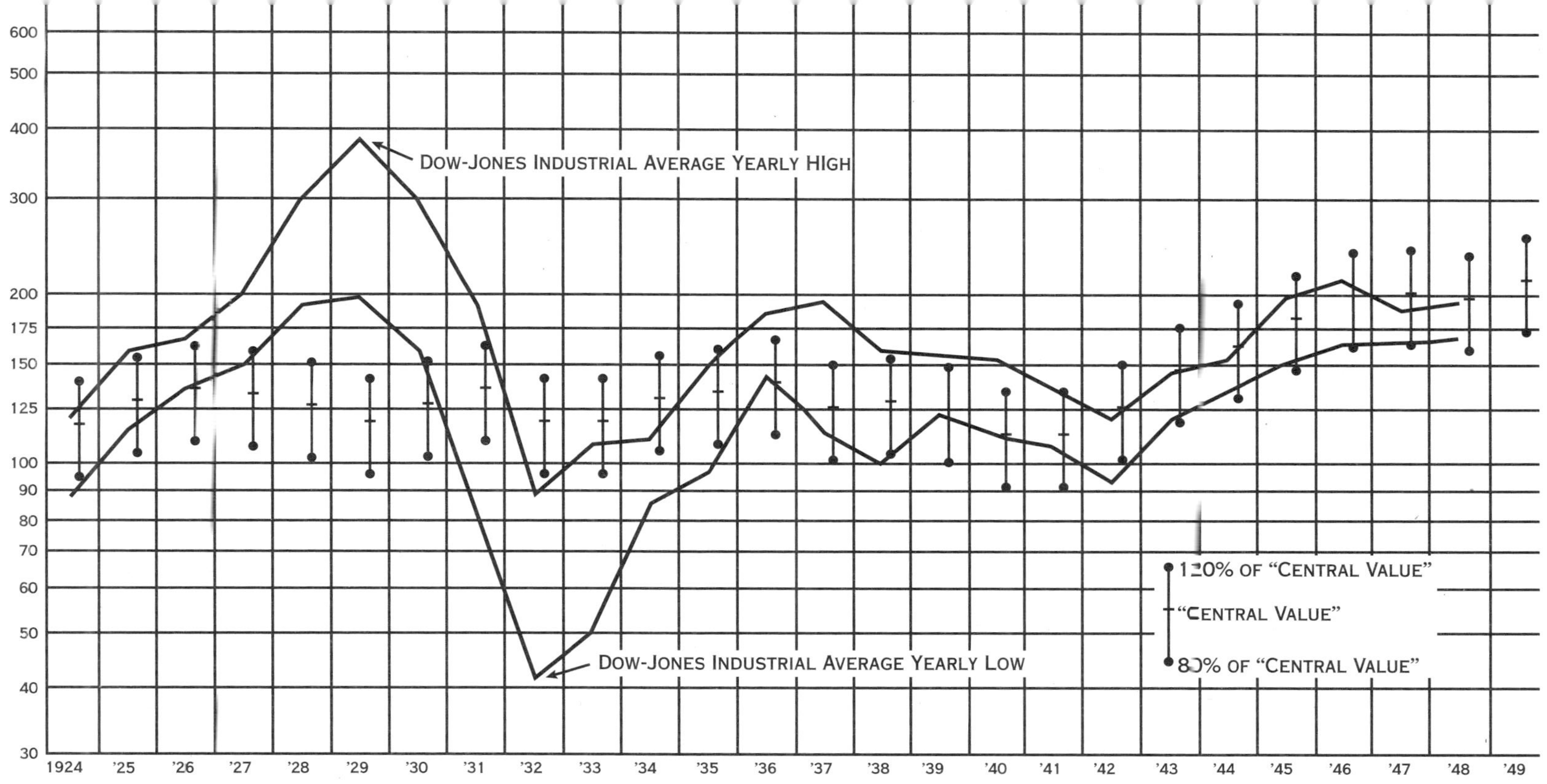

600
500
400
300
200
175
150
125
100
90
80
70
60
50
40
30
1924
'25
'26
'27
'28
'29
'30
'31
'32
'33
'34
'35
'36
'37
'38
'39
'40
'41
'42
'43
'44
'45
'46
'47
'48
'49
Dow-Jones Industrial Average Yearly High
Dow-Jones Industrial Average Yearly Low
120% of "Central Value"
"Central Value"
80% of "Central Value"

CHART C

INDEX

ABOUT BENJAMIN GRAHAM

1894–1976

BENJAMIN GRAHAM WAS born in 1894 in London. Upon migration to America, his father started an importing business—unfortunately, he died shortly thereafter, and the business failed. More bad news was to follow when an economic crisis in 1907 resulted in the loss of the family savings. Through hard work, Graham, a bright student, enrolled in Columbia University and was offered a teaching position there upon graduation. However, he chose instead to take a job as a chalker on Wall Street with the firm Newburger, Henderson and Loeb. Recognizing his innate skills, he was soon made a financial researcher for the firm and quickly became a partner, earning over $500,000 a year—a princely sum at that time, especially for a twenty-five-year-old.

In 1926, Graham formed an investment partnership with Jerome Newman. He also began lecturing on finance at Columbia, and continued to maintain his scholastic ties with the school and academia until he retired in 1956.

The Crash of 1929 proved to be a turning point for Graham. The dark days almost wiped him out, but the partnership survived largely through the aid of friends and the sale of most of the partners' personal assets. Graham was able to get back on his feet but the experience taught him valuable lessons that he would soon share with the world through his books.

In 1934, Benjamin Graham partnered with another academic from Columbia, David Dodd, to publish the classic *Security Analysis*—a book, like *The Intelligent Investor*, that has never been out of print. Despite the recent stock market crash, the book proposed that it was possible to successfully invest in common stocks as long as sound investment principles were applied.

In 1949, Graham wrote *The Intelligent Investor,* a book widely considered the bible of value investing. It was published to unanimous acclaim, and the principles it espouses have been widely read and taught throughout the world for more than fifty years.

Clearly, Graham took his own words to heart. Graham and Newman's partnership continued until 1956 and never again lost money for its investors. He continued as a partner, while simultaneously writing and lecturing at Columbia. Graham retired from both institutions in 1956.

Benjamin Graham died in 1976, with the reputation of being the "Father of Security Analysis."

About John C. Bogle

—◆◇◆—

BORN IN 1929, John C. Bogle grew up in a family whose wealth had vanished during the Great Depression. Bogle was a responsible young man, who worked steadily to support himself as waiter, post-office clerk, reporter, and through other jobs. He earned a scholarship to Blair Academy (N.J.), where he was captain of the student waiters and voted "most likely to succeed," graduating in 1947.

With the help of another scholarship, he entered Princeton University, working his way through with jobs of increasing responsibility. In December 1949, he received what he called "the lucky break of a lifetime." Reading *Fortune* magazine in the university library, he stumbled on an article that described the "tiny but contentious" mutual fund industry. He decided to make it the subject of his senior thesis.

After exhaustive study of the industry, Bogle concluded that "the principal function of mutual funds is the management of their investment portfolios. Everything else is incidental . . . that future industry growth can be maximized by a reduction of costs," that funds could "make no claim for superiority over the market averages," and that funds should operate "in the most efficient, honest, and economical way possible." Entitled *The Economic Role of the Investment Company*, the thesis enabled Bogle to graduate magna cum laude in June 1951.

Largely on the basis of his thesis, Bogle was immediately hired by fund industry pioneer Walter L. Morgan, founder of Philadelphia's Wellington Fund. He rose quickly through the ranks and by 1965 was leading the firm.

In a move he describes as opportunistic and naïve, Bogle merged Wellington with a Boston investment firm that had achieved spectacular results during the "Go-Go Era" of the mid-1960s. The once-happy marriage was not to last, and in the midst of the 1973–1974 bear market, Bogle was fired from the firm that he considered "his."

Heartsick but determined, Bogle seized a well-disguised opportunity to create the firm that would embody the idealism of his senior thesis. In founding The Vanguard Group in 1974, he created a unique mutual fund firm: one that was owned not by an external management company as was (and is) the industry standard but one that was owned by its mutual fund shareholders—a truly *mutual* mutual fund organization. At the outset, Vanguard was responsible for just $1.4 billion of mutual fund assets. Thirty-one years later, assets under management approach $850 billion.

Bogle's innovations did not stop with Vanguard's ownership structure, which has allowed the firm to operate at costs that are less than one-fifth the industry average. In 1975, just a year after he founded the firm, Vanguard launched the world's first index mutual fund. (Today, the 500 Index Fund is the world's largest mutual fund.) Two years later, Vanguard created the first multi-series bond fund, whose then-novel structure—comprised of separate short-, intermediate-, and long-term portfolios—quickly became the industry standard. His 1977 decision to eliminate broker distribution and abandon sales loads sharply accelerated the growth of no-load mutual funds.

Ever since he first read *The Intelligent Investor* in 1965, Bogle has been an admirer of Benjamin Graham, citing Graham's work and espousing his principles. *In John Bogle on Investing: New Perspectives for the Intelligent Investor* (1993), Bogle honored Graham's book in his own book's title and identified Graham as one of "the giants on whose shoulders I have stood" in writing the book.

In 1999, exactly a half century after the magazine had introduced him to the mutual fund industry, *Fortune* named John C. Bogle one of the financial industry's four "Giants of the Twentieth Century." In 2004, *Time* magazine named him to the "Time 100: The World's 100 Most Powerful and Influential People." Former Federal Reserve Chairman Paul A. Volcker has praised Bogle for his "fiduciary responsibility, objectivity of analysis, and willingness to take a stand," and former Chancellor of the Delaware Court of Chancery,

William T. Allen, described him as "a man of high virtue." Bogle has dedi-
cated his long career to the notion that the human beings who own mutual
fund shares deserve a fair shake. His fifth and latest book, with a working title of *The Battle for the Soul of Capitalism—Owners vs Managers* will be published by Yale University Press in the fall of 2005.